Law Express

CRIMINAL LAW

6th edition

Emily Finch

Stefan Fafinski

PEARSON

Harlow, England • London • New York • Boston • San Francisco • Toronto • Sydney • Auckland • Singapore • Hong Kong
Tokyo • Seoul • Taipei • New Delhi • Cape Town • São Paulo • Mexico City • Madrid • Amsterdam • Munich • Paris • Milan

Pearson Education Limited
Edinburgh Gate
Harlow CM20 2JE
United Kingdom
Tel: +44 (0)1279 623623
Web: www.pearson.com/uk

First published 2007 (print)
Second edition 2009 (print)
Third edition 2011 (print)
Fourth edition 2013 (print)
Fifth edition published 2015 (print and electronic)
Sixth edition published 2017 (print and electronic)

ISBN: 978-1-292-08679-8 (print)
  978-1-292-08736-8 (PDF)
  978-1-292-08735-1 (ePub)

British Library Cataloguing-in-Publication Data
A catalogue record for the print edition is available from the British Library

10 9 8 7 6 5 4 3 2 1
20 19 18 17 16

Front cover bestseller data from Nielsen BookScan (2009–2014, Law Revision Series).

Back cover poll data from a survey of 16 UK law students in September 2014.

Print edition typeset in 10 pt and Helvetica Neue LT W1G by SPi Global
Print edition printed and bound in Malaysia (CTP-PJB)

NOTE THAT ANY PAGE CROSS REFERENCES REFER TO THE PRINT EDITION

Contents

Have your say!

What do you think of LawExpress?

We're really keen to hear your opinions about the series and how well it supports your studies. Your views will help inform the future development of Law Express and ensure it is best suited to the revision needs of law students.

Please log on to the website and leave us your feedback. It will only take a few minutes and your thoughts are invaluable to us.

www.pearsoned.co.uk/lawexpressfeedback

Acknowledgements

This book is dedicated to STG.

We are, as ever, grateful to all who have offered feedback on the last edition of *Law Express: Criminal Law,* particularly the anonymous academic reviewers who provided some suggestions for improvement. We have been pleased to incorporate these as best we could. We would really like to hear what you think of the book, which you can do by visiting www.finchandfafinski.com, Twitter at @FinchFafinski or via email to hello@finchandfafinski.com.

Emily Finch and Stefan Fafinski

Publisher's acknowledgements

Our thanks go to all reviewers who contributed to the development of this text, including students who participated in research and focus groups, which helped to shape the series format.

Introduction

Criminal law is one of the core subjects required for a qualifying law degree, so is a compulsory component on most undergraduate law programmes. Aspects of criminal law also appear in other subjects, such as environmental law, family law and company law, as well as relating more directly to the study of criminal justice, evidence and criminology. As such, a thorough understanding of criminal law is vital for law students.

Crime is an integral part of everyday life. It is a prominent feature in the news and is a popular subject for fictional portrayal. Most students commencing legal studies will have some experience of crime, whether directly, as a victim of crime or indirectly through exposure to media coverage. This means that most offences covered on the syllabus, such as murder, theft and rape will be familiar terms. This tends to give students the impression that they know more about criminal law than they do about other subjects on the syllabus. This can be a real disadvantage in terms of the academic study of criminal law because it tends to lead students to rely on preconceived notions of the nature and scope of the offences and to reach instinctive, but often legally inaccurate, conclusions. It is absolutely essential to success in criminal law that you put aside any prior knowledge of the offences and focus on the principles of law derived from statutes and cases. By doing this, you will soon appreciate just how much difference there is between everyday conceptions of crime and its actuality.

This revision guide will help you to identify and apply the law and it also provides frequent reminders of the importance of abandoning preconceptions about the offences. It is written to be used as a supplement to your course materials, lectures and textbooks. As a revision guide, it should do just that – guide you through revision; it should not be used to cut down on the amount of reading (or thinking) that you have to do in order to succeed. Criminal law is a vast and complex subject – you should realise this from looking at the size of your recommended text (which, incidentally, covers only a fraction of the criminal law that exists 'out there'). It follows that this revision guide could never be expected to cover the subject in the depth and detail required to succeed in exams and it does not set out to do so. Instead, it aims to provide a concise overall picture of the key areas for revision – reminding you of the headline points to enable you to focus your revision and identify the key points that you need to know.

REVISION NOTE

- Do not be misled by the familiarity of the offences; learn each topic afresh and focus on the legal meanings of the words that you encounter
- Do rely on this text to guide you through the revision process
- Do not rely on this text to tell you everything you need to know about criminal law
- Make sure you consult your own syllabus frequently to check which topics are covered and in how much detail
- Make use of your lecture notes, handouts, texts and other materials as you revise, as these will ensure that you have sufficient depth of knowledge
- Take every possible opportunity to practise your essay-writing and problem-solving techniques; get as much feedback as you can
- Be aware that many questions in criminal law combine different topics; selective revision could leave you unable to answer questions that include reference to material that you have excluded from your revision

Before you begin, you can use the study plan available on the companion website to assess how well you know the material in this text and identify the areas where you may want to focus your revision.

Guided tour

How to use features in the book and on the companion website

Understand quickly

Topic maps – Visual guides highlight key subject areas and facilitate easy navigation through the chapter. Download them from the companion website to pin on your wall or add to your revision notes.

Key definitions – Make sure you understand essential legal terms.

Key cases and key statutes – Identify and review the important elements of essential cases and statutes you will need to know for your exams.

Read to impress – These carefully selected sources will extend your knowledge, deepen your understanding, and earn better marks in coursework and exams.

Glossary – Forgotten the meaning of a word? This quick reference covers key definitions and other useful terms.

Test your knowledge – How well do you know each topic? Test yourself with quizzes tailored specifically to each chapter.

Podcasts – Listen as your own personal Law Express tutor guides you through a step-by-step explanation of how to approach a typical but challenging question.

Revise effectively

Revision checklists – Identify essential points you should know for your exams. The chapters will help you revise each point to ensure you are fully prepared. Print the checklists from the companion website to track your progress.

Revision notes – These boxes highlight related points and areas where your course might adopt a particular approach that you should check with your course tutor.

Study plan – Assess how well you know a subject prior to your revision and determine which areas need the most attention. Take the full assessment or focus on targeted study units.

Flashcards – Test and improve recall of important legal terms, key cases and statutes. Available in both electronic and printable formats.

Take exams with confidence

Sample questions with answer guidelines – Practice makes perfect! Consider how you would answer the question at the start of each chapter then refer to answer guidance at the end of the chapter. Try out additional sample questions online.

Assessment advice – Use this feature to identify how a subject may be examined and how to apply your knowledge effectively.

Make your answer stand out – Impress your examiners with these sources of further thinking and debate.

Exam tips – Feeling the pressure? These boxes indicate how you can improve your exam performance when it really counts.

Don't be tempted to – Spot common pitfalls and avoid losing marks.

You be the marker – Evaluate sample exam answers and understand how and why an examiner awards marks.

Table of cases and statutes

■ Cases

TABLE OF CASES AND STATUTES

Statutes

■ European legislation

Elements of
criminal liability

1

Revision checklist

Essential points you should know:

☐ The relationship between *actus reus* and *mens rea*

☐ The problems surrounding the need for coincidence of *actus reus* and *mens rea*

☐ The nature of strict liability

☐ The role and operation of defences

■ Topic map

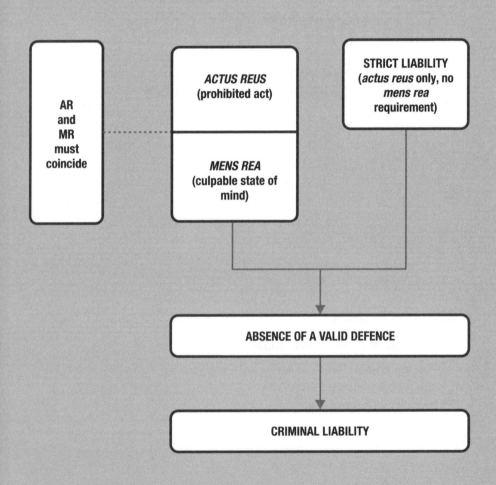

AR and MR must coincide

ACTUS REUS (prohibited act)

MENS REA (culpable state of mind)

STRICT LIABILITY (*actus reus* only, no *mens rea* requirement)

ABSENCE OF A VALID DEFENCE

CRIMINAL LIABILITY

A printable version of this topic map is available from **www.pearsoned.co.uk/lawexpress**

■ Introduction

Criminal liability is based upon a combination of actions (*actus reus*) and thoughts (*mens rea*).

This is expressed by the maxim *actus non facit reum nisi mens sit rea,* which means that an act alone will not give rise to criminal liability unless it was done with a guilty state of mind.

If **actus reus** and **mens rea** are established and there is no valid defence, the defendant is guilty. The onus is on the prosecution (burden of proof) to establish the elements of the offence beyond reasonable doubt (standard of proof).

It is important not to overlook the foundations of criminal liability as part of the revision process, as a grasp of this material provides an essential foundation upon which an understanding of the operation of the substantive offences is based. There is also potential for exam questions that tackle these basic issues.

ASSESSMENT ADVICE

Essay questions

Essay questions focusing on the relationship between the *actus reus* and *mens rea* are quite common and require the student to have a good grasp of basic principles as well as an ability to discuss the underlying rationale of the law. Questions on strict liability are also common and involve discussion of why such offences depart from the general principle that criminal liability requires a culpable state of mind.

Problem questions

Problem questions involving the coincidence of *actus reus* and *mens rea* are common and require an understanding of the various ways that the courts have dealt with lack of coincidence as well as the ability to tackle the substantive offences themselves (often murder or criminal damage). Knowledge of the elements of criminal liability and their operation is essential, even if it does not arise directly in a question, as it would be impossible to answer any problem without understanding how *actus reus, mens rea* and defences work in combination.

■ Sample question

Could you answer this question? Below is a typical essay question that could arise on this topic. Guidelines on answering the question are included at the end of this chapter, whilst a sample problem question and guidance on tackling it can be found on the companion website.

ESSAY QUESTION

How accurately is the maxim *actus non facit reum nisi mens sit rea* reflected in criminal law?

■ *Actus reus* and *mens rea*

These are the building blocks of criminal liability. In simple terms, *actus reus* (AR) is the guilty act and *mens rea* (MR) is the guilty mind, both of which are required for criminal liability.

The precise nature of the *actus reus* and *mens rea* are determined by the particular offence. For example, the *actus reus* of criminal damage is the damage/destruction of property belonging to another whilst the *mens rea* of **murder** is intention to kill or cause **grievous bodily harm** (GBH). The definition of the offence, in statute or common law, will contain the elements of the offence.

✎ EXAM TIP

Failing to state the specific *mens rea* of the particular offence is a common mistake. Intention is a category of *mens rea*; it is *not* the *mens rea* of any offence. Many offences include intention within their *mens rea* but always in relation to the *actus reus*.

WRONG: The *mens rea* of murder is intention.

CORRECT: The *mens rea* of murder is intention to kill or cause GBH.

Always be sure that you can state the full and correct *mens rea* of each offence.

□ REVISION NOTE

A more detailed account of *actus reus* and *mens rea* will be found in the chapters that follow.

◼ Coincidence of *actus reus* and *mens rea*

It is not enough that the defendant has committed the guilty act and then later formed the guilty state of mind (or vice versa): the two must coincide. This means that the defendant must possess the guilty state of mind *at the time* that the *actus reus* is committed (see Figure 1.1).

Problems arise in fixing liability if there is a lapse in time after the *actus reus* before the *mens rea* comes into being and, equally, in situations where the *mens rea* precedes the *actus reus*.

Actus reus occurring before *mens rea*

This means that the defendant completes the prohibited act before he forms the prohibited state of mind. The scenario in Figure 1.1 is an example of this.

Two distinct approaches have been used to secure a conviction in situations where the *actus reus* is complete prior to the formation of *mens rea*:

◼ treating the *actus reus* as a *continuing act* (*Fagan*) (see below); and

◼ basing liability on *failure to act* after creating a dangerous situation (*Miller*) (see below).

✎ EXAM TIP

Lack of coincidence is a popular examination topic. You will need to be able to explain why lack of coincidence is a problem and how the courts have tackled this. A good grasp of cases such as *Fagan, Miller* and *Church* is important, as the facts demonstrate the problems with lack of coincidence and the judgments illustrate the creativity of the judiciary in overcoming this impediment to conviction.

KEY CASE

Fagan v *Metropolitan Police Commissioner* [1969] 1 QB 439 (DC)

Concerning: coincidence of actus reus *and* mens rea *as a continuing act*

Facts

The defendant accidentally stopped his car on a policeman's foot, but then refused to move when he realised this. He appealed against his conviction for assaulting a police officer in the execution of his duty on the basis that at the time of the *actus reus* (when his car made contact with the policeman's foot) he had no *mens rea* (because it was accidental) and, by the time he formed *mens rea* (refusing to move), there was no act upon which to base liability (he merely refused to undo that which he had already done). ▶

Figure 1.1

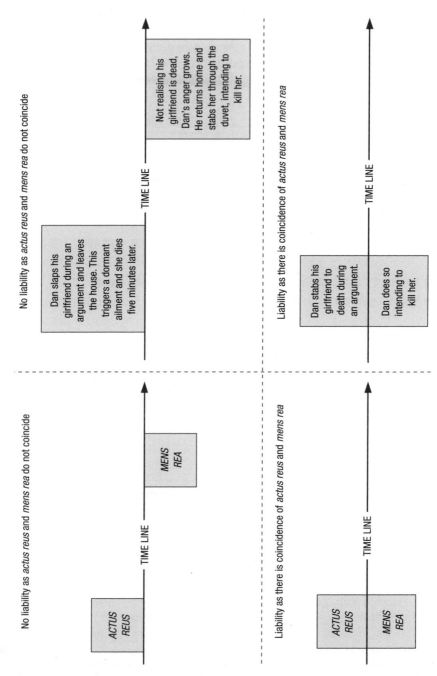

No liability as *actus reus* and *mens rea* do not coincide

Dan slaps his girlfriend during an argument and leaves the house. This triggers a dormant ailment and she dies five minutes later.

Not realising his girlfriend is dead, Dan's anger grows. He returns home and stabs her through the duvet, intending to kill her.

TIME LINE

No liability as *actus reus* and *mens rea* do not coincide

ACTUS REUS

MENS REA

TIME LINE

Liability as there is coincidence of *actus reus* and *mens rea*

Dan stabs his girlfriend to death during an argument.

Dan does so intending to kill her.

TIME LINE

Liability as there is coincidence of *actus reus* and *mens rea*

ACTUS REUS

MENS REA

TIME LINE

Legal principle

It was held that the *actus reus* of assault (in the sense of a battery) came into being when contact was first made between the car and the policeman's foot. This *actus reus* continued for the whole time that the car remained on the foot, ending only when the car was moved. At the point in time that the defendant became aware of the contact and refused to move, he developed the requisite *mens rea* and liability was complete.

Figure 1.2

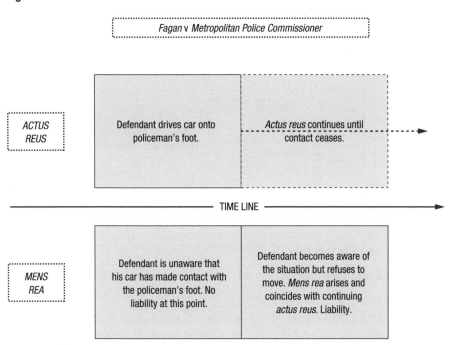

Fagan v *Metropolitan Police Commissioner*

| ACTUS REUS | Defendant drives car onto policeman's foot. | *Actus reus* continues until contact ceases. |

TIME LINE →

| MENS REA | Defendant is unaware that his car has made contact with the policeman's foot. No liability at this point. | Defendant becomes aware of the situation but refuses to move. *Mens rea* arises and coincides with continuing *actus reus*. Liability. |

✎ **EXAM TIP**

It can be useful to scribble down a timeline of events to clarify when the *actus reus* and *mens rea* occurred, as Figure 1.2 demonstrates in relation to *Fagan*. This is particularly useful when facing a problem question on coincidence, as it can be difficult otherwise to determine 'what happened when' from the mass of facts included in the question.

The use of a continuing *actus reus* can provide a solution only if there is some ongoing conduct (the car remained on the foot). It cannot overcome lack of coincidence if the *actus reus* is complete (if the defendant had driven over the foot).

An alternative approach was formulated in *Miller* to deal with a situation in which the *actus reus* was complete prior to formation of *mens rea* (see Figure 1.3).

Figure 1.3

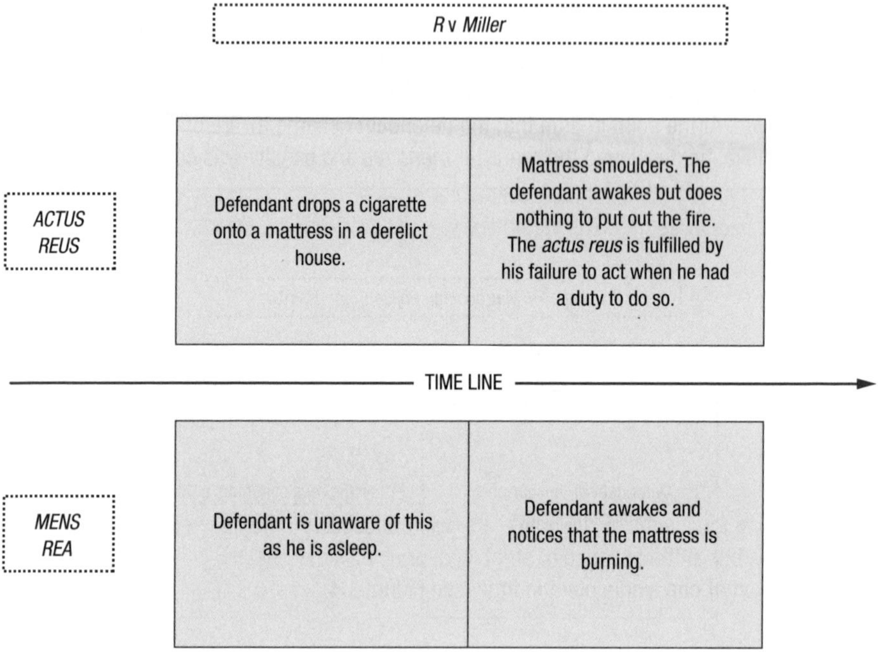

> R v Miller

ACTUS REUS	Defendant drops a cigarette onto a mattress in a derelict house.	Mattress smoulders. The defendant awakes but does nothing to put out the fire. The actus reus is fulfilled by his failure to act when he had a duty to do so.

————————— TIME LINE —————————➤

MENS REA	Defendant is unaware of this as he is asleep.	Defendant awakes and notices that the mattress is burning.

KEY CASE

R v Miller [1983] 2 AC 161 (HL)

Concerning: coincidence of actus reus and mens rea in relation to a failure to act

Facts

The defendant fell asleep in a derelict house whilst smoking a cigarette. He awoke to find the mattress smouldering, but merely moved to a different part of the house. The house was damaged in the ensuing fire. Here, the act causing the *actus reus* (dropping the cigarette) occurred when the defendant was asleep and the *mens rea* (recklessness as to the damage or destruction of property) arose when he awoke.

Legal principle

The House of Lords held that the defendant had created a dangerous situation that gave rise to a duty to act. Therefore, the *actus reus* was satisfied by the defendant's failure to deal with the fire and this coincided with the relevant *mens rea,* thus he was liable.

Mens rea occurring before actus reus

Neither of the solutions formulated in *Fagan* or *Miller* is able to deal with situations in which the *mens rea* occurs prior to the *actus reus,* so further judicial creativity was necessary. This resulted in the *single transaction* view.

KEY CASE

R v *Church* [1966] 1 QB 59 (CA)

Concerning: coincidence of actus reus *and* mens rea *as part of a single transaction*

Facts

The defendant attacked a woman intending to cause her GBH (*mens rea*). She lapsed into unconsciousness, but the defendant believed she was dead so he threw her body into a river in order to dispose of it. The victim subsequently drowned (*actus reus*).

Legal principle

A defendant will be liable if the entire incident viewed as a whole could be regarded as a 'series of events' designed to cause death or GBH. The elements of the offence will be satisfied, provided the *actus reus* and *mens rea* occur somewhere during a single transaction.

A defendant cannot have an intention to kill a person if he believes that person is already dead. By viewing the events as a whole – a single transaction – the courts were able to impose liability, but at the expense of strict legal principles that require the *actus reus* and *mens rea* to exist at one single point in time (see Figure 1.4).

Figure 1.4

	R v *Church*	

		Defendant throws unconscious woman into river to dispose of the body. As a result, the victim drowned thus fulfilling the *actus reus* of murder.
ACTUS REUS	Defendant attacks victim. She does not die. No *actus reus* of murder.	

————————————————— TIME LINE —————————————————▶

		Defendant did not intend to kill the victim at this point as he believed she was already dead. It was held that he was liable as the whole incident was a 'series of events' designed to cause death.
MENS REA	Defendant intends to cause GBH thus satisfying the *mens rea* of murder.	

■ Strict liability

Strict liability offences do not require *mens rea* in relation to all parts of the *actus reus*. This means that a defendant can be convicted, even if he was unaware of essential matters relevant to the offence. For example:

- A defendant can be convicted of driving whilst disqualified, even if he believes his disqualification period has ended: *Bowsher* [1973] RTR 202 (CA).
- Liability can be imposed for selling a lottery ticket to a person under 16, even if the defendant did not realise the age of the customer: *Harrow LBC* v *Shah* [2000] 1 WLR 83 (DC).

Strict liability offences are, almost inevitably, created by statute and often are regarded as 'regulatory offences' where there is no moral content to the offence, such as laws relating to trading standards and road traffic offences. Strict liability offences are seen as a way of enforcing particular standards of behaviour and thus protecting the public from harm.

❗ Don't be tempted to . . .

Neglect the debate about whether strict liability offences should exist at all. This is a difficult area and one that could form the subject of a tricky essay question. Do not assume that the reasons for their existence are clear-cut. The arguments in favour of their existence include:

- □ *promotion of care:* enforce regulations to protect people from harm;
- □ *deterrent value:* ensures compliance to avoid criminal prosecution;
- □ *easier enforcement:* no need to establish *mens rea,* particularly useful in respect of corporations;
- □ *no risk to liberty:* as offences generally are regulatory and lead to the imposition of fines rather than imprisonment.

However, strong arguments exist that it is contrary to fundamental principles of criminal law to impose liability without fault, i.e. in the absence of a culpable state of mind. The European Court of Human Rights suggests strict liability is not appropriate in offences conferring serious criminal liability (*Salabiaku* v *France* (1988) 13 EHRR 379 (ECHR)). Equally, the House of Lords emphasised that there should be a presumption of *mens rea* (or a presumption against strict liability) in all statutory offences: *B* v *DPP* [2000] 2 AC 428 (HL); *R* v *K* [2002] 1 AC 462 (HL).

An excellent outline of the opposing arguments that incorporates discussion of recent case law developments and an examination of the theoretical justification for strict liability can be found in Horder, 2002.

It is unusual to encounter a problem question involving strict liability, but essays are commonplace. Some will make it clear that a discussion of strict liability is required, such as 'Discuss the role of strict liability offences in modern criminal law'. Others, however, are less direct, so be alert for references to 'fault' or 'mental states' as a clue that an essay involves strict liability: for example, 'There should be no criminal liability without fault. Discuss.' (Note that this question could involve other issues raised in this chapter, such as the coincidence of AR and MR.)

◼ Defences

Strictly speaking, a defence is a means by which the defendant is able to avoid criminal liability even if the *actus reus* and *mens rea* have been established. However, some things that are described often as defences are actually *denials* of part of the offence. Defences fall into four categories (see Figure 1.5).

Defences may be:

- general (available for any offence), e.g. **insanity**;
- particular (limited to specific offences), e.g. loss of control is a defence only to murder;
- complete (results in an acquittal), e.g. **automatism**;
- partial (results in reduction of liability), e.g. diminished responsibility reduces murder to manslaughter.

Figure 1.5

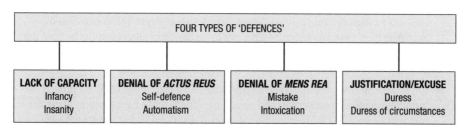

FOUR TYPES OF 'DEFENCES'			
LACK OF CAPACITY Infancy Insanity	**DENIAL OF *ACTUS REUS*** Self-defence Automatism	**DENIAL OF *MENS REA*** Mistake Intoxication	**JUSTIFICATION/EXCUSE** Duress Duress of circumstances

Individual defences, their operation and effect are considered in more detail in later chapters.

■ Putting it all together

Answer guidelines

See the essay question at the start of the chapter. A diagram illustrating how to structure your answer is available on the companion website.

Approaching the question

This is a typical example of an essay question on the elements of law. It is a straightforward question, but it could appear off-putting, as it is not immediately clear what it requires. The key to answering questions like this is to unpick them and work out what they want from you. If you do not know what the Latin phrase means, there is no point in attempting this question, as you cannot work out what it is asking you to discuss. A rough translation of the phrase is that there is no criminal liability unless the defendant has a guilty mind: in other words, no liability without *mens rea.*

Important points to include

- The starting point should be an explanation of the meaning of the Latin phrase. This should not be limited to a rough translation but should also include a consideration of why it is seen as important that a defendant is not convicted for his actions unless he has a guilty mind. Remember that there is credit available for doing simple things well, so your answer should include a simple description of *actus reus* and *mens rea.*

- Having established the general rule (the liability is imposed when there is both a pro-hibited act and a guilty mind), you can go on to explore the accuracy of the maxim by considering exceptions to the general rule.

- Explain strict liability offences as an exception to the rule and consider the justi-fications for their existence. Your answer will be strengthened by the inclusion of examples from case law but remember not to go too far in describing the facts of the cases: include sufficient information to make the case work as an illustration of your point but do not weaken your focus by including excessive detail.

- You could also cover the situations in which there was no *mens rea* at the time of the *actus reus* (lack of coincidence) and outline the efforts made by the courts to create coincidence so that liability could be imposed. A good knowledge of relevant case law is essential here.

- Make sure that you reach a conclusion: it is a common problem that essays just stop abruptly without reaching some conclusion. This is unfortunate, as a strong conclu-sion can really add strength to your essay. In this instance, you should draw together the strands of your answer and consider whether, given the number of exceptions that you have identified, the maxim still has an important role in criminal law. You might conclude, for example, that the way that the courts strive to find coincidence illustrates how important the maxim is considered to be, as the courts will be creative in order to comply with it.

 Make your answer stand out

The ability to deal with underlying theoretical principles of criminal law will impress your examiners. Incorporate reference to concepts such as fault, blame and culpability throughout your answer to demonstrate the depth of your understanding of the criminal law.

The ability to explain the rationale for the existence of strict liability offences by reference to their role in the criminal law will add depth to your answer and allow you to engage in more intricate consideration of whether their existence offends the maxim.

READ TO IMPRESS

Horder, J. (2002) Strict Liability, Statutory Construction and the Spirit of Liberty. *Law Quarterly Review,* 118: 458.

www.pearsoned.co.uk/lawexpress

 Go online to access more revision support, including quizzes to test your knowledge, sample questions with answer guidelines, podcasts you can download and more!

Actus reus

2

Revision checklist

Essential points you should know:

- [ ] The different types of *actus reus*
- [ ] The role of *actus reus* in establishing criminal liability
- [ ] The relationship between factual and legal causation
- [ ] The circumstances when intervening acts will break the chain of causation
- [ ] The situations giving rise to liability for failing to act

■ Topic map

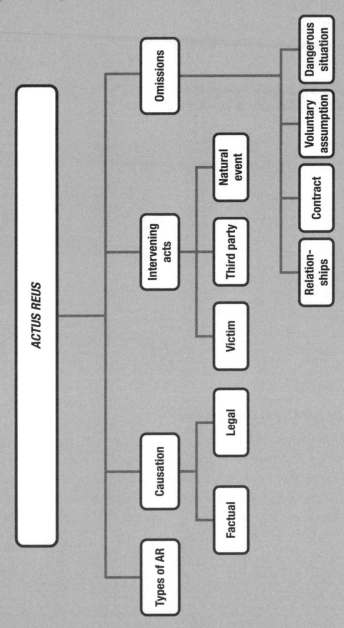

A printable version of this topic map is available from **www.pearsoned.co.uk/lawexpress**

■ Introduction

Actus reus **is often described as the 'guilty act' or 'conduct element' of an offence but is more correctly described as** *all the external elements of the offence.*

In other words, the *actus reus* covers everything apart from the defendant's state of mind.

All offences have an *actus reus,* so the issues covered in this chapter could arise in relation to any offence, making this an important revision topic. Revising issues, such as causation and omissions, provides an excellent foundation for coursework or exam problem questions, so make sure you have a firm grasp of these before revising the substantive offences.

ASSESSMENT ADVICE

Essay questions

Essay questions involving the *actus reus* of criminal liability fall into two general categories:

1　Broad questions dealing with the nature of *actus reus* and its role in establishing criminal liability. These require *breadth* of knowledge and the ability to select relevant examples in support of your argument.

2　Narrower questions focusing on particular issues, such as the policy underlying causation or the rationale for imposing liability for omissions. These require greater *depth* of knowledge. Make sure you know *enough* about a topic before attempting to answer a question.

Problem questions

Problem questions involving issues of *actus reus* arise in conjunction with substantive offences. For example, you might encounter a question on homicide that includes a tricky issue of causation or a question on, say, criminal damage that bases liability on failing to act.

■ Sample question

Could you answer this question? Below is a typical problem question that could arise on this topic. Guidelines on answering the question are included at the end of this chapter, whilst a sample essay question and guidance on tackling it can be found on the companion website.

Darius attacks Veronica, leaving her unconscious. Adam and Bernard walk past. Adam does nothing, but Bernard, experienced in first aid, attempts to treat Veronica but gives up after a few moments because he is late for a meeting. At the hospital, Dr Eric fails to spot Veronica's head injuries and assumes she is unconscious because she is drunk. Veronica dies from her injuries two hours later. The inquest determines that she would have survived had she received prompt treatment.

Discuss the criminal liability of the parties.

Types of *actus reus*

The *actus reus* covers all external elements of an offence, going far beyond its common characterisation as a 'guilty act' (see Figure 2.1).

✎ EXAM TIP

Understanding the different types of *actus reus* should ensure that you are able to look for all the elements of the *actus reus* in the facts of a problem question, ensuring that no aspect of the offence is omitted from your answer.

Causation

KEY DEFINITION: Result crimes and conduct crimes

Result crimes are those in which the *actus reus* is defined in terms of prohibited consequences, irrespective of how these are brought about, e.g. causing death (murder). This differs from conduct crimes.

Conduct crimes are those in which the *actus reus* is concerned with prohibited behaviour, regardless of its consequences, e.g. driving whilst disqualified.

As **result crimes** are concerned with consequences, the nature of the act that brought the consequences about is unimportant, provided it caused the consequence. For example, in relation to homicide offences, there is no requirement that death is caused by unlawful means, just a requirement that death is caused. Therefore, the *actus reus* of murder is

Figure 2.1

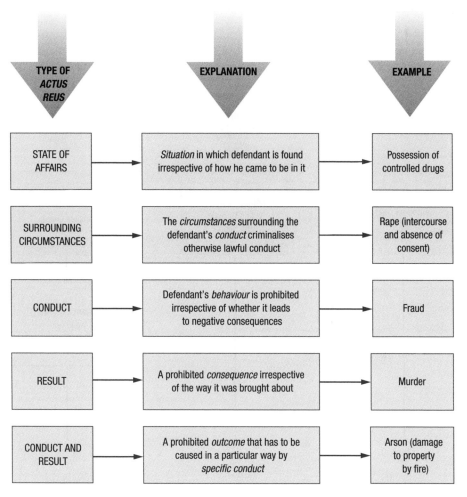

TYPE OF ACTUS REUS	EXPLANATION	EXAMPLE
STATE OF AFFAIRS	*Situation* in which defendant is found irrespective of how he came to be in it	Possession of controlled drugs
SURROUNDING CIRCUMSTANCES	The *circumstances* surrounding the defendant's *conduct* criminalises otherwise lawful conduct	Rape (intercourse and absence of consent)
CONDUCT	Defendant's *behaviour* is prohibited irrespective of whether it leads to negative consequences	Fraud
RESULT	A prohibited *consequence* irrespective of the way it was brought about	Murder
CONDUCT AND RESULT	A prohibited *outcome* that has to be caused in a particular way by *specific conduct*	Arson (damage to property by fire)

equally satisfied if the defendant shoots the victim (unlawful act) or gives him a piece of cake that induces an extreme allergic reaction (lawful act), provided that death results.

This is why *causation* plays such a central role in criminal law.

KEY DEFINITION: Chain of causation

This provides a link between the initial act of the defendant (which need not be unlawful) and the prohibited consequence that has occurred. This is why it forms part of the *actus reus*: it is not enough that the prohibited consequence has occurred, it must be caused by the defendant.

2 *ACTUS REUS*

This chapter will focus on causation in murder, but the principles are applicable to all result crimes (see Figure 2.2).

Figure 2.2

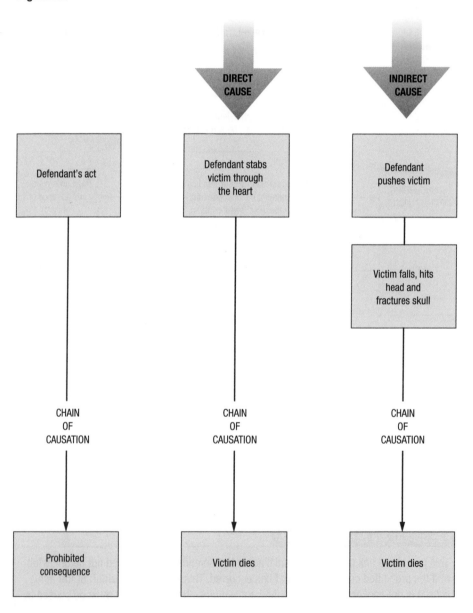

Figure 2.3

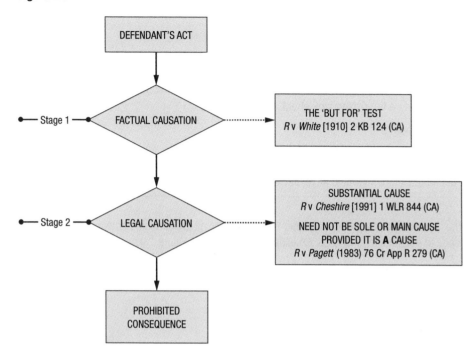

A defendant will be liable for causing death, even if it is an indirect consequence of his act, provided the **chain of causation** between act and consequence is unbroken.

Causation is established using a two-stage test (see Figure 2.3):

1. Factual causation.
2. Legal causation.

Factual causation

KEY DEFINITION: Factual causation

The defendant's act must be a *sine qua non* of the prohibited consequence. This means that the consequence would not have occurred without the defendant's actions. Factual causation is established using the 'but for' test.

KEY CASE

R v *White* [1910] 2 KB 124 (CA)

Concerning: 'but for' test, factual causation

Facts

The defendant wanted to kill his mother. He poisoned her drink but she died of natural causes before the poison took effect.

Legal principle

Factual causation is established by asking whether the victim would have died 'but for' the defendant's conduct. If the answer is 'yes', the defendant did not cause death. The defendant's mother would have died anyway, thus he is not the factual cause of death.

The 'but for' test is a preliminary filter that eliminates all unconnected acts/events, leaving a range of potential legal causes. Consider the scenarios in Figure 2.4.

Figure 2.4

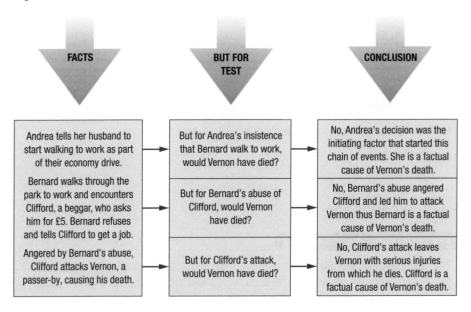

The 'but for' test establishes multiple factual causes of death. Not all factual causes make a meaningful contribution to death nor do factual causes imply blameworthiness. Look again at the example in Figure 2.4. All three parties are a 'but for' cause of death, but not all of them are regarded as equally to blame for Vernon's death. Factual causes merely establish a preliminary connection between act and consequence.

Legal causation

It would be unthinkable to base liability on factual causes alone, as these are often too remote from the prohibited consequence. For example, in the illustration in Figure 2.4, Andrea should not be criminally liable for Vernon's death merely because she told Bernard to walk to work. Legal causation as a policy-driven notion uses notions of culpability, responsibility and foreseeability to select the most appropriate, i.e. blameworthy, factual cause as the basis for liability, even if this is not the most immediate cause of death.

KEY CASE

R v Pagett (1983) 76 Cr App R 279 (CA)

Concerning: legal causation, multiple causes

Facts

To avoid arrest, the defendant used his pregnant girlfriend as a shield and fired at armed police. The police returned fire, hitting and killing the girl. The defendant was held to be the legal cause of death, despite causing no physical injury himself, as he set in motion the chain of events that led to death and it was foreseeable that the police would return fire.

Legal principle

It was held that the defendant's act need not be the sole cause, or even the main cause, of death, provided it is a cause in that it 'contributed significantly to that result' (*per* Robert Goff LJ at 290).

Pagett is a good illustration of the policy underlying legal causation. He did not fire the shot that killed the victim, but he was liable for her death as his was the most *blameworthy* act in the events leading to her death. This approach is reflected in the medical negligence cases in which only 'palpably wrong' medical treatment will relieve the person inflicting the initial **wound** of liability (see Figure 2.5).

The defendant in *Cheshire* remained liable, despite the contribution of the negligent treatment to the victim's death because the defendant's wrongdoing put the victim in the position where medical treatment was needed. As the House of Lords said in *Cheshire*, misdiagnosis and routine errors are inevitable and it is therefore foreseeable as a result of causing a person to suffer injury. Only in cases such as *Jordan* where the treatment given to the victim was 'palpably wrong' would it break the chain of causation and remove liability for causing death from the defendant.

Figure 2.5

R v Jordan (1956) 40 Cr App R 152 (CA)	**R v Cheshire [1991] 1 WLR 844 (CA)**
↓	↓
FACTS The defendant stabbed the victim, who was taken to hospital. The wound healed but the victim died following an allergic reaction to drugs administered at the hospital.	**FACTS** The defendant shot the victim in the leg and stomach, necessitating hospital treatment. The victim suffered complications following a tracheotomy which the hospital failed to recognise.
↓	↓
DEFENDANT'S CONTRIBUTION TO DEATH The initial stab wound.	**DEFENDANT'S CONTRIBUTION TO DEATH** The initial gunshot wounds.
↓	↓
OTHER CONTRIBUTION(S) TO DEATH The hospital's failure to note the victim's allergy and the administration of drugs that prompted an allergic reaction.	**OTHER CONTRIBUTION(S) TO DEATH** The poor standard of care following the tracheotomy which caused respiratory complications from which the victim died.
↓	↓
OUTCOME The defendant was not liable as the original wound had healed and the medical treatment was 'palpably wrong' thus breaking the link between the defendant's act and the victim's death.	**OUTCOME** It was accepted that the original injuries were no longer life-threatening and that the victim would not have died had he received appropriate care following the tracheotomy. However, the need for the tracheotomy flowed from the defendant's original act, thus he remained liable.

! Don't be tempted to . . .

Assume that the most immediate cause of death will be the legal cause. As *Pagett* and *Cheshire* demonstrate, this is not always the case. To put it another way, supervening acts that contribute to death will not necessarily absolve the defendant from liability for causing death. Therefore, it is not always a straightforward matter to select which of the causes of death will be the legal cause. This is an area that often causes confusion in exams.

Glanville Williams describes legal causation as a 'moral reaction' that determines 'whether the result can fairly be said to be imputable to the defendant'. In cases involving multiple causes, you should follow the chain of events backwards from death in search of the *most culpable act* as this usually will be the legal cause.

Intervening acts

KEY DEFINITION: Intervening act

An intervening act (*novus actus interveniens*) is something that occurs after the defendant's act that breaks the chain of causation and relieves the defendant of responsibility for the prohibited consequence. As *Cheshire* demonstrates, not all events that occur after the defendant's act will break the chain of causation. Circumstances will break the chain of causation only if they are:

(a) an overwhelming cause of death; and

(b) an unforeseeable occurrence.

Intervening acts fall into three categories:

1. Acts of the victim.
2. Acts of third parties.
3. Naturally occurring events.

Victim's actions

The general rule of causation is that the defendant is liable for the foreseeable consequences of his actions. Therefore, the victim may break the chain of causation if his reaction to the defendant's initial act is extreme and unforeseeable.

KEY CASE

R v *Roberts* (1972) 56 Cr App R 95 (CA)

Concerning: intervening acts, victim's reaction

Facts

The defendant interfered with the victim's clothing whilst she was a passenger in his car. She jumped from the moving vehicle and sustained serious injuries in the fall. The defendant denied causing these injuries but his conviction was upheld as it was foreseeable that the victim would attempt to escape and could be injured in doing so.

Legal principle

The chain of causation will be broken only if the victim's actions were 'so daft' as to be unforeseeable.

Roberts makes it clear that only extreme acts of the victim will break the chain of causation and relieve the defendant of liability. This must be considered in conjunction with the **thin-skull rule**.

KEY DEFINITION: Thin-skull rule

This provides that a defendant is liable for the full extent of the victim's injuries even if, due to some abnormality or pre-existing condition, the victim suffers greater harm as a result of the defendant's actions than the 'ordinary' victim would suffer.

The thin-skull rule is an exception to the rule that the defendant is liable only for the foreseeable consequences of his actions.

The leading case is *Blaue* [1975] 1 WLR 1411 (CA). The defendant stabbed the victim, puncturing her lung. She refused a blood transfusion as it was contrary to her religious beliefs. The defendant was convicted of manslaughter, even though the victim had refused treatment that would have saved her life. It was held that the thin-skull rule was not limited to physical conditions but included an individual's psychological make-up and beliefs.

Third parties

Third parties may intervene between the defendant's act and the victim's death in a number of ways. There may be a subsequent attack on the victim, for example, or an unsuccessful attempt to assist the victim that worsens his condition or causes fresh injuries.

✎ EXAM TIP

In a problem question involving third-party intervention, consider (1) how significant their contribution was to death and (2) whether their actions were foreseeable.

For example, if the defendant inflicted minor burns upon the victim and the ambulance driver accidentally drove into a river causing the victim to die, it is arguable that this rendered the defendant's initial injury insignificant and was wholly unforeseeable, thus breaking the chain of causation. Always remember the powerful counter-argument that the victim would not have needed the ambulance without the defendant's actions.

Naturally occurring events

Again, principles of foreseeability determine whether a naturally occurring event will amount to an intervening act that breaks the chain of causation. For example, imagine that the defendant punches the victim, knocking him unconscious on the beach above the tide line. If a freak wave washes the unconscious victim out to sea, this is likely to be regarded as an unforeseeable occurrence that would amount to an intervening act. Compare this to a situation in which an unconscious victim is left below the tide line and drowns when the tide comes in. This is a wholly foreseeable occurrence so it will not break the chain of causation. Even though the defendant did not drown the victim directly, he put the victim in a position where it was foreseeable that the victim would drown, so liability would be established.

▉ Omissions

The general rule is that there is no liability in criminal law for omissions. There are exceptions to that rule if there is a duty to act. Such a duty can arise in various ways:

Statute

A duty to act is an onerous burden that is imposed by statute in only a narrow range of circumstances, generally requiring action in situations where inaction would be unreasonable. For example, section 170(4) of the Road Traffic Act 1988 imposes a duty upon a driver involved in an accident to report it to the police or provide his details to other parties involved.

Contract

If a person fails to do something they are bound by contract to do, they will be criminally liable if harm or injury arises from their omission, even though the person harmed was not a party to the contract.

KEY CASE

R v *Pittwood* (1902) 19 TLR 37 (Assizes)

Concerning: duty to act, contract

Facts

The defendant was contracted to open and close level-crossing gates to ensure that nobody was harmed by the trains. He failed to close the gates and the victim was killed by a train.

Legal principle

A person under contract will be liable for the harmful consequences of his failure to perform his contractual obligations. This duty extends to those reasonably affected by the omission, not just the other party to the contract.

✎ EXAM TIP

If a problem question involves someone with a particular job, consider what it is that his contract will oblige him to do and whether his failure to do this contributed to death.

Special relationships

Certain relationships can create a duty to act: for example, parent/child, husband/
wife and doctor/patient. These are relationships where there is dependence, reliance
and responsibility; for example, in *Gibbins and Proctor* (1919) 13 Cr App R 134 (CA),
the first defendant failed to provide food for his child who starved to death. His liability
was based upon his omission to fulfil the duty established by the special relationship of
father/child.

Voluntary assumption of care

The second defendant in *Gibbins and Proctor* was the partner of the child's father. She was
also liable for her omission to provide food, but liability was based not on the nature of the
relationship but because she had previously fed the child but had ceased to do so. A person
cannot cast off the duty to act that the voluntary assumption of care imposes.

> **✎ EXAM TIP**
>
> In problem questions, look out for individuals who have started to provide assistance then
> ceased to do so, as this is likely to be indicative of a voluntary assumption of care that
> creates a duty to act.

Dangerous situations

The categories of duty are based on common principles of knowledge (that the victim is
in need) and reliance (the victim relies upon the defendant for help; the rest of the world
relies upon the defendant to be responsible, thus precluding their intervention). It is these
principles that lead to the expansion of the situations in which there is a duty to act, to
include the creation of a dangerous situation.

> **📖 REVISION NOTE**
>
> The leading case on the creation of a dangerous situation is *Miller* [1983] 2 AC 161 (HL).
> See the last chapter to remind yourself of the facts and legal principle.

> **✎ EXAM TIP**
>
> Liability for creating a dangerous situation usually arises from an initially lawful act.
> Look out for situations where the defendant has done something potentially dangerous,
> but otherwise lawful, but has failed to act when the situation has escalated out of
> control.

Further expansion?

This extension of the categories of duty in *Miller* left the door open for further expansion. In *Khan* [1998] Crim LR 830 (CA), consideration was given to whether a drug-dealer, whose 'customer' had collapsed following self-administration of drugs, was under a duty to act by summoning medical assistance. However, this could be seen as the application of the *Miller* principle rather than a new category of duty.

 Make your answer stand out

Essays on omissions require more than an outline of the categories of duty. In order to make your answer stronger, think about the underlying rationale for the categories (knowledge and reliance). Also, consider why there is no general duty to act. Glanville Williams states: 'If there is an act, someone acts; but if there is an omission, everyone (in a sense) omits. We omit to do everything in the world that is not done. Only those of us omit in law who are under a duty to act.'

■ Putting it all together

Answer guidelines

See the problem question at the start of the chapter. A diagram illustrating how to structure your answer is available on the companion website.

Approaching the question

This is a typical example of a problem question involving causation in homicide. One person (Veronica) has died but there are four potential defendants – Adam, Bernard, Darius and Dr Eric – each of whom have played some part in events. The key to success in answering such a question is to give consideration to each party in a methodical manner rather than making an instinctive assessment of who is liable.

Important points to include

- Causation is a two-stage process, so establish both factual and legal causation.
- Start by considering the liability of the primary party (Darius) and consider whether any of the other parties have broken the chain of causation. ▶

- Having reached a conclusion in relation to Darius, go on to consider whether any of the parties would incur criminal liability, too: remember that more than one person can be liable for causing the death of a single victim:

  - ☐ Adam: did nothing – did he have a duty to act? There is nothing in the facts to suggest that he falls into the category of duty to act.

  - ☐ Bernard: tried to administer first aid and then gave up. Potentially liable on the basis of a voluntary assumption of care.

  - ☐ Dr Eric: medical negligence is a potential break in the chain of causation, but consider his liability for homicide on the basis of the quality of his medical treatment (see Chapter 8 and gross negligence manslaughter).

- Incorporate references to case law, remembering that the legal principle is more important than the facts of the case.

- Reach a conclusion that summarises your findings rather than ending your answer after a discussion of the last party's liability without drawing the strands of your answer together.

 Make your answer stand out

Problem questions involving causation typically involve several parties who have contributed, to a greater or lesser degree, to the end result (typically, the death of the victim). The ability to create a well-organised answer that deals with each party in a methodical manner will draw attention to your problem-solving skills and help you to present a clear picture of each party's liability.

Draw a time line of events to help you to identify each party's contribution to the death that occurred. You will find an example on the companion website that will help you to understand how to do this. Remember that there is credit to be gained in the exam for presenting a logical, structured answer as well as for the legal content, so it is worth spending some time planning the structure of your answer.

The straightforward way to deal with Adam is to assume that he has no duty to act, as there is no information that suggests otherwise. However, you could make your answer stronger by speculating about his identity: can you think of any facts that would give him a duty to act? For example, he might be a policeman or a security guard paid to patrol the area where Veronica was found. This sort of speculation allows you to demonstrate a good grasp of the situations in which a duty may arise.

READ TO IMPRESS

Ashworth, A. (1989) The Scope of Criminal Liability for Ommissions. *Law Quarterly Review,* 104: 424.

Ormerod, D. and Fortson, R. (2005) Drug suppliers as manslaughterers (again). *Criminal Law Review,* 819.

Stannard, J.E. (1993) Medical Treatment and the Chain of Causation. *Journal of Criminal Law,* 75: 88.

www.pearsoned.co.uk/lawexpress

 Go online to access more revision support, including quizzes to test your knowledge, sample questions with answer guidelines, podcasts you can download and more!

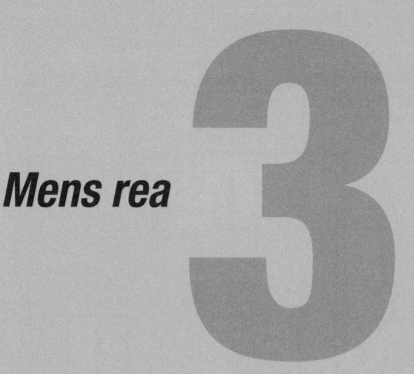

Mens rea

Revision checklist

Essential points you should know:

- [ ] The types of *mens rea* and their role in establishing liability
- [ ] The distinction between direct and oblique intention
- [ ] The distinction between subjective and objective recklessness
- [ ] The current tests on intention and recklessness to be applied in problem scenarios
- [ ] The evolution of the current law on intention and recklessness
- [ ] The operation of transferred malice

Topic map

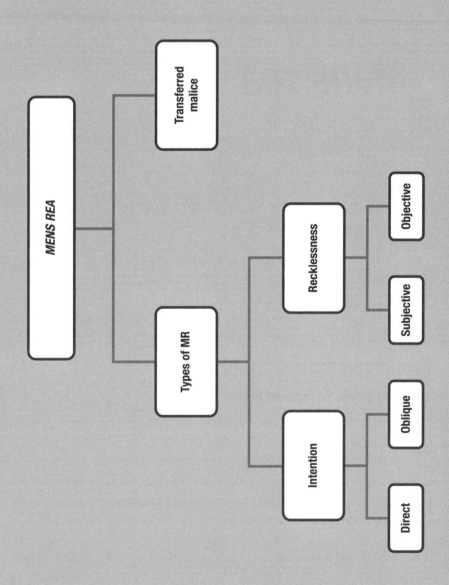

◼ Introduction

***Mens rea* refers to the guilty mind required for criminal liability.**

This chapter concentrates on intention and **recklessness** as these forms of *mens rea* are part of most offences and have been the subject of judicial scrutiny. The volume of case law on intention and recklessness can seem daunting, but this demonstrates the problems the courts have had in perfecting an appropriate definition.

The judicial approach to intention and recklessness can be tricky to grasp. *Mens rea* is concerned with the defendant's state of mind at the time of the *actus reus.* It is difficult to prove what was in someone's mind, which partially explains why the courts struggled with these words. Remember that the words have a *legal meaning.* Students often struggle because intention in law can mean something different from its ordinary meaning. Accept that this is the result of judicial interpretation of the words and that legal and dictionary definitions do not always match.

ASSESSMENT ADVICE

Essay questions

Essay questions either require a *broad* knowledge of the types of *mens rea,* their relationship to each other and their role in ascribing criminal liability, or they will take a *narrow* focus, requiring examination of a particular type of *mens rea,* such as the difficulty in defining oblique intention. Either type of question requires understanding of the development of the law, i.e. earlier cases as well as the current law.

Problem questions

Problem questions involving *mens rea* always include substantive offences, often murder (intention) and criminal damage (recklessness). Problem questions that include an issue of recklessness are particularly likely, given the relatively recent change in the law in *R* v *G* [2004] 1 AC 1034 (HL). Remember that the only test that you should state in an answer to a problem question is the applicable current law – there is no credit available for including an essay-style outline of the history of the law.

■ Sample question

Could you answer this question? Below is a typical problem question that could arise on this topic. Guidelines on answering the question are included at the end of this chapter, whilst a sample essay question and guidance on tackling it can be found on the companion website.

PROBLEM QUESTION

Donald cuts the brakes on Andrew's car, hoping that this will frighten him into repaying the £5,000 that he owes. Andrew's wife, Vera, borrows the car and is killed when the brakes fail and the car crashes into a brick wall.

Discuss Donald's liability for murder and criminal damage.

■ Types of *mens rea*

Intention is the most culpable form of *mens rea*. This is because it is more blameworthy to cause harm deliberately (intention) than it is to do so carelessly (recklessness). Therefore, intention is used in more serious offences: murder requires intention to kill or cause GBH which sets it apart from other, less culpable, forms of homicide.

Intention

Direct intention

KEY DEFINITION: Direct intention

Direct intention corresponds with the everyday meaning of intention. A person who has causing death as his aim, purpose or goal has direct intention to kill.

It was defined in *Mohan* [1976] QB 1 (CA) as 'a decision to bring about . . . the commission of an offence . . . no matter whether the defendant desired the consequences of his act or not'.

Oblique intention

This is broader than **direct intention** and includes the foreseeable and inescapable consequences of achieving a desired result, even if the consequence itself is not desired.

! Don't be tempted to . . .

Avoid oblique intention because it is difficult – it is a very important concept that makes frequent appearance in homicide problem questions. It can be a challenging topic, probably because it differs from the ordinary meaning of intention, being a broader concept. Be careful not to confuse the legal meaning with the everyday meaning. It may help to think about the reason why the courts expanded the definition of intention – to widen the net to catch more defendants, particularly in relation to murder. As murder has no alternative *mens rea* of recklessness, defendants cannot be liable unless they fall within the scope of intention. If this is limited to direct intention, a defendant would be liable only if his purpose was to cause death. A defendant who caused death in pursuit of some other end would not be liable for murder, even if achieving his primary purpose rendered death inevitable.

For example, if the defendant wants to destroy a package on an aeroplane to collect the insurance, he would not be liable for murder if he planted a bomb timed to go off in mid-flight unless the definition of intention went beyond direct intention.

Formulating a definition that captured the appropriate level of fault proved difficult. The courts tried on several occasions, only to have their definition revised by subsequent courts. The challenge was producing a test that was sufficiently narrow so as to reserve liability for murder to only the most serious manifestations of homicide. The matter is largely decided since *Woollin,* but awareness of the journey to this point is essential (see Figure 3.1).

Figure 3.1

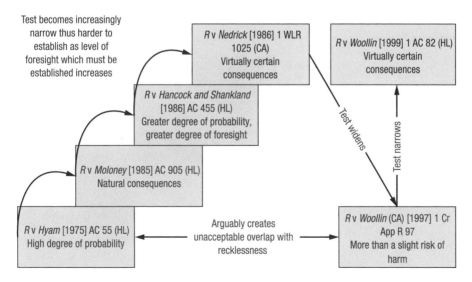

The cases shown in Figure 3.1 aimed to formulate a test that conveyed an appropriate degree of inevitability:

■ *Hyam* (HL): held that if the defendant knew that it was 'highly probable' that his act would cause death or serious bodily harm then the prosecution will have established the necessary intent.

■ *Moloney* (HL): used 'natural consequences' to describe something that necessarily followed the defendant's pursuit of his primary purpose. This was ambiguous, as natural consequences need not be inevitable: for example, pregnancy is a natural consequence of intercourse but it is by no means inevitable.

■ *Hancock and Shankland* (HL): addressed this ambiguity, stating that reference should be made to the degree of probability that the prohibited outcome would result from the defendant achieving his primary purpose. Their reasoning was as shown in Figure 3.2.

Figure 3.2

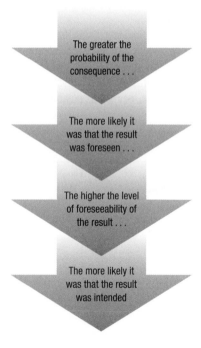

- *Moloney* and *Hancock and Shankland* conflicted in their formulation of an appropriate test of **oblique intention**.

- *Nedrick* (CA): addressed the conflict and formulated the virtual certainty test that conveyed inevitability (*Moloney*) and foreseeability (*Hancock and Shankland*).

- As *Nedrick* lacked the authoritative status of a House of Lords decision, subsequent case law eroded the narrow virtual certainty test. Ultimately, the Court of Appeal in Woollin accepted a test based upon 'substantial risk', which created a dangerous overlap with recklessness (therefore blurring the line between murder and manslaughter).

- *Woollin* (HL): reversed the CA decision, restored the virtual certainty test and set to rest much of the uncertainty.

KEY CASE

R v Woollin [1999] 1 AC 82 (HL)

Concerning: oblique intention, virtual certainty

Facts

The defendant threw his baby in exasperation when it would not stop crying. The baby died from head injuries. It was accepted that the defendant did not intend to cause harm to the child. His conviction for murder was upheld by the Court of Appeal on the basis that it was not a misdirection to explain oblique intention to the jury in terms of 'appreciation of a substantial risk of injury'. His appeal was allowed by the House of Lords.

Legal principle

The appropriate test for oblique intention was that formulated in *Nedrick*. A jury may find that a defendant intended an outcome if it was a virtually certain consequence of his actions and he realised this was the case.

 Make your answer stand out

It will help your essay on oblique intention to stand out if you can demonstrate understanding of the progression of the case law and an ability to engage with the reasoning underlying the decisions. You will find that good articles on the topic help you to do this: Simister and Chan (1997) provide a clear evaluation of the case law leading up to *Woollin*, whilst Norrie (1999) explores the state of the law after the House of Lords decision in *Woollin*.

✎ EXAM TIP

An ability to distinguish direct and oblique intention is crucial. Try answering the following questions to identify the type of intention:

1 *What was the defendant trying to achieve?* If the answer is 'death' or 'GBH', then it is an issue of direct intention and it should be straightforward to establish liability for murder (this may lead to issues of voluntary manslaughter, see Chapter 7). If the answer is 'something other than death or GBH', turn to oblique intention.

2 *Was death an inevitable consequence of achieving his primary purpose?* If so, this is likely to be oblique intention, so apply the 'virtual certainty' test from *Woollin.* If you are not sure, think about whether the facts suggest that the defendant must have seen death 'out of the corner of his eye' when embarking on his primary objective, as this also points towards oblique intention.

If the facts raise neither direct nor oblique intention but the defendant caused death, the issue becomes involuntary manslaughter (Chapter 8).

Recklessness

Recklessness is a less culpable form of *mens rea* based on unjustified risk-taking. The law on recklessness has been subject to change over the years as the courts have fluctuated between a subjective and an objective approach.

Date	Test	Scope
1957	Subjective *Cunningham* recklessness	Applied to all offences at the time
1982	Subjective *Cunningham* recklessness and objective *Caldwell* recklessness	*Caldwell* applies to criminal damage, *Cunningham* applies to all other offences involving recklessness
2004	Subjective *Cunningham* recklessness and subjective *R* v *G* recklessness	*R* v *G* applies to criminal damage, *Cunningham* applies to all other offences involving recklessness

Subjective recklessness

In *Cunningham,* a subjective test of recklessness was applied that asks 'did the defendant foresee a risk that his actions would cause the *actus reus* of the relevant offence?' In other words, a person would be liable for an offence that can be committed recklessly only if he (a) caused the *actus reus* and (b) realised that there was a risk that he would cause the *actus reus*. As such, liability for offences involving recklessness was based on the defendant's foresight of the consequences of his actions.

KEY CASE

R v Cunningham [1957] 2 QB 396 (CA)

Concerning: interpretation of malicious, subjective recklessness

Facts

The defendant fractured a gas pipe during an attempt to steal money from the meter. This caused gas to leak into an adjoining property where it was inhaled by the woman sleeping there, endangering her life. He was charged under section 23 of the Offences Against the Person Act 1861 for maliciously administering a noxious substance. The issue in the case was the correct interpretation of the word 'maliciously'.

Legal principle

It was held that 'maliciously' meant foresight of consequences, so an offence that requires maliciousness requires either that the defendant intended the consequences or foresaw the consequences and recklessly took the risk that these would occur. In relation to recklessness, Judge Byrne J approved a definition that gave rise to a subjective test: the accused has foreseen that a particular type of harm might be done and yet has gone on to take the risk of it.

The essence of the test of subjective recklessness is that it requires that the defendant is aware that his actions might cause the *actus reus* of a particular offence (foreseen that a particular type of harm might be done), but goes ahead with his actions in the light of this awareness (has gone on to take the risk of it) so, if the *actus reus* does occur, then he will have been reckless in bringing it about.

This means that a defendant who has not foreseen the risk cannot be liable. For example, in *Cunningham,* the defendant's conviction was quashed because he had not foreseen any risk that the gas would escape and be inhaled by others.

The requirement that the defendant foresaw the risk of harm was seen as a limitation to the *Cunningham* test of recklessness because it allowed defendants to argue that they had not realised that a risk existed, even if the risk was an obvious one. For example, in *Stephenson* [1979] QB 695 (CA) the defendant took shelter in a haystack and lit a fire because he was cold. He was charged with arson when the fire spread and destroyed the haystack, but the defendant avoided conviction on the basis that he had not foreseen that this could happen, as he suffered from schizophrenia. In other words, the subjective nature of the test – the requirement that the defendant must foresee the risk rather than that the risk was one that could be foreseen by an ordinary person – could enable defendants to avoid liability.

Objective recklessness

It was this feature of *Cunningham* recklessness that the House of Lords sought to eliminate in *Caldwell*.

KEY CASE

R v *Caldwell* [1982] AC 341 (HL)

Concerning: objective test of recklessness

Facts

The defendant set fire to a hotel whilst he was drunk, as revenge for being fired. He was charged with arson with intent to endanger life or being reckless as to whether life was endangered. The focus of the case was the interpretation of recklessness.

Legal principle

The House of Lords held that failure to recognise an obvious risk was just as culpable as recognising a risk and deciding to take it, so formulated a test of recklessness based upon the objective standards of the reasonable man. A person would be reckless if (1) he created an obvious risk that property would be destroyed or damaged and (2) he recognised that risk and went on to take it (advertent recklessness) or he failed to recognise that risk (inadvertent recklessness). A risk would be obvious if it was one that the reasonable man would foresee.

Caldwell overruled

Until the House of Lords decision in *R* v *G* (see Key case, below), subjective and objective recklessness operated side by side, with *Caldwell* (objective) recklessness applying to criminal damage and *Cunningham* (subjective) recklessness applying to all other offences, albeit often in a modified form, for example, the test of recklessness applied to section 20 of the Offences Against the Person Act 1861 (see Chapter 9).

The operation of two tests was problematic, as it was far easier to establish objective recklessness as this required only that there was an obvious risk whereas subjective recklessness required that the defendant had foreseen a risk.

In the example shown in Figure 3.3, it seems questionable that Jimmy can cause the *actus reus* of two offences from a single action but be liable for only one of them because of the different tests of recklessness applicable to these offences. The position is also problematic because it suggests that the law protects interests in property more rigorously than it protects against harm to the person (because it is easier to convict a defendant of criminal damage than it is to convict of offences that use *Cunningham* recklessness).

Figure 3.3

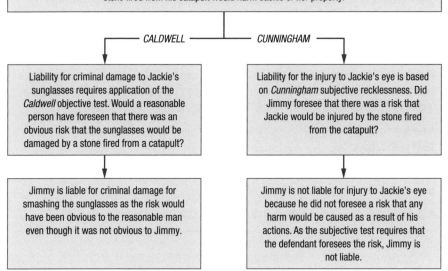

The decision in *R* v *G* resolved some of the difficulties associated with a dual standard of recklessness by overruling *Caldwell* and removing objective recklessness from criminal law.

As you read the details of *R* v *G* in the key case box overleaf, make sure that you understand its impact and the difference that it makes.

✎ EXAM TIP

Make sure that you have grasped the sphere of operation of the two forms of recklessness. Remember that *R* v *G* replaces *Caldwell* so applies only to criminal damage whilst *Cunningham* (often in a modified form) applies to all other offences involving recklessness. It is a common mistake to say that *R* v *G* replaces all previous tests of recklessness: the House of Lords in *R* v *G* went to lengths to emphasise that this was not the case, as it was only considering recklessness in criminal damage.

KEY CASE

R v *G* [2004] 1 AC 1034 (HL)

Concerning: recklessness, criminal damage

Facts

Two boys (11 and 12) set fire to a bin outside a supermarket during the night. The fire spread, destroying the supermarket. They were convicted of criminal damage following application of objective *Caldwell* recklessness, despite the fact that their youth and inexperience prevented them from recognising the risk of the fire spreading and property being damaged.

Legal principle

The House of Lords overruled *Caldwell* because it imposed liability upon those who were incapable, through no fault of their own, of operating at the standards of the reasonable man. They formulated a subjective test based upon the Draft Criminal Code:

A person acts recklessly within the meaning of section 1 of the Criminal Damage Act 1971 with respect to:

■ a circumstance when he is aware of a risk that it exists or will exist;

■ a result when he is aware of a risk that it will occur;

and it is, in the circumstances known to him, unreasonable to take the risk.

 Make your answer stand out

A good grasp of the problems of the position prior to *R* v *G*, the ruling in *R* v *G* and the reasons for it are essential for success in an essay on recklessness.

Consider the following justifications for Lord Bingham's ruling:

1 Criminal liability for serious offences should be based upon culpability; this requires a guilty mind as well as a guilty act. Failing to appreciate an obvious risk through no fault of one's own is not a sufficiently culpable state of mind.

2 *Caldwell* applied a common standard of foresight (the reasonable man) that did not take account of an individual's ability to operate at that level. This created manifest injustice to the young and those with mental disabilities who were incapable of operating at this standard.

3 There was a strong dissenting voice in *Caldwell* and it has since attracted widespread judicial and academic criticism.

Consider *Elliot* v *C* [1983] 1 WLR 939 (DC). A 14-year-old girl with learning difficulties was out at night. She sheltered in a shed and lit a fire for warmth, using white spirit. The shed was destroyed in the ensuing blaze.

Make sure that you understand how the case was decided using *Caldwell* recklessness and how it would be decided now following *R* v *G*. Which outcome do you consider to be preferable?

Caldwell (objective) recklessness	*R* v *G* (subjective) recklessness
Test: did the defendant create an obvious and serious risk that property would be damaged or destroyed? If so, did she fail to recognise a risk that would have been obvious to the reasonable man?	Test: was the defendant aware of a risk of the damage/destruction of property and, in the circumstances, was it unreasonable for her to take that risk?
The risk of damage from an out-of-control fire would be obvious to the reasonable man. As such, the defendant failed to recognise an obvious risk and thus falls within the remit of *Caldwell* recklessness and was convicted of criminal damage. This position was heavily criticised and contributed to the demise of *Caldwell* recklessness.	This test is subjective so focuses on what this particular defendant knew and expected to result from her actions. As the defendant was young with learning difficulties, it may well be that she was unable to recognise the risks posed by her actions. If so, she would not be reckless and thus would not be liable for criminal damage.

✎ **EXAM TIP**

R v *G* formulates a test of subjective recklessness that differs from *Cunningham* subjective recklessness. Therefore, the law has moved from having one objective and one subjective test (*Caldwell* and *Cunningham*) to having two subjective tests (*R* v *G* and *Cunningham*).

■ Transferred malice

Transferred malice is a means of imposing liability for the unplanned consequences of deliberate wrongdoing. If the defendant has the *mens rea* of murder in relation to A but brings about the *actus reus*, i.e. causes death, in relation to B he may still be liable. Transferred malice operates only if the *actus reus* of the offence committed matches the *actus reus* of the offence planned.

R v *Pembliton* (1872–75) LR 12 CCR 119 (CCR) and *Latimer* (1886) LR 17 QBD 359 (CCR) illustrate the principle in operation (Figure 3.4).

Figure 3.4

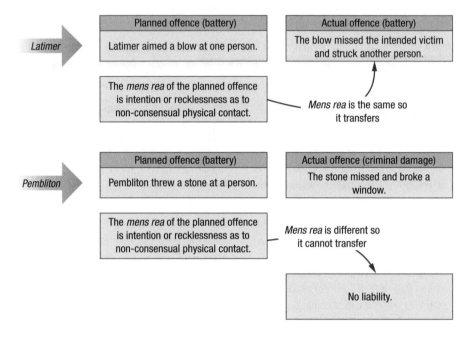

■ Putting it all together

Answer guidelines

See the problem question at the start of the chapter. A diagram illustrating how to structure your answer is available on the companion website.

Approaching the question

This is a typical example of a problem question that involves simple facts but contains a couple of tricky legal issues:

1   The test of intention in murder.
2   The correct approach to recklessness in criminal damage.

There is also a relatively straightforward transferred malice issue that should not be overlooked. Marks can be lost when answering questions such as this by not following the instructions: murder and criminal damage are specified by the question, so there is no merit in discussing other offences as no marks will be awarded for such a discussion. Remember to start by discussing the more serious offence, so deal with murder before considering liability for criminal damage.

Important points to include

- Start by defining murder and stating the *actus reus* and *mens rea* of the offence (see Chapter 6). Deal with the *actus reus* first and remember not to 'over-egg' straightforward issues: in other words, there are no complicated issues surrounding causation (see Chapter 2) so you should not devote any great detail to this issue. Simply state and apply both tests of causation before moving on to consider *mens rea,* which merits far more detailed attention.

- Think carefully about which of the tests of intention is needed here by asking yourself 'What did Donald want to achieve?' He wanted to frighten rather than to kill or cause GBH, so you should provide a concise explanation of why direct intention cannot be used here, making reference to relevant facts, and then move on to consider oblique intention. State the *Woollin* test and apply it to the facts in order to reach a conclusion about *mens rea.*

- Consider whether a reference to transferred malice is needed, remembering that it can be used only when the planned *actus reus* and the actual *actus reus* match.

- Move on to consider liability for criminal damage (see Chapter 11). State the *actus reus* and *mens rea* and apply these to the facts, ensuring that you state the correct (*R* v *G*) test of recklessness. Note that there are two potential events that might give rise to liability for criminal damage:

  ☐ cutting the brakes of the car;

  ☐ damaging the wall.

 Make your answer stand out

Remember that you are answering a problem question not writing an essay. When answering a problem question, you should state the current law and apply it to the facts. There is no scope for a discussion of how the law used to be. In other words, make sure that you rely on *Woollin* as a test for oblique intention and *R* v *G* for the correct test of recklessness in criminal damage. There is no need to explore the line of cases that led to these decisions and you would not get any credit for doing so. In fact, it could be something that has a negative impact on the marks awarded to your work because the inclusion of irrelevant detail would weaken the focus of your answer. ▶

Students often get confused about what test of intention to apply in relation to murder. Remember that direct intention to kill should be considered first, followed by direct intention to cause GBH and, only if neither of these are satisfied, should there be a discussion of oblique intention and reference to the *Woollin* test.

Similarly, it is often the case that students select the wrong test of recklessness in relation to criminal damage. Try to remember that *Caldwell* has been overruled by *R* v *G* but that *Cunningham* continues to apply to all offences other than criminal damage.

READ TO IMPRESS

Amirthalingham, M. (2004) *Caldwell* Recklessness is Dead: Long Live *Mens Rea's* Fecklessness. *Modern Law Review,* 67: 491.

Horder, J. (2006) Transferred Malice and the Remoteness of Unexpected Outcomes From Intentions. *Criminal Law Review,* 383.

Norrie, A. (1999) After *Woollin. Criminal Law Review,* 532.

Simister, A.P. and Chan, W. (1997) Intention Thus Far. *Criminal Law Review,* 740.

www.pearsoned.co.uk/lawexpress

Go online to access more revision support, including quizzes to test your knowledge, sample questions with answer guidelines, podcasts you can download and more!

Inchoate offences

4

Revision checklist

Essential points you should know:

☐ The nature of each of the offences: attempt, conspiracy and assisting/encouraging

☐ The *actus reus* and *mens rea* of the three inchoate offences

☐ The reasons why liability is imposed for inchoate offences

☐ The meaning of 'more than merely preparatory'

☐ The relationship between conspiracy, assisting and encouraging

■ Topic map

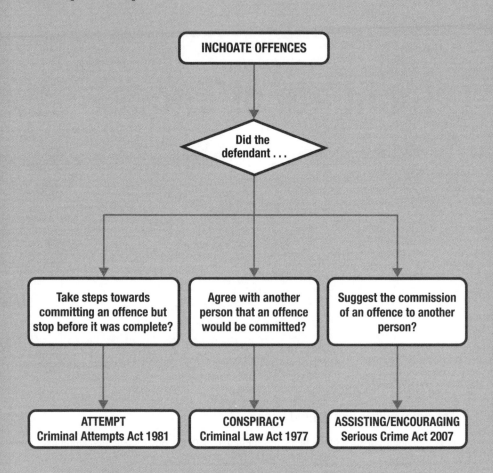

■ Introduction

Inchoate means incomplete or unfinished.

Inchoate offences are a means of imposing liability on a defendant who started to take steps towards the commission of an offence but stopped before the offence was complete. For example:

- attempt penalises thwarted or abandoned efforts to complete an offence;
- conspiracy criminalises the planning stage at which defendants agree to commit an offence; and,
- assisting/encouraging imposes liability on those who encourage others to commit offences whilst not taking an active part themselves.

The key to understanding inchoate offences is to think about why they exist at all. What is the law trying to achieve when it imposes liability on those who have not actually brought about the *actus reus* of an offence? By addressing the rationale for their existence, inchoate offences become more explicable. Think also about whether you agree with their existence. Should a person who agreed to commit an offence be liable for conspiracy to commit that offence if he decides not to go ahead? Try to incorporate notions of 'harm' into your thoughts about inchoate offences by considering why the preliminary stages that precede the actual offence are harmful.

ASSESSMENT ADVICE

Essay questions

Essay questions dealing with inchoate offences often raise issues concerning the justification for the imposition of criminal liability on defendants who have not completed the *actus reus* of a substantive offence. An essay should address the rationale for the existence of inchoate offences in general and then consider the rationale for each of the inchoate offences. It is useful to be able to answer the question 'why' about each of these: Why do we have inchoate offences? Why do we criminalise conspiracy, incitement and attempt?

Problem questions

Problem questions usually involve inchoate offences in combination with substantive offences. It is common for students to focus on the substantive offences (which are easier to spot) and to miss issues of inchoate liability. Make sure that you look out for inchoate offences and are able to deal with them effectively. Remember that conspiracy and incitement involve two parties, so cannot arise in a problem question that involves only one defendant. Attempt does not necessarily involve collaboration, so can arise with a single defendant or multiple defendants.

■ Sample question

Could you answer this question? Below is a typical problem question that could arise on this topic. Guidelines on answering the question are included at the end of this chapter, whilst a sample essay question and guidance on tackling it can be found on the companion website.

PROBLEM QUESTION

Alfred tells Bernard and Charles that he wishes that Victor was dead. Bernard and Charles later agree to kill Victor to gain favour with Alfred. They agree to meet at 8 pm to carry out the murder. Bernard does not turn up as planned, so Charles takes an axe and goes to wait in an alley outside Victor's house. By 10 pm, Victor has not appeared so Charles gives up and goes home.

Discuss the criminal liability of Alfred, Bernard and Charles.

■ Attempt

Liability for attempt is governed by the Criminal Attempts Act 1981. This covers attempts to commit indictable offences only; it is not an offence to attempt a summary offence, i.e. there can be no offence of attempted **battery**.

KEY STATUTE

Criminal Attempts Act 1981, section 1(1)

If, with intent to commit an offence to which this section applies, a person does an act that is more than merely preparatory to the commission of the offence, he is guilty of attempting to commit the offence.

Two *actus reus* elements	The *mens rea* element
An act (not omission)	Intention to commit the substantive offence
that is more than merely preparatory to the commission of an offence	

Actus reus elements

More than merely preparatory

Liability for attempt is based upon a demarcation between planning/preparation (not an offence) and embarkation on an active endeavour to commit an offence (attempt) that stops short of the substantive offence (substantive liability). This is demonstrated in Figure 4.1.

Attempt requires that the defendant has done something *more than merely preparatory*. Movement between these stages will depend on the nature of the substantive offence as some offences require more planning and preparation than others.

Think about the steps towards committing a robbery. At what stage would Dennis incur liability for attempted robbery?

- Dennis decides to rob a bank.
- He visits it to familiarise himself with the layout of the building.
- He purchases a balaclava and gloves.
- He acquires and modifies a shotgun.
- He steals a car to use as a getaway vehicle.
- He drives to the bank.
- He goes into the bank and approaches the counter.
- He points the shotgun at the cashier.
- He passes the cashier a note demanding money.

Figure 4.1

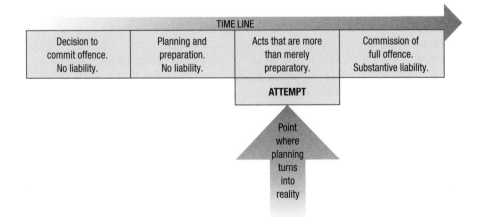

It is easy to dismiss some of these stages as planning and preparation, but is it straightforward to decide at which stage the defendant's conduct becomes more than merely preparatory?

The meaning of 'more than merely preparatory' is something on which the courts have not always taken a consistent approach. The initial test was *proximity* between the defendant's act and the completed offence. This required that the defendant had completed the final act of preparation: having 'crossed the Rubicon and burned his boats': *Stonehouse* [1978] AC 55 (HL). This restricted liability for attempt. For example, a jeweller who faked a burglary was not liable for attempting to make a fraudulent insurance claim because he had not obtained and completed a claim form: *Robinson* [1915] 2 KB 342 (CA).

Case law after the enactment of the Criminal Attempts Act 1981 has placed less emphasis on proximity, leading to a broadening of liability for attempt.

KEY CASE

R v *Griffen* [1993] Crim LR 515 (CA)

Concerning: more than merely preparatory

Facts

The defendant planned to remove her children from the custody of their father. She booked ferry tickets and told the school that she would collect the children to take them to the dentist. Her conviction for attempting to abduct the children was upheld, even though she was apprehended before she collected the children from school.

R v *Geddes* [1996] Crim LR 894 (CA)

Facts

The defendant was in the school toilets without lawful reason, with masking tape and a knife in his possession. His conviction for attempting to falsely imprison a child was overturned as he had not moved beyond preparation; he was in a position where he *could* commit the offence but he had not started to do so. As he had not approached a child, he had not 'moved from the realm of intention, preparation and planning into ... execution and implementation'.

Legal principle

'More than merely preparatory' is characterised not by physical conduct but in a psychological commitment to the commission of the substantive offence. The defendant in *Geddes* may not have continued to complete the substantive offences, despite having put himself in a position where he could do so, whereas the defendant in *Griffen* had no such ambiguity of commitment to carrying the substantive offence to fruition; she was implementing her plan but was interrupted before its completion.

The cases may seem inconsistent as the defendant in *Geddes* was within reach of children but not liable, whilst the defendant in *Griffen* was liable despite not being anywhere near her children. However, they demonstrate the shift from the 'final act' proximity approach to a focus on the psychological commitment of the defendant to completing the offence.

Mens rea of attempt

The *mens rea* of attempt is variable because it is an intention to commit the substantive offence: a defendant charged with attempted robbery must have intended to commit robbery, whilst a defendant charged with attempted rape must have intended to commit rape.

This remains true even if the substantive offence can be committed recklessly. For example, criminal damage requires *either* intention *or* recklessness (to destroy/damage property belonging to another: Chapter 11) but intention to damage/destroy another's property is required for attempted criminal damage.

> **! Don't be tempted to . . .**
>
> The *mens rea* of attempted murder is a tricky area that often gives rise to confusion in exams. The *mens rea* for murder is intention to kill or cause GBH (Chapter 6) but the *mens rea* for attempted murder is limited to intention to kill. This is because an attempted offence involves a failed outcome, i.e. the victim is not dead. If the victim is alive and the defendant intended to cause only GBH, he is liable for a non-fatal offence (Chapter 9); he cannot be liable for attempted murder unless he intended to kill the victim.

> **✎ EXAM TIP**
>
> The *actus reus* of attempt is directly referable to the *actus reus* of the substantive offence. Therefore, the 'more than merely preparatory' conduct will vary according to the nature of the substantive offence that the defendant has attempted. The *mens rea* of attempt is not referable to the substantive offence; it remains consistent as an intention to commit the substantive offence irrespective of the type of offence or its *mens rea*.

■ Conspiracy

There are two types of conspiracy, with different sets of rules:

1. Common law conspiracy (to defraud, to corrupt public morals).
2. Statutory conspiracy (to commit any other offence).

This chapter deals with statutory conspiracy.

Criminal Law Act 1977, section 1(1)

If a person agrees with any other person or persons that a course of conduct shall be pursued which, if the agreement is carried out in accordance with their intentions, either

(a)   will necessarily amount to or involve the commission of any offence or offences by one or more of the parties to the agreement; or

(b)   would do so but for the existence of facts which render the commission of the offence or any of the offences impossible,

he is guilty of conspiracy to commit the offence or offences in question.

Three *actus reus* elements	Two *mens rea* elements
Agreement	Intention to be a party to an agreement (to commit an offence)
Between the parties	Intention that the substantive offence be carried out by one of the conspirators (even if it is impossible and even if D knew what was planned and failed to stop it)
Specified course of conduct	

Actus reus elements

Agreement

Agreement is the essence of conspiracy. The parties need not commit the agreed offence or take steps towards doing so as their liability is complete once the agreement is reached.

The agreement need be only general. If the parties have agreed to kill someone, it is irrelevant that they have not yet decided when or how they will carry out the murder.

The parties

Conspiracy requires at least two people (a person cannot conspire alone!). Certain categories of people are excluded from this calculation:

■ husband and wife: section 2(2)(a);

■ those under the age of criminal responsibility: section 2(2)(b);

■ the intended victim: section 2(2)(c).

A person may conspire with 'person or persons unknown' if the identity of the other parties is not known. Therefore, a single defendant can be convicted of conspiracy if it is clear that he or she planned an offence with others but those others have been acquitted or cannot be identified.

Course of conduct

The course of conduct agreed between the parties must be one that would necessarily amount to an offence by one of the conspirators if the plan was carried to fruition. Focus on what the conspirators plan to do even if their plans are conditional on the circumstances being favourable.

KEY CASE

R v ***Jackson*** **[1985] Crim LR 442 (CA)**
Concerning: conspiracy, contingent plans

Facts

The defendant and another agreed to shoot a third man in the leg, if he was convicted of an offence for which he was on trial, so that he would attract leniency in sentencing. The defendant appealed against his conviction for conspiracy to pervert the course of justice because he had planned to do something that might never happen (there would be no need to shoot the third party if he was acquitted).

Legal principle

The Court of Appeal rejected this argument and held that a contingent plan to commit an offence if it was necessary (or possible) was still a plan to commit an offence.

Consider the 'best case scenario' of the conspirators to determine what they plan to achieve. If their plan would be a failure without achieving this aim, then this is what they have conspired to achieve. For example:

Facts	Liability
Alison and Brenda have no money. They decide to steal a gift for their mother from a shop, if it is so busy that they can do so without being spotted.	The parties will be liable for conspiracy to steal, despite the contingent nature of their plan. If their plan is successful, they will have committed theft, so they are liable for conspiracy to commit theft, even though the shop may not be sufficiently busy for them to go ahead with their plan.

Complex conspiracies

It is not always the case that a conspiracy involves two or more people who, at the same time, meet to discuss the commission of an offence. It may be the case that there are larger, more complex conspiracies in which not all of the conspirators meet each other or even know of each other's existence. In such a case, there are two options: either to treat the conspiracy as a single whole event, even though it involves people who have not had a 'meeting of minds', or to treat it as a series of separate conspiracies which, inevitably, may result in a series of separate conspiracy prosecutions.

KEY CASE

R v *Shillam* [2013] EWCA Crim 160
Concerning: complex conspiracies

Facts

The appellant and others were charged with conspiracy to supply cocaine after they each purchased drugs from a single supplier with the intention of selling it on. None of the defendants who purchased cocaine knew each other but they all knew the supplier.

Legal principle

The Court of Appeal upheld the appeal on the basis that the appellant was not part of a conspiracy with the other defendants. Conspiracy requires a single joint design between all of the conspirators. It is not necessary that all the conspirators know the identity or even the existence of all of the others but there must be a shared criminal purpose to which they have all agreed rather than a series of separate but similar plans.

It seems, then, that the crucial factor is to determine whether there was one common plan involving a number of people or whether a single core individual had a series of separate agreements with several individuals. In the latter instance, there would be several successful prosecutions for conspiracy offences involving the core individual and each of those with whom he has an agreement, but there cannot be a single successful conspiracy prosecution involving all of those involved in the separate agreements. This is because there is no common purpose that links the individual conspirators with each other, only with the core individual.

Mens rea elements

The *mens rea* of conspiracy is based upon the intentions of the conspirators. They must intend to agree to commit the offence. It is not necessary for all of the conspirators to participate in the commission of the actual offence, provided that it is intended that at least one of them will do so. There does not have to be an intention on the part of each conspirator that the offence should be committed: it is sufficient that there was knowledge that the course of conduct would amount to the commission of an offence and intention to play some part in the conduct in furtherance of that offence (*R* v *Anderson* [1986] AC 27). However, in *Yip Chiu-Cheung* v *R* [1995] 1 AC 111, the Privy Council held that the crime of conspiracy requires an agreement between two or more persons to commit an unlawful act with the intention of carrying it out, even if this was a conditional intent, i.e. only to do so in certain circumstances.

In the leading case of *Saik,* the House of Lords clarified that the parties must intend every element of the principal offence, even if the offence itself could be satisfied by a mental state short of intention.

KEY CASE

R v *Saik* [2006] UKHL 18
Concerning: mens rea *of conspiracy*

Facts

The appellant ran a Bureau de Change whose income had increased from £1,000 a month to £8 million a year. Undercover police operations discovered that the appellant was undertaking financial transactions in parked cars rather than in his business premises and he was charged with conspiracy to launder the proceeds of crime. It was accepted that the appellant only suspected that the money was the proceeds of crime – he did not know for sure that this was the case. A suspicion that money is the proceeds of crime is enough to establish liability for the substantive offence but the question for the House of Lords was whether such suspicion would be sufficient to give rise to a conviction for conspiracy.

Legal principle

The House of Lords allowed the appeal and quashed the conviction, confirming that the *mens rea* for conspiracy required that the defendant must have the intention or knowledge in relation to every element of the planned offence. In this case, a conviction would be possible only if the appellant had known that the money was the proceeds of crime; a suspicion that it might be the proceeds of crime would not suffice.

■ Assisting/encouraging

The three offences of assisting or encouraging an offence were introduced by sections 44–46 of the Serious Crime Act 2007. These offences are based upon the recommendations of the Law Commission Report No. 300 *Inchoate Liability for Assisting and Encouraging Crime* (2006) and replace the common law offence of incitement which, according to the

Law Commission Report, was unclear in scope and application, particularly in relation to the *mens rea,* as a result of a series of contradictory Court of Appeal decisions.

In particular, there was concern that there was a gap in the law because a person who provided assistance but not encouragement would not be liable for any offence if the principal did not go on to commit the offence. If the principal committed the offence, the person who provided assistance would be liable as a secondary party for **aiding** and **abetting** the offence (see Chapter 5); and, if the offence was not committed but the person who provided assistance had also encouraged the principal to commit the offence, then he would be liable for inciting the offence, even if it was not committed. However, there was no offence that covered the situation in which assistance but not encouragement was provided in relation to an offence that was never committed.

This can be quite tricky to grasp, so let us look at a factual example. Imagine that Ron wants to kill his wife, Agatha. He expresses his wish to Harold, who wordlessly passes him a gun. Harold does so thinking that Ron will never have the nerve to go through with the killing and, in fact, he is correct, as Ron makes no attempt to kill Agatha. What liability can Harold face? He did nothing to encourage the commission of the offence, other than providing the means by which it could be committed (which would not be sufficient to give rise to liability for inciting the offence); there was no agreement between Ron and Harold that the offence would be committed, so he cannot be liable for conspiracy to commit murder; and he cannot be liable as an **accessory** to murder as the killing did not take place.

 Make your answer stand out

Make sure that you understand what was wrong with the previous law of incitement as you will then be in a position to evaluate whether the new provisions have addressed the problems and closed the gap that was believed to exist. It might be useful to read Chapter 3 of the Law Commission Report No. 300, as this provides a good overview of the weaknesses of incitement.

The three offences

The three offences created to replace the common law offence of incitement are:

- intentionally encouraging or assisting an offence (s. 44);
- encouraging or assisting an offence believing that it will be committed (s. 45); and
- encouraging or assisting offences believing that one or more will be committed (s. 46).

It is useful to compare the *actus reus* and *mens rea* of the three offences (see Figure 4.2) as this demonstrates the scope of each offence. The *actus reus* of section 44 and section 45 is the same, as both require an act that encourages or assists an offence. There is no requirement that the offence that is assisted or encouraged is ever committed. Remember,

Figure 4.2

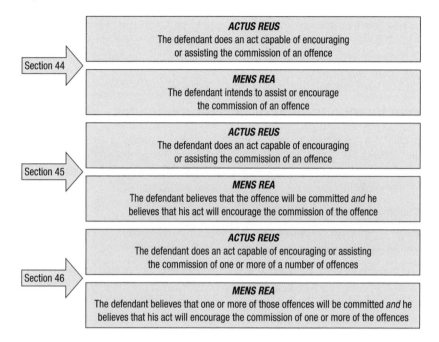

this is an inchoate (incomplete) offence: it exists to penalise the steps leading up to the commission of a complete offence.

The difference lies in the *mens rea* of the two offences. Section 44 requires an intention to encourage or assist the commission of an offence. In other words, to be liable under section 44, the defendant must provide encouragement or assistance with the purpose of causing an offence to be committed: the offence is one of direct intent and it excludes oblique intent (see Chapter 3). Section 44(2) makes it clear that it is not enough that the defendant foresees that his actions will encourage or assist: he must want the offence to occur. By contrast, the *mens rea* of section 45 covers two beliefs, both of which must be established:

1. A belief that the act will assist or encourage.
2. A belief that an offence will be committed.

The third offence is also based upon belief but differs from section 45 in terms of how specific the defendant's beliefs are regarding the outcome of his assistance or encouragement.

Section 46 covers situations in which the defendant believes his assistance or encouragement will facilitate one or more of a range of offences whereas section 45 covers the situation in which the defendant has only one offence in mind that he believes will be assisted or encouraged by his act.

For example, if Luke lends John a knife, believing that John is going to use the knife to break into Abigail's house so that he can defecate on her bed, then this is covered by section 45. However, if Luke knows that John is furious with Abigail and believes that he will either use the knife to break into her house, to scratch the paintwork of her car or to stab her, then the situation falls under section 46 and each of the possible offences must be stipulated in the charge.

Defences to encouraging or assisting offences

Section 50 creates a defence of reasonableness that will allow a person to avoid liability if they either knew (s. 50(1)) or believed (s. 50(2)) that circumstances existed that made it reasonable for them to act as they did. Section 50(3) lists factors that are to be considered when determining whether it was reasonable for a person to act as he did:

■ the seriousness of the anticipated offence or offences;

■ the purpose for which the defendant claims to have been acting; and

■ any authority by which he claims to be acting.

Following on from the example used above, if Luke realises that John is going to take the knife and stab Abigail, he may persuade John to slash the tyres of her car instead. He may then seek to rely on the defence of reasonableness on the basis that he encouraged the lesser offence in order to prevent a more serious offence and with the purpose of preventing injury to Abigail.

Of course, it may be that the courts would not accept that this situation fell within the defence of reasonableness: it is a matter of waiting for cases based upon the new law to reach the appellate courts so that insight into their operation can be gained.

The Explanatory Notes that accompany the legislation make it clear that these are factors that the court could consider when determining whether a person's acts were reasonable, but the list is not exhaustive so it is open to the defendant to raise other issues.

 Make your answer stand out

It is often the case that essay questions ask whether a new piece of legislation has been effective. This sort of question requires knowledge of the perceived defects of the old law as well as an ability to engage in critical evaluation of the new law. An excellent article to read that will help you to prepare for such a question is Ormerod and Fortson (2009) as it outlines the old and new laws and presents an argument that the new offences are too complex, too broad and were unnecessary.

■ Putting it all together

Answer guidelines

See the problem question at the start of the chapter. A diagram illustrating how to structure your answer is available on the companion website.

Approaching the question

This question covers all three inchoate offences so presents quite a test of knowledge of this topic. In this respect, it may not represent a typical problem question as these tend to combine liability for inchoate offences with substantive offences. This question has grouped the inchoate offences together in order to provide an illustration of how each of them should be tackled. This approach will be effective irrespective of whether the inchoate offences are grouped together in a single question, as they are in this example, or whether you encounter individual inchoate offences in a question concerning substantive offences. You might find that you are able to spot inchoate offences more easily if you think about how each of them is characterised: look for facts that indicate (1) the parties have agreed that they will commit an offence (conspiracy), (2) one party suggests the commission of an offence to others (assisting/encouraging) and (3) the parties started to commit an offence but did not complete it (attempt).

Important points to include

- The key to success is to be methodical and to untangle the facts into a series of straightforward issues. Take each party separately and work through the facts chronologically to identify the issues that need to be addressed in your answer.

- Albert: expresses his wish that Victor would die. Bernard and Charles act upon this. Albert has no further involvement so his only possible liability could be for assisting or encouraging murder but has he done enough to satisfy the requirements of the offence?

- Bernard: agrees with Charles that they should kill Victor so has potential liability for conspiracy to commit murder. A good answer would consider whether there is any possibility that Bernard and Charles are excluded parties who cannot be liable for conspiring with each other.

- Charles: waits for Victor with an axe but gives up and goes home. The planned murder has not been carried out so your answer will need to consider whether Charles has gone far enough to be liable for attempted murder. The key question here will be whether waiting for Victor with an axe was part of the planning of the offence or whether it crossed over into an act that could be said to be 'more than merely preparatory'.

▶

Make your answer stand out

Students do not always tackle inchoate offences effectively. It is often the case that the inchoate offence is not spotted and there is no discussion of it whatsoever. When these offences are discussed, it is often in far less detail than substantive offences. Make sure that you are equipped to deal with each of the inchoate offences so that you do not fall into the trap of missing them or dealing with them at an extremely superficial level:

■ *Intentionally* doing an act *knowing* that it is capable of assisting the principal.

■ Doing the act with the *intention* of *assisting/encouraging* the principal.

■ Doing the act *in contemplation of the commission* of the substantive offence.

READ TO IMPRESS

Child, J. (2012) Exploring the *Mens Rea* Requirements of the Serious Crime Act 2007 Assisting and Encouraging Offences. *Journal of Criminal Law,* vol. 76: pp. 220–231.

Ormerod, D. (2006) Making Sense of *Mens Rea* in Statutory Conspiracies. *Current Legal Problems,* vol. 59: pp. 185–230.

Ormerod, D. and Fortson, R. (2009) Serious Crime Act 2007: The Part 2 Offences. *Criminal Law Review,* 389.

Child, J. (2014) The Structure, Coherence and Limits of Inchoate Liability: The new ulterior element. *Legal Studies,* vol. 34: pp. 537–559.

www.pearsoned.co.uk/lawexpress

 Go online to access more revision support, including quizzes to test your knowledge, sample questions with answer guidelines, podcasts you can download and more!

Accessorial liability

Revision checklist

Essential points you should know:

- [ ] The distinction between joint principals and principal/accessories
- [ ] The meaning of 'aid, abet, counsel and procure'
- [ ] The intention and knowledge required by an accessory
- [ ] The steps needed for effective withdrawal
- [ ] The consequences of departure from a common plan

■ Topic map

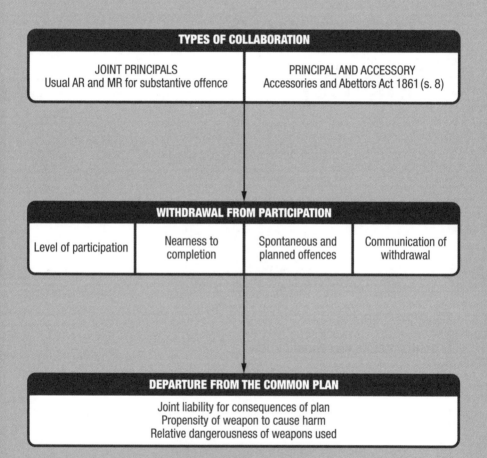

■ Introduction

Not everyone involved in the commission of a crime plays an active part in the *actus reus*.

Accessorial liability recognises the contribution of 'behind the scenes' assistance, such as provision of weapons, advice or moral support, and penalises those who play an indirect role in the complete offence.

It is important to be able to establish liability of those who play a peripheral part in the commission of an offence and to understand how and why the law imposes liability on these 'supporting actors'.

ASSESSMENT ADVICE

Essay questions

Accessorial liability is a relatively unsettled area of law and thus a fertile area for essay questions. Despite this, such questions are not common, possibly due to the complexity of the issues raised by the case law. Pay particular attention to recent developments to ensure that you are well prepared to provide an up-to-date account of the law in an essay.

Problem questions

Problems involving accessories are easily identified as they involve more than one defendant. Accessorial liability can combine with any substantive offence, making it a dangerous omission from revision that could seriously limit the number of questions you could answer in an exam.

■ Sample question

Could you answer this question? Below is a typical problem question that could arise on this topic. Guidelines on answering the question are included at the end of this chapter, whilst a sample essay question and guidance on tackling it can be found on the companion website.

PROBLEM QUESTION

Adam finds out that Vernon has been embezzling money from their company. He tells Bernard, who lends Adam a knife to 'sort him out'. Adam shows the knife to Callum and Derek, both of whom agree to accompany Adam to confront Vernon. Adam and Callum meet as agreed but Derek lost his nerve and failed to turn up. Bernard left a message for Adam saying, 'I want my knife back straight away'. Adam and Callum confront Vernon, who laughs. Enraged, Adam takes out a gun and shoots Vernon, killing him outright.

Discuss the liability of the parties.

■ Types of collaboration

When two (or more) parties embark on a criminal enterprise, their liability will depend upon the extent of their involvement with the *actus reus* of the main offence (see Figure 5.1).

The situation is more straightforward when the parties are joint principals as both must have the *actus reus* and *mens rea* of the offence in question. Accessorial liability is based upon the assistance provided to the principal, which may take a variety of different forms. For example, Arnold assisted by providing a gun, but others may have helped Ben commit the

Figure 5.1

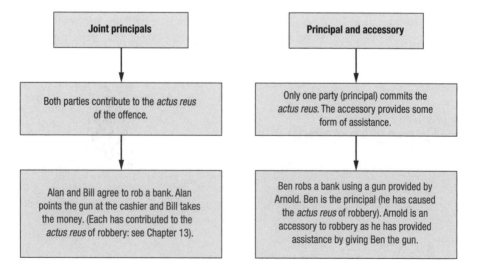

robbery: Conrad drove the getaway car, David kept lookout and Eric attacked the security guard. All these activities may give rise to accessorial liability.

! **Don't be tempted to . . .**

Avoid this topic because of its complexity – it could combine with any of the offences in a problem question. Students do sometimes struggle with accessorial liability. There are so many different ways that one person could assist another to commit an offence and the line between joint principals and principal/accessory is not always clear. A further complication occurs if the liability of the principal and accessory do not match or if the principal is acquitted and the accessory remains liable, something that we will consider now.

■ The principal is acquitted but the accessory remains liable

The principal has a defence. In *Bourne* (1952) 36 Cr App R 125 (CA), the defendant was convicted as accessory to buggery after forcing his wife to have intercourse with a dog. She was acquitted by virtue of duress (Chapter 18).

The principal lacks *mens rea*. In *DPP* v *K and B* [1997] 1 Cr App R 36 (DC), the defendants (girls of 14 and 11) encouraged the principal to have intercourse with the victim, a 14-year-old girl they had been holding captive by threats. They were convicted as accessories to rape, despite failure to establish that the principal (who had not been identified or traced) had the *mens rea* of the rape (he may have been unaware that the victim was not consenting). He committed the *actus reus* (non-consensual intercourse) which was sufficient to found accessorial liability. This also demonstrates that a person can be an accessory to an offence that he or she cannot commit as principal (both defendants were female – rape can only be committed by a male).

■ Principal and accessory are liable for different offences

This may arise if offences have the same *actus reus* but different *mens rea,* e.g. Offences Against the Person Act 1861, sections 18 and 20 (see Chapter 9). Alternatively, the principal may have a defence that reduces his liability such as the reduction of murder to manslaughter by virtue of diminished responsibility (see Chapter 7).

■ Accessorial liability

Accessories and Abettors Act 1861, section 8

Whoever shall aid, abet, counsel or procure the commission of any indictable offence . . . shall be liable to be tried, indicted and punished as a principal offender.

Magistrates' Courts Act 1980, section 44

Comparable provision for summary offences.

Four *actus reus* elements	Three *mens rea* elements
Aid	Intention to do an act with knowledge that
or	it will assist the principal
Abet	and
or	Intention to assist the principal
Counsel	and
or	Knowledge of the circumstances surrounding the offence
Procure	

Actus reus elements

Aid, abet, counsel and procure

KEY DEFINITIONS: Aiding, abetting, counselling, procuring

In *Attorney-General's Reference (No. 1 of 1975)* [1975] QB 773 (CA), Lord Widgery stated that each word must have a different meaning otherwise Parliament would not have used four different words.

This prompted a search for distinctions in the meaning between the words with the classic statement being from Smith and Hogan (Smith, J.C. (2002) *Smith and Hogan Criminal Law,* 10th edition. London: Butterworths, pp. 145–6):

Procuring implies causation not consensus.

Abetting and counselling imply consensus not causation.

Aiding requires actual assistance but neither consensus nor causation.

Make your answer stand out

Smith and Hogan's approach received judicial approval in *Attorney-General* v *Able* [1984] QB 795 (DC). It was also stated in *Bryce* [2004] 2 Cr App R 35 (CA) that there were shades of difference between aid, abet, counsel and procure but that all required 'some form of causal connection' between the assistance and the offence. The Court of Appeal in *Bryce* recommended that accessories should be charged using a 'catch-all' composite phrase (aid, abet, counsel or procure) to avoid acquittals, based upon the difference of meaning between the words.

This difference of opinion is unresolved. In problem questions, it should suffice to identify the nature of the assistance provided by the accessory and adopt the *Bryce* recommendation of a composite phrase.

An essay question might pick up on this uncertainty, so a sound understanding of the definitional debate and the departure from the accepted position in *Bryce* would be needed. It would be useful to read a case comment on *Bryce* as a means of understanding its implications in preparation for essay writing (Rees and Ashworth, 2004).

Mens rea elements

The *mens rea* of accessorial liability is a combination of intention and knowledge. It was summed up in *Bryce* as having three elements (see Figure 5.2).

The first two of these requirements are summed up in the following quotation from *Bryce*:

> An intention to assist (and not to hinder or obstruct) [the principal] in acts which [the accessory] knows are steps taken by [the principal] towards the commission of the offence.

Figure 5.2

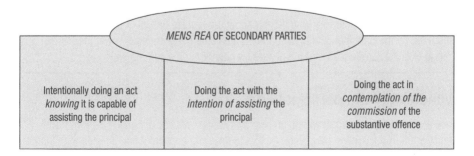

MENS REA OF SECONDARY PARTIES		
Intentionally doing an act *knowing* it is capable of assisting the principal	Doing the act with the *intention of assisting* the principal	Doing the act in *contemplation of the commission* of the substantive offence

Contemplation of the offence

An accessory need not know precisely what the principal intends. However, he must have some knowledge of the criminal purpose of the principal.

> **KEY CASE**
>
> ### *R* v *Bainbridge* [1960] 1 QB 129 (CA)
>
> *Concerning: accessories, knowledge*
>
> **Facts**
>
> The defendant supplied some cutting equipment suspecting it would be used for illegal purposes. He argued that he did not know the specifics of the offence, i.e. the precise location and timing of the offence.
>
> **Legal principle**
>
> It was held that knowledge that the cutting equipment was going to be used for a particular type of offence, i.e. burglary, would suffice to establish the *mens rea* of secondary liability.

The House of Lords approved this approach in *Maxwell* and extended it further.

> **KEY CASE**
>
> ### *Maxwell* v *DPP for Northern Ireland* [1978] 1 WLR 1350 (HL)
>
> *Concerning: accessories, knowledge*
>
> **Facts**
>
> The defendant drove people he knew to be involved in a terrorist organisation to a pub. He was unsure of exactly what they would do there but knew it would involve some sort of terrorist attack. He argued that this was insufficiently precise knowledge to render him liable as an accessory for their crimes arising from the throwing of a pipe bomb into the pub.
>
> **Legal principle**
>
> It was held that an accessory who did not know the precise nature of the offence intended by the principal would, nonetheless, be liable if the principal committed one of a range of possible offences that the accessory had within his contemplation.

Withdrawal from participation

Once assistance has been provided, an accessory can avoid liability only if he withdraws from the enterprise. There are several factors to take into account when considering whether there has been successful withdrawal:

- How much assistance has been provided and can its contribution be neutralised?
- How far has the plan progressed? Are the defendants close to completion of the offence?
- What has the defendant done to communicate his withdrawal to the other parties to the offence?
- Was the offence planned or spontaneous?

Level of participation

The rule is that the more assistance that accessory has provided, the more he must do to withdraw from the criminal enterprise.

✎ EXAM TIP

In a problem question, balance the level of the defendant's involvement against measures he has taken to withdraw, taking into account other characteristics of effective withdrawal (below) to determine whether he has severed himself from the principal's actions.

 Make your answer stand out

In an essay, you may want to discuss whether it is reasonable to distinguish active assistance and passive assistance/advice. In *Whitefield* (1984) 79 Cr App R 36 (CA), the defendant provided information that enabled the burglary to take place: nothing that he said or did, short of informing the authorities, could negate his contribution to the offence. Is it acceptable that those who provide information are more able to detach themselves from liability? Smith's (2001) article on withdrawal from participation provides an interesting discussion of the issues, and incorporation of academic comment will always strengthen the answer to an essay question.

Nearness to completion

The level of participation often will depend on the closeness of the accessory to the completion of the offence. It seems reasonable to say that the nearer the offence is to completion, the harder it will be for the accessory to withdraw. For example, the defendant in *Whitefield* provided advice prior to the commencement of the offence and sought to withdraw before the principal offenders had embarked upon the planned burglary, whereas the defendant in *Becerra* (see next page) was held not to have made an effective withdrawal by fleeing the scene whilst a burglary was in the midst of being committed.

Communication of withdrawal

A defendant may be able to withdraw from participation if he gives 'timely and unequivocal' notice to the other(s) that he is not going to be involved.

KEY CASE

R v *Rook* [1993] 1 WLR 1005 (CA)

Concerning: withdrawal from participation

Facts

The defendant changed his mind about involvement in a plan to kill the wife of a friend. He failed to meet the others, as planned, to commit the offence.

Legal principle

The Court of Appeal held that this would not suffice to absolve the defendant of liability as he had made no attempt to communicate his withdrawal to the other parties. Accordingly, he remained liable (as there is no requirement that a person actually be present at the commission of the crime in order to attract accessorial liability).

Case law also makes it clear that it is not enough for an accessory to inform others that he is not taking part; it must be clear that he is disassociating himself from the enterprise.

KEY CASE

R v *Becerra* [1975] 62 Cr App R 212 (CA)

Concerning: withdrawal from participation

Facts

The defendant provided a knife and went with another to commit a burglary. When they were disturbed, he jumped out of a window. The principal stabbed the householder with the defendant's knife.

Legal principle

Communication of withdrawal must be timely and 'serve unequivocal notice upon the other party that if he proceeds upon it he does so without further aid and assistance of those who withdraw'.

Spontaneous and planned offences

There is less time to communicate withdrawal if an offence occurs spontaneously. In *Mitchell* [1999] Crim LR 496 (CA), it was held that the necessity of communication was waived in relation to spontaneous violence. This was discussed in *Robinson*.

R v *Robinson* [2000] EWCA Crim 8

Concerning: withdrawal of accessories

Facts

The defendant was one of a group involved in an unplanned attack. He struck the first blow but thereafter took little part, ultimately intervening to protect the victim. The issue was whether this amounted to withdrawal.

Legal principle

This situation was characterised as a 'build-up of tension culminating in violence' rather than a truly spontaneous attack (as in *Mitchell*). A defendant who initiated an attack would be able to withdraw only in exceptional circumstances and must give unequivocal communication to others that he was withdrawing.

■ Departure from the common plan

Parties who agree to a criminal enterprise become liable for unplanned offences committed by others during the enterprise. In *Anderson and Morris* [1966] 2 QB 110 (CA), Lord Parker stated:

> Where two persons embark on a joint enterprise, each is liable for the acts done in pursuance of that joint enterprise [and] . . . that includes liability for unusual consequences if they arise from the execution of the agreed joint enterprise.

✎ EXAM TIP

The key to determining each party's liability is to work out the scope of the common plan, i.e. what the parties have agreed to do. With this in mind, consider whether what has actually happened is within this or arose directly from this.

If there is a gap, it may be that one party has departed from the common plan in a way that renders him solely liable for events that occurred.

The courts are reluctant to separate the liability of parties who embark on a criminal enterprise together. The 'liability includes unusual consequences' rule stated in *Anderson and Morris* usually means all parties are equally liable. The exception to this occurs if one party has done something so different from what was agreed that it is unreasonable to hold the others responsible.

R v *Powell; R* v *English* [1999] 1 AC 1 (HL)

Concerning: departure from common plan

Facts

Powell: The defendant went with others to buy drugs, knowing that one of his companions was carrying a gun. The drug-dealer was shot and the defendant was convicted as accessory to murder, as he was aware of the presence of the weapon and thus knew its use was a possibility.

English: The defendant took part in an attack where it was agreed that fencing posts would be used to inflict injury. Another attacker produced a knife and stabbed the victim. The defendant's conviction was quashed, as he was unaware of the presence of the weapon so its use was an unexpected and unforeseeable departure from the plan.

Legal principle

The House of Lords held:

(1) Defendants who realised that another party might kill with the necessary *mens rea* during an agreed offence would be accessories to murder. Knowledge that a companion had a weapon was strong evidence that the accessory had considered the possibility that killing might occur.

(2) There will be no liability as accessory to a killing caused by a weapon that the accessory did not know the principal possessed.

(3) If the accessory knew that the principal had a weapon but the killing was caused by a different weapon of equal dangerousness, accessorial liability for the killing will arise.

The implications of the unexpected production of a weapon were re-examined in *Uddin* [1999] QB 431 (CA) where the questions were reframed in terms of the *propensity of the weapon to cause death* (the plan involved snooker cues but one party unexpectedly produced a knife). It was held in *Greatrex* [1999] 1 Cr App R 126 (CA) that the dangerousness of different weapons should be determined by the jury.

This issue was re-examined by the House of Lords in *R* v *Rahman* [2008] UKHL 45 in a case involving the fatal stabbing of the victim after an attack by a large group of Asian youths including the four appellants. It was accepted that none of the appellants inflicted the knife wound, carried a knife or took an active part in inflicting blows on the victim during the attack that led to his death. Seeking to rely on the principles set out in *Powell* and *English,* the appellants sought to avoid liability as accessories to murder on the basis that they had contemplated, at most, serious bodily harm as the outcome of the joint enterprise and the unforeseen and undisclosed intention to kill possessed by the principal offender (who had not been identified) took the killing outside of the common plan.

Their appeals against conviction were rejected by the Court of Appeal and this decision was upheld by the House of Lords, with Lord Bingham of Cornill approving the questions posed by the trial judge (after omitting one question as too favourable to the appellants) as suitable to be asked in such cases (see Figure 5.3).

Figure 5.3

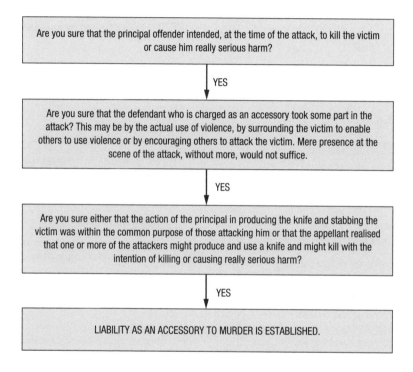

The question that Lord Bingham rejected as being too favourable to the defendants concerned their foresight of the principal's intentions: in essence, this would have opened the door for the appellants to avoid liability on the basis that they did not share or foresee the principal offender's murderous intentions. Lord Bingham stated that this would add a 'highly undesirable level of complexity' to an 'already very complex' area of law (Para. 24). He explained:

> Given the fluid, fast-moving course of events in incidents such as that which culminated in the killing of the deceased . . . it must often be very hard for jurors to make a reliable assessment of what a particular defendant foresaw as likely or possible acts on the part of his associates. It would be even harder, and would border on speculation, to judge what a particular defendant foresaw as the intention with which his associates might perform such acts. It is safer to focus on the defendant's foresight of what an associate might do, an issue to which knowledge of the associate's possession of an obviously lethal weapon such as a gun or a knife would usually be very relevant.

In essence, then, this case confirms that liability for the unplanned consequences of a joint enterprise arises on the basis of what the accessory foresaw the principal might *do* and not on foresight of the state of mind with which the principal might carry out that act. This was followed by the Court of Appeal in *R* v *A, D, C and B* [2010] EWCA Crim 1622.

It follows from this that it is only in circumstances where the common plan does not involve causing death and the accessory does not foresee any possibility that his associate might intentionally set about causing death that liability may be avoided by arguing that the principal did something fundamentally different to that which was agreed by producing an unknown weapon.

There are three possible outcomes if a principal uses a weapon when this was not part of the common plan (see Figure 5.4).

Figure 5.4

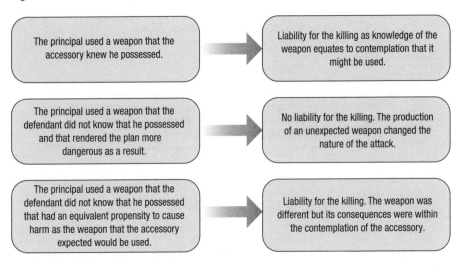

The Supreme Court has held that a defendant could be guilty of murder in circumstances where he was the intended victim of the offence:

KEY CASE

R v *Gnango* [2011] UKSC 59

Concerning: accessorial liability for murder

Facts

The victim was talking to her sister on her mobile phone as she walked through a car park on her way home from work when she was killed by a single shot to the head. The shot came from crossfire between the 17-year-old defendant, Gnango, and another, referred to at the trial as 'Bandana Man', who were engaged in a violent dispute. It was common ground that both Gnango and Bandana Man were shooting at each other. Both the defendant and Bandana Man fled the scene of the killing. Scientific evidence established that the fatal shot had come from Bandana Man's gun and not that of the defendant. The defendant was convicted of murder. On appeal, the Court of Appeal overturned his conviction on the basis that there was no joint enterprise upon which liability for murder could rest. The existence of a joint enterprise was essential to liability. Simple participation in the affray with foresight that the other might kill someone other than the immediate target but without a joint enterprise was not a basis for criminal liability.

On further appeal by the Crown, the Supreme Court was asked to consider the following point of law certified as being of general public importance:

If (1) D1 and D2 voluntarily engage in fighting each other, each intending to kill or cause grievous bodily harm to the other and each foreseeing that the other has the reciprocal intention, and if (2) D1 mistakenly kills V in the course of the fight, in what circumstances, if any, is D2 guilty of the offence of murdering V?

Legal principle

The Supreme Court held (by a 6–1 majority, Lord Kerr dissenting) that either:

■ by a combination of the common law principles relating to aiding and abetting and the common law doctrine of transferred malice, or;

■ as a principal to a joint enterprise to engage in unlawful violence specifically designed to cause death or serious injury from which death had resulted;

■ the defendant's conviction for murder would be restored.

The defendant had aided and abetted the killing through his presence and by shooting at the principal (Bandana Man, who fired the fatal shot) with death or serious injury in his contemplation.

✎ **EXAM TIP**

In a problem question, think about the different weapons and consider whether the weapon used is (a) more, (b) less or (c) equally dangerous, compared to the weapon contemplated.

Make your answer stand out

In an analytical essay, you could question the approach of determining liability of accessories for deaths caused by others. Is relative dangerousness of weapons a useful approach or is it preferable to base liability upon knowledge of the presence of a weapon irrespective of its dangerousness? What happens, for example, if a defendant knows that another party has a gun so has contemplated that someone might be shot but the other party actually uses the gun to bludgeon the victim to death? Given that the gun was used as a blunt instrument, does this make it sufficiently different to absolve the defendant of liability? It is a difficult question.

■ Putting it all together

Answer guidelines

See the problem question at the start of the chapter. A diagram illustrating how to structure your answer is available on the companion website.

Approaching the question

This problem scenario involves a tangled set of facts in which there are four parties – Adam, Bernard, Callum and Derek – each of whom makes a direct or indirect contribution to Vernon's death. In order to deal with this question effectively, you would need to untangle the facts in order to determine what each party has done and consider whether this makes him a principal offender or an accessory. It is useful to work out who has carried out the *actus reus* of the substantive offence as this will enable you to identify the principal offender. From this, you can work out what assistance has been provided. Remember to keep a particular lookout for facts that seem to suggest that a party has tried to withdraw or that there has been a departure from the common plan.

Important points to include

■ Adam has shot and killed Vernon. This is the *actus reus* of murder (see Chapter 6) so Adam is the principal offender. As such, his liability will be determined by reference to the *actus reus* and *mens rea* of murder.

- Bernard gave Adam a knife so that he could 'sort out' Vernon. The provision of a weapon is a form of assistance so consider the *actus reus* and *mens rea* of secondary liability in relation to Bernard. Make sure that you note the potential withdrawal here as Bernard has left a telephone message asking for his knife back. Consider whether this is a timely and unequivocal withdrawal. There is also an issue of departure from the common plan as Adam uses a gun to kill Vernon rather than the knife that he borrowed from Bernard.

- Callum is present at the scene when Adam shoots Vernon. Consider whether this is sufficient to make him liable as an accessory to murder. Callum knows that Adam has a knife but Adam does not use this to kill Vernon. Remember that the general rule is that there is liability for unusual consequences unless the principal has departed from the common plan. As there is the use of a different weapon here, consideration of the principles from leading cases – *Powell, English, Uddin* and *Greatrex* – is needed.

- Derek agreed to accompany Adam and Callum but lost his nerve and failed to show up. The issue here is whether this would amount to a withdrawal from participation. Reference should be made to *Rook*.

 ## Make your answer stand out

Be organised and methodical. These are tangled facts and students often struggle with such questions as they jump straight in to deal with the obvious issues without taking time to identify all the issues. Take time to create order from the chaos. Your marker will be able to follow your answer if you present a clear and structured account. A methodical approach will help you to ensure that you deal with all the issues and do not overlook any key facts.

Make sure that you consider both sides of the argument: for example, make an argument that Bernard has withdrawn from participation and then counter that with an argument that he has not done enough for there to be an effective withdrawal. You can then evaluate the relative strengths of the two positions in order to reach a conclusion. If it is too close to call, your conclusion can be something along the lines of 'it will depend upon whether the jury considers that Bernard's attempts to withdraw amounted to an effective and timely communication'.

The issue of the use of a different weapon from that planned is a complex one that has generated a fair amount of case law. Make sure that you are familiar with each of the key cases and that you can provide a clear and simple statement of the legal principle from each case. Look back at the key case boxes to help you with this.

READ TO IMPRESS

Reed, A. (1996) Joint Participation in Criminal Activity. *Journal of Criminal Law,* 60: 310.

Rees, T. and Ashworth, A. (2004) Aiding and abetting: *Mens Rea* and intention to assist. *Criminal Law Review,* 936.

Smith, K.J.L. (2001) Withdrawal in Complicity: A Restatement of Principles. *Criminal Law Review,* 769.

Sullivan, G.R. (2008) Participating in Crime: Law Com 305 – Joint Criminal Ventures. *Criminal Law Review,* 19.

www.pearsoned.co.uk/lawexpress

Go online to access more revision support, including quizzes to test your knowledge, sample questions with answer guidelines, podcasts you can download and more!

Murder

Revision checklist

Essential points you should know:

☐ The *actus reus* and *mens rea* of murder

☐ The role of causation and omissions

☐ The distinction between implied and express malice

☐ The scope of direct and oblique intention

☐ The relationship between murder and manslaughter

Topic map

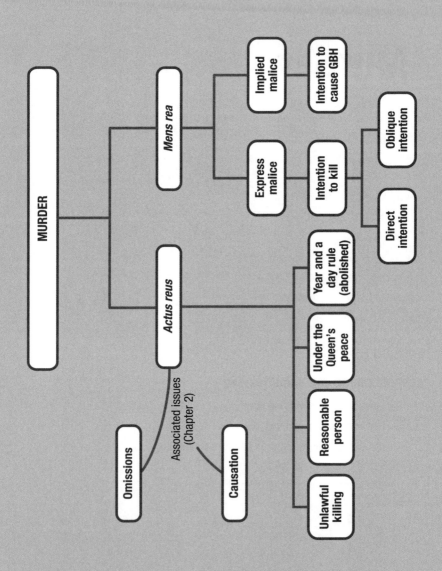

■ Introduction

Murder is the most culpable form of homicide which carries a mandatory life sentence.

It is almost certain to feature on exam papers either as an essay topic or in a problem question (possibly both). It raises little that has not been covered in the chapters on *actus reus* and *mens rea*, so it may be useful to regard this chapter as a consolidation exercise as well as touching upon points specific to murder.

Murder overlaps with voluntary and involuntary manslaughter as all homicide offences share a common *actus reus* (unlawful killing). They differ only in terms of the *mens rea* requirement.

ASSESSMENT ADVICE

Essay questions

Essay questions tend to require engagement with underlying policy issues such as:

- relationship between murder and other homicide offences;
- abolition of the murder/manslaughter distinction;
- introduction of discretion in sentencing;
- removal of the mandatory life sentence.

Problem questions

Problem questions on murder often combine with other topics, particularly voluntary manslaughter (Chapter 7), involuntary manslaughter (Chapter 8) or non-fatal offences (Chapter 9), so these other topics will need thorough revision. Causation, omissions (Chapter 2) and oblique intention (Chapter 3) are common issues.

■ Sample question

Could you answer this question? Below is a typical problem question that could arise on this topic. Guidelines on answering the question are included at the end of this chapter, whilst a sample essay question and guidance on tackling it can be found on the companion website.

PROBLEM QUESTION

Doreen sets fire to her former employer's house. Adam, a fireman, was badly burned in the fire and kills himself a week later. Adam's wife, Deborah, decides to kill Doreen to avenge her husband's death. She shoots Maureen, Doreen's twin sister, by mistake, killing her outright.

Discuss Doreen and Deborah's liability for murder.

Murder

KEY DEFINITION: Murder

Murder is when a man of sound memory, and of the age of discretion, unlawfully killeth within any country of the realm any reasonable creature *in rerum natura* under the King's peace, with malice aforethought, either expressed by the party or implied by law [so as the party wounded, or hurt, die of the wound or hurt within a year and a day of the same].

Coke, 3 Inst. 47

The definition has undergone some modification since its inception in 1797. Of particular note is the abolition of the requirement that the victim's death must occur within one year and a day of the injury inflicted.

Actus reus elements	Two alternative *mens rea* elements
Act/omission	Intention to kill (express malice)
Unlawful killing	Intention to cause GBH (implied malice)
Reasonable person	
Within Queen's peace	

Students often fail to recognise that murder is a common law offence. This means that it has its origin in, and owes its development to, case law rather than statute. It is very common for students to state, incorrectly, that 'murder is an offence under section 1 of the Homicide Act 1957' or 'murder is defined by the Homicide Act 1957'. If you look at the actual wording of the Homicide Act 1957, you will find that very little of it remains in force and it contains no prohibition of murder and no definition of its elements, although it does state the requirement that killing be done with **malice aforethought**. Make sure that you avoid this error, as it is often taken to be a sign of poor preparation for the exam or lack of understanding of the law.

Actus reus of murder

The *actus reus* of murder generally is stated as unlawful killing, but there are other elements to be taken into account (see Figure 6.1). Note the abolition of the year-and-a-day rule.

Figure 6.1

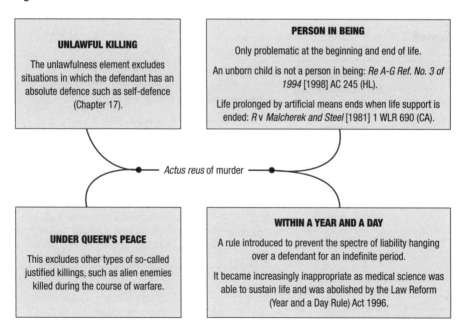

UNLAWFUL KILLING

The unlawfulness element excludes situations in which the defendant has an absolute defence such as self-defence (Chapter 17).

PERSON IN BEING

Only problematic at the beginning and end of life.

An unborn child is not a person in being: *Re A-G Ref. No. 3 of 1994* [1998] AC 245 (HL).

Life prolonged by artificial means ends when life support is ended: *R v Malcherek and Steel* [1981] 1 WLR 690 (CA).

Actus reus of murder

UNDER QUEEN'S PEACE

This excludes other types of so-called justified killings, such as alien enemies killed during the course of warfare.

WITHIN A YEAR AND A DAY

A rule introduced to prevent the spectre of liability hanging over a defendant for an indefinite period.

It became increasingly inappropriate as medical science was able to sustain life and was abolished by the Law Reform (Year and a Day Rule) Act 1996.

📖 **REVISION NOTE**

In addition to these requirements, it is essential that the defendant's act (or, in certain circumstances, omission) caused the victim's death. Causation and omissions are covered in the chapter on *actus reus,* which you may like to revisit to refresh your memory (Chapter 2).

Mens rea of murder

KEY DEFINITION: Malice aforethought

Killing shall not amount to murder unless done with . . . malice aforethought (section 1, Homicide Act 1957). Malice aforethought was defined in *Cunningham* [1982] AC 566 (HL) as intention to kill (express malice) or cause GBH (implied malice).

There are three alternative mental states in relation to murder (see also Figure 6.2):

1. Direct intention to kill (express malice): causing death is the defendant's main aim/purpose.
2. Direct intention to cause GBH (implied malice): causing GBH is the defendant's purpose but death occurs as a result.

Figure 6.2

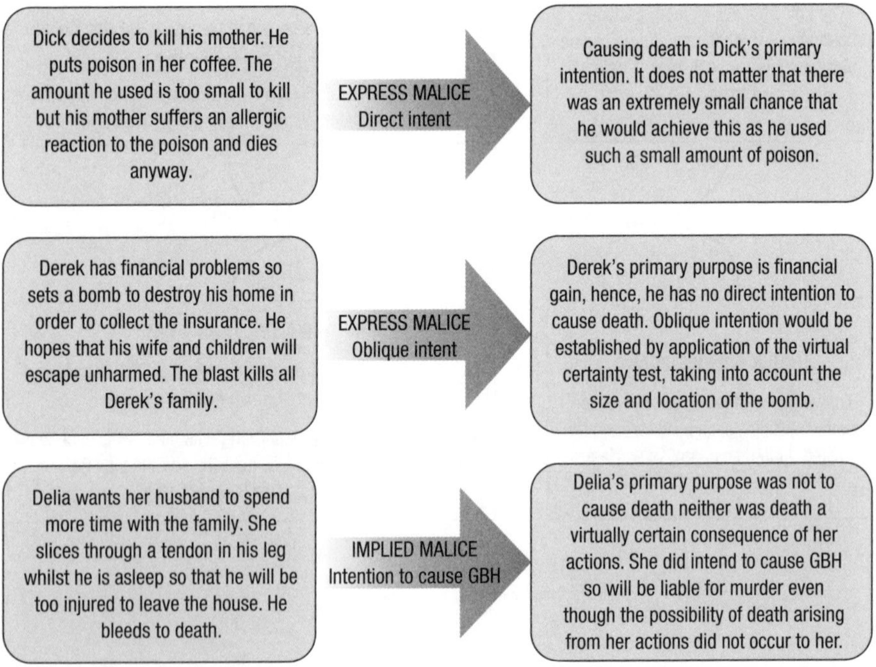

Dick decides to kill his mother. He puts poison in her coffee. The amount he used is too small to kill but his mother suffers an allergic reaction to the poison and dies anyway.

EXPRESS MALICE
Direct intent

Causing death is Dick's primary intention. It does not matter that there was an extremely small chance that he would achieve this as he used such a small amount of poison.

Derek has financial problems so sets a bomb to destroy his home in order to collect the insurance. He hopes that his wife and children will escape unharmed. The blast kills all Derek's family.

EXPRESS MALICE
Oblique intent

Derek's primary purpose is financial gain, hence, he has no direct intention to cause death. Oblique intention would be established by application of the virtual certainty test, taking into account the size and location of the bomb.

Delia wants her husband to spend more time with the family. She slices through a tendon in his leg whilst he is asleep so that he will be too injured to leave the house. He bleeds to death.

IMPLIED MALICE
Intention to cause GBH

Delia's primary purpose was not to cause death neither was death a virtually certain consequence of her actions. She did intend to cause GBH so will be liable for murder even though the possibility of death arising from her actions did not occur to her.

3. Oblique intention to kill or cause GBH: the defendant had some other aim in mind other than causing death or GBH but his actions rendered death or serious injury a virtual certainty and he realised that this was the case.

📖 **REVISION NOTE**

The *mens rea* of murder is broken down further into two types of express malice: direct intention and oblique intention. (These are covered in Chapter 3.) You might like to familiarise yourself with these concepts before moving on, paying particular attention to *Woollin* [1999] 1 AC 82 (HL) (the current test for oblique intention).

Figure 6.3

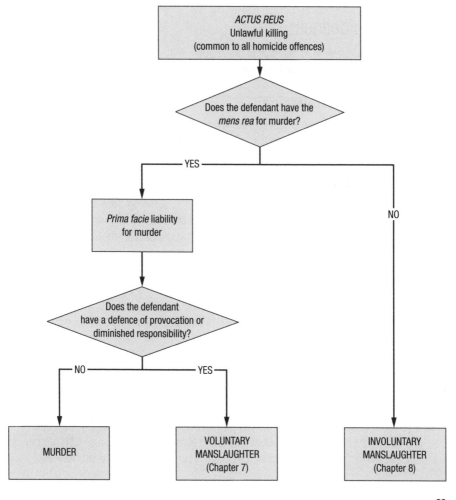

Relationship with manslaughter

All homicide offences have a common *actus reus,* so the distinction between murder and the two forms of manslaughter lies in (a) the availability of partial defences (voluntary manslaughter) and (b) the presence or absence of *mens rea* (involuntary manslaughter). The flow chart (see Figure 6.3) captures the murder/manslaughter relationship.

Putting it all together

Answer guidelines

See the problem question at the start of the chapter. A diagram illustrating how to structure your answer is available on the companion website.

Approaching the question

This question raises a range of issues relevant to murder but, unusually for a problem question dealing with homicide, does not involve any issues of voluntary or involuntary manslaughter. If the question did not limit the scope of the answer to a consideration of murder, it may have been relevant to consider defences that reduced liability to voluntary manslaughter: it would have been possible to argue that Deborah had lost control due to the death of her husband or that she was suffering from an abnormality of mind (diminished responsibility). (These defences are covered in Chapter 7.) For the purposes of this chapter, the answer will focus only on issues relevant to murder.

Important points to include

- Doreen started a fire in which a fireman, Adam, was badly burned. He killed himself the following week. Start by considering the *actus reus* of murder, as there is a tricky causation issue that will involve discussion of whether Adam's suicide is an intervening act that breaks the chain of causation.

- If causation is established, move on to address the *mens rea* of murder. If you concluded that Adam's suicide has broken the chain of causation, then you must conclude that Doreen is not liable for murder and move on to consider Deborah's liability.

- If you are considering Doreen's liability for murder, take care to select the appropriate test of *mens rea* by asking whether Doreen intended to kill or cause GBH when she set fire to the house. It is difficult to reach a conclusion on this point from the information provided so it would be sensible to base liability on oblique intention. This requires that you state the *Woollin* test and apply it to the facts.

■ Deborah's liability for murder is more straightforward. Causation is uncomplicated and it is not difficult to establish that she had a direct intention to cause death, thus establishing the elements of murder. Do not overlook the transferred malice point.

 Make your answer stand out

Do the simple things well. Students often jump straight to the central issues without providing a basic framework for discussion. For example, although the issue of Adam's suicide as a potential intervening act requires discussion, this should follow on from an outline of the elements of murder and take its place in a consideration of legal causation. Failure to define the offence and set out the *actus reus* and *mens rea* is a major weakness that is easily avoided by the use of a methodical problem-solving strategy.

Do not allow instinctive reactions to get in the way of legal reasoning. You may sympathise with Deborah as she has lost her husband in such tragic circumstances but that is irrelevant to whether or not she is liable for murder. Arguments based upon emotional notions of fairness attract little (or no) credit from examiners.

READ TO IMPRESS

Ashworth, A. (2007) Principles, Pragmatism and the Law Commission's Recommendations on Homicide Law. *Criminal Law Review*, 333.

www.pearsoned.co.uk/lawexpress

 Go online to access more revision support, including quizzes to test your knowledge, sample questions with answer guidelines, podcasts you can download and more!

Voluntary manslaughter

7

Revision checklist

Essential points you should know:

☐ The relationship between murder and voluntary manslaughter

☐ The circumstances in which a defendant can rely upon diminished responsibility

☐ The nature and operation of the defence of loss of control

☐ The difference between loss of control and the old defence of provocation that it replaced

☐ The rationale for the changes introduced to these defences by the Coroners and Justice Act 2009

Topic map

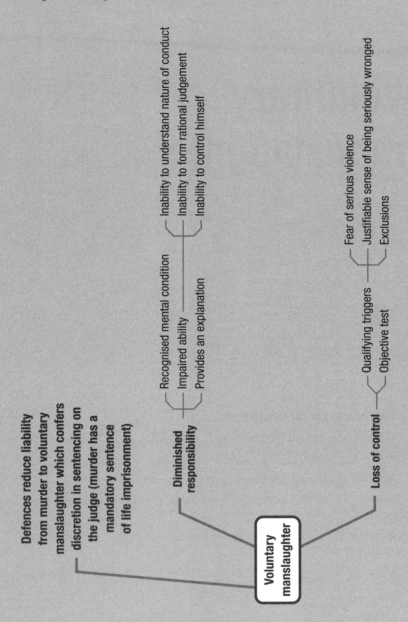

Voluntary manslaughter

Defences reduce liability from murder to voluntary manslaughter which confers discretion in sentencing on the judge (murder has a mandatory sentence of life imprisonment)

Diminished responsibility
- Recognised mental condition
- Impaired ability
  - Inability to understand nature of conduct
  - Inability to form rational judgement
  - Inability to control himself
- Provides an explanation

Loss of control
- Qualifying triggers
  - Fear of serious violence
  - Justifiable sense of being seriously wronged
  - Exclusions
- Objective test

A printable version of this topic map is available from **www.pearsoned.co.uk/lawexpress**

◼ Introduction

Not all killings that fall within the scope of murder are regarded as equally culpable, yet the mandatory penalty of life imprisonment will apply to them all unless one of the partial defences is available.

The Homicide Act 1957 contained three defences that operated to reduce liability from murder to voluntary manslaughter, giving the judge discretion in sentencing as a reflection of the lower level of culpability attached to certain killings. These forms of manslaughter are described as voluntary because the defendant had the *mens rea* for murder as opposed to involuntary manslaughter, discussed in the next chapter, where the defendant did not have the necessary *mens rea* for murder.

This chapter focuses on diminished responsibility and loss of control, which replaced the defence of provocation from 4 October 2010. The third defence, suicide pacts, are not covered in this chapter, as they do not feature often on the syllabus, occur rarely in practice and do not raise any contentious issues.

ASSESSMENT ADVICE

Essay questions

Essay questions on voluntary manslaughter are likely to be popular following the changes introduced by the Coroners and Justice Act 2009. Make sure that you are aware of how the law was prior to these changes, what the perceived problems with the law were and how the new provisions have changed the defences. This should provide you with a good basis upon which to engage in a critical assessment of the effectiveness of the new law in an essay question.

Problem questions

Problem questions featuring provocation and diminished responsibility were always very popular with examiners, but this may not be the case with the new defence of loss of control and the modified defence of diminished responsibility – at least for a few years after the new statutory provisions have been introduced, as there will be a lack of case law to act as a guide in the operation of the new law. However, some examiners will still include this area and expect students to apply the statutory provisions to the facts without the aid of case law, so it would still be worth ensuring that you were prepared for a problem question on this topic.

Sample question

Could you answer this question? Below is a typical essay question that could arise on this topic. Guidelines for answering this question are included at the end of this chapter. Another sample question and guidance on tackling it can be found on the companion website.

ESSAY QUESTION

'The demise of the defence of provocation is not to be mourned because the defence has been resurrected, albeit with minor modifications, in the guise of loss of control. The name is different but the essential nature of the defence is the same.'

Discuss this comment, explaining whether or not you agree with the view expressed.

Diminished responsibility

The defence of diminished responsibility recognises that it is less culpable to kill when the mind is disturbed than it is to kill when the mind is operating normally. The essence of this defence is that some form of transient disruption to the defendant's mental state has rendered the defendant less blameworthy than otherwise would be the case.

The law on diminished responsibility can be found in section 2 of the Homicide Act 1957 as substituted by section 52 of the Coroners and Justice Act 2009, which came into force on 4 October 2010.

KEY STATUTE

Homicide Act 1957, section 2 (as substituted by Coroners and Justice Act 2009, section 52)

(1) A person ('D') who kills or is a party to the killing of another is not to be convicted of murder if D was suffering from an abnormality of mental functioning which –

    (a) arose from a recognised medical condition,

    (b) substantially impaired D's ability to do one or more of the things mentioned in subsection (1A), and

    (c) provides an explanation for D's acts and omissions in doing or being a party to the killing.

The newly created section 2(1A) specifies that the reference made to impairment in section 2(1)(b) refers to the ability of the defendant:

(a)   to understand the nature of his conduct;

(b)   to form a rational judgement; or

(c)   to exercise self-control.

There is further elaboration in the new section 2(1B) that explains that 'an abnormality of mental functioning provides an explanation for D's conduct if it causes, or is a significant contributory factor in causing, D to carry out that conduct'.

The following table provides a quick reference guide to the differences between the old and new definition of diminished responsibility. Each of the significant changes will be discussed in greater detail in the sections that follow.

Old law	New law	Comment
Where a person kills or is party to the killing of another, he shall not be convicted of murder	A person (D) who kills or is party to the killing of another is not to be convicted of murder	No significant difference here. These words just introduce the defence and specify its application to murder only.
if he was suffering from such abnormality of mind	if D was suffering from an abnormality of mental functioning	Notice the change in wording here. The Explanatory Notes that accompany that Act state that this is just a modernisation of terminology.
(whether arising from a condition of arrested or retarded development of mind of any inherent causes or induced by disease or injury)	which (a) arose from a recognised medical condition;	The new law is narrower as it only permits reliance on diminished responsibility if D's abnormality of mental functioning arose from a recognised medical condition. Lord Bach, introducing the Second Reading of the Bill, stated that expert evidence will be crucial in establishing whether diminished responsibility is established.

Old law	New law	Comment
as substantially impairs his mental responsibility for his acts and omissions in doing . . . the killing	(b) substantially impaired D's ability to do one or more of the things mentioned in subsection (1A), namely, to understand the nature of his conduct, to form a rational judgement or to exercise self-control;	The old law required that D's responsibility for his actions was impaired. This was quite vague and general, whereas the new law specifies which of D's capabilities must be impaired: his understanding of his actions or his ability to exercise judgement or self-control. It is likely that this will reduce the scope of the defence, excluding some situations that would have fallen within the old definition.
	and (c) provides an explanation for D's acts and omissions in doing or being party to the killing in the section that, according to section 2(1B), it causes or makes a significant contribution to D's conduct.	This provision has no parallel under the old law so, as with the previous elements of the defence, narrows its availability. Not only must the defendant have a recognisable mental condition that has a specific effect on his understanding, reasoning or control, this must also be at least a significant factor in the killing that has occurred.

Recognised medical condition

The requirement that diminished responsibility is based upon a recognised medical condition was based upon the response of the Royal College of Psychiatrists to the Law Commission consultation on proposals to change the law of homicide. The Royal College of Psychiatrists sought a defence of diminished responsibility 'grounded in valid medical diagnosis', preferably by reference to one of the two accepted classification systems of mental conditions (Law Com. No. 304, Para. 5.114). This would lead to greater concordance between the law and the medical profession, thus avoiding the strange situation that has arisen with regard to the disparity of meaning of insanity that exists in law and medicine (see Chapter 15).

It was not clear initially whether conditions such as alcohol and drug dependency will fall within the meaning of a recognised medical condition but the issue has now been considered by the courts. In *R* v *Dowds* [2012] EWCA Crim 281, the Court of Appeal refused to accept that extreme intoxication was a recognised medical condition for the purposes of diminished responsibility, even though the World Health Organization categorisation includes this in the International Classification of Diseases. Hughes LJ stated that 'the presence of a recognised medical condition is a necessary, but not always a sufficient, condition to raise diminished responsibility'. He further stated that the reformulation of the defence should not change the established position that intoxication, by alcohol or other substance, is not the basis for a defence of diminished responsibility.

It is also possible that difficulties may arise in relation to defendants who are in the early stages of developing a recognised medical condition, particularly if there is some difference of opinion between medical experts on the issue. As with other issues arising from the modified definition of diminished responsibility, these points will be resolved only once cases reach the appellate courts.

Impaired ability

Section 2(1A) of the Homicide Act 1957 (as amended) specifies what sorts of impairment must arise from the defendant's medically recognised disorder in order for his situation to fall within the scope of diminished responsibility.

Inability to understand the nature of his conduct

This category covers situations in which the defendant has a mental impairment that affects his ability to understand the nature of his conduct. It is likely that this covers an inability to understand that his acts or omissions could have fatal consequences, as well as a fundamental inability to comprehend the nature of death. The example given by the Law Commission (Law Com. No. 304, Para. 5.121) concerns a young child who has spent a protracted period of his short life playing violent computer games without adult supervision. He kills another child in anger when they interrupt his game but it is clear that he expected the dead child to come back to life like the characters in a computer game. Here, the child understands that he has caused death but does not understand that the nature of death is irreversible.

Inability to form rational judgement

This category focuses on the reasoning processes underlying the defendant's actions and their ability to engage in logical decision making. The examples given in Law Com. No. 304 (at Para. 5.121) are:

- An abused wife suffering from post-traumatic stress disorder who kills her abusive husband in the belief that only his death will rid the world of his sins.

- A mentally subnormal boy who obeys his older brother's order to kill someone as he cannot comprehend that his brother would tell him to do something wrong.

- A depressed husband who, after years of caring for his terminally ill wife, finally gives in to her repeated requests that he kill her to end her suffering because the requests dominate his thoughts.

Remember, though, that these are only examples given by the Law Commission and that it may be that the courts will reach different decisions about the sorts of situations that amount to an inability to form rational judgement. It will be particularly interesting to see how case law develops in relation to battered women who kill and people who kill their terminally ill spouses, as these were issues that received a great deal of attention during the passage of this legislation.

Inability to control himself

It is interesting that diminished responsibility now explicitly covers the defendant's inability to control his actions. The similar concept of a 'sudden and temporary loss of self-control' was part of the now abolished defence of provocation. However, even though the old section 2 did not explicitly refer to a lack of control, case law did bring the inability to control one's actions within the defence. For example, in *R* v *Byrne* [1960] 2 QB 396, the Court of Appeal quashed the murder conviction of a sexual psychopath who had strangled and mutilated his victims as a result of his uncontrollable perverted sexual desires. It was held that diminished responsibility could cover situations in which a defendant suffered from uncontrollable urges.

The example given in Law Com. No. 304 is of a man who believes that he is controlled by the devil who implants within him a desire to kill that he has to act upon. This is an interesting example, as Peter Sutcliffe, the so-called Yorkshire Ripper, who murdered 13 women in the 1970s and claimed that voices from God told him to kill prostitutes, was denied a defence of diminished responsibility at his trial in 1981. It may be that the amended definition of diminished responsibility would now provide a partial defence in such situations but, again, it will not be until cases reach the courts that the ambit of the provisions of the defence will become clear.

Provides an explanation

The final element of the defence requires that there is a causal link between the defendant's abnormality of mental functioning and the acts or omissions that caused death. In other words, it is not enough that the defendant has killed and suffers from a mental impairment: he must kill *because* he has a mental impairment. As such, the defendant's mental impairment will provide an explanation for the killing that justifies the decision to grant him a partial defence and treat the killing as one that is less blameworthy than murder.

It is important to note that the mental impairment must either cause or make a significant contribution to the defendant's acts or omissions. This may leave scope for the defence to operate in conjunction with some other causal factor. This would mirror the position under the old law that was recognised by the House of Lords in *Dietschmann.*

KEY CASE

R v *Dietschmann* [2003] 1 AC 1209 (HL)

Concerning: intoxication, multiple causes of abnormality of mind

Facts

The defendant killed whilst heavily intoxicated and suffering from an adjustment disorder (depressed grief reaction following bereavement) that amounted to an abnormality of mind. The trial judge directed the jury that diminished responsibility was available only if the defendant would have killed even if he had not taken a drink; in other words, only if the adjustment disorder was the sole cause would he be able to rely on the defence.

Legal principle

The House of Lords looked at the requirements of section 2(1) prior to the amendments made by the Coroners and Justice Act 2009 and concluded that there was no requirement that the abnormality of mind was the sole cause of the killing. Even if the defendant would not have killed if he had been sober, the contribution of the alcohol did not necessarily prevent the abnormality of mind from substantially impairing his mental responsibility and giving rise to diminished responsibility.

■ Loss of control

Loss of control is a defence to murder that was introduced by sections 54 and 55 of the Coroners and Justice Act 2009. It replaces the defence of provocation that was previously to be found in section 3 of the Homicide Act 1957 and that was abolished by section 56(1) of the 2009 Act with effect from 4 October 2010. If successful, loss of control will reduce the defendant's liability from murder to manslaughter: section 54(7).

KEY STATUTE

Coroners and Justice Act 2009, section 54

(1) Where a person ('D') kills or is party to a killing of another ('V'), D is not to be convicted of murder if –

  (a) D's acts and omissions in doing or being a party to the killing resulted from D's loss of self-control,

  (b) the loss of self-control had a qualifying trigger, and

  (c) a person of D's sex and age, with a normal degree of tolerance and self-restraint and in the circumstances of D, might have reacted in the same or in a similar way to D.

In essence, section 54 replicates the two-stage nature of the old test of provocation in that first it asks a subjective question – did the defendant lose control – and, second, it weighs the defendant's actions against an objective benchmark that provides a measure of the self-control that is expected of members of society. As with the old law of provocation, the second limb of the loss of control defence is not purely objective but takes into account some characteristics of the defendant and the situation in which he found himself when the loss of control occurred.

These elements of the defence will be examined in greater detail in the sections that follow. However, before looking in detail at the structure, content and scope of loss of control, it will be useful to compare the old and the new defences to determine the extent to which they differ.

! Don't be tempted to . . .

Borrow principles from the old defence of provocation. The Court of Appeal made it clear in *R* v *Clinton, Parker and Evans* [2012] EWCA Crim 2 (discussed in detail later in this chapter) that loss of control operates under an entirely new statutory regime and that no guidance on its operation can be taken from prior case law. The old law is included here for comparative purposes only so that you can consider whether the current law is an improvement. You should not assume that legal principles from provocation cases will automatically apply to loss of control.

At first glance, the old defence of provocation and its replacement, the defence of loss of control, appear similar but there are some significant differences in the two defences that were introduced in order to overcome weaknesses associated with the defence of provocation (see Figure 7.1).

Figure 7.1

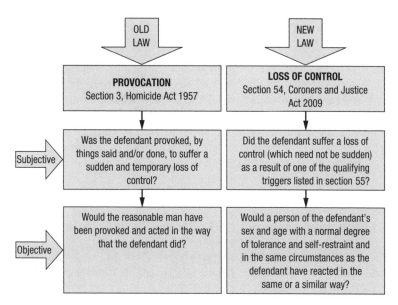

Loss of control – a comparison with provocation

One of the most obvious differences in the wording of the two defences is that provocation
required a 'sudden and temporary loss of self-control' (*Duffy* [1949] 1 All ER 932) whereas
the definition in section 54(1) refers only to 'loss of self-control' and section 54(2) makes it
clear that the requirement for this to be sudden has been abandoned.

KEY STATUTE

Coroners and Justice Act 2009, section 54(2)

For the purposes of subsection (1)(a), it does not matter whether or not the loss of control
was sudden.

The requirement of the old law that the loss of self-control must be sudden was based upon the nature of the defence in that it was developed to take account of killings that took place 'in the heat of the moment' rather than those that occurred some time after the provocation had occurred.

This caused particular problems in cases involving abused women who killed their abusive husbands, as case law demonstrates that often they involved a lapse in time between the provocation and the killing (*Ahluwalia* [1992] 4 All ER 889). Subsequent cases sought to extend the defence to battered women by accepting the notion of cumulative provocation and acknowledging that provocation might still be operating on the defendant's mind, even after a lapse of time. Irrespective of this, there were still concerns that the requirement of a sudden and temporary loss of control made it too difficult for battered women to rely on this defence.

 Make your answer stand out

Concerns about the ability of abused women who killed their abusers to rely upon provocation were a significant issue in the debate leading up to the reform of the law and the abolition of the defence of provocation. Great emphasis was placed on the need to ensure that the new defence was equally 'user-friendly' to male and female defendants in recognition that men and women respond differently to provocation and kill in different circumstances (Law Com. No. 304, Para. 5.62). Quick and Wells (2006) explore this in their article, saying 'women do not often kill from anger, while anger is what fuels many male killings'. An ability to engage in detail with the arguments put forward about the nature of male and female anger and violence would be advantageous in preparing to answer a question that required a discussion of the old and the new law.

The loss of control defence seeks to accommodate what was previously known as 'slow burn' or cumulative provocation: that is, a situation that has built up over a period of time and is composed of a series of separate incidents, one of which 'broke the camel's back' causing the defendant to lose control and kill. The removal of the suddenness requirement does go some way towards achieving that objective, but the issue of timing may, to a certain extent, be relevant under the new law. This is because of the stipulation found in section 54(4) regarding revenge killings.

KEY STATUTE

Coroners and Justice Act 2009, section 54(4)

Subsection (1) does not apply if, in doing or being a party to the killing, D acted in a considered desire for revenge.

It seems reasonable to say that a person who kills another in a planned and cold-blooded attack should not have a defence that reduces liability from murder to manslaughter, but is it a desire for revenge that enables a distinction to be made between a premeditated killing and one carried out in the heat of the moment? It is not difficult to imagine a situation in which a person has both lost control *and* wants revenge.

For example, imagine a defendant who was confronted and mocked by the person who had raped his young daughter and who responded by attacking the rapist and inflicting fatal injuries. This instantaneous reaction to a pressured and emotional situation seems to be one in which the law should extend the defence of loss of control, but would the defence be unavailable to the defendant if he declared 'I had to get revenge for what he had done to my daughter'? Although it is fair to say that revenge killings are often premeditated, it does seem possible that removing the defence from defendants who acted out of a desire for revenge might be problematic.

How will the courts interpret 'considered'?

The *Oxford English Dictionary* defines 'considered' as 'characterised by careful thought'.

If this or a similar interpretation is adopted by the courts in relation to the exclusion of a 'considered desire for revenge', then perhaps the law will be able to accommodate situations in which revenge forms part of the motivation for a fatal attack. A distinction would be made between a heat-of-the-moment, emotion-charged attack in which the defendant thinks 'I'll make you pay for what you've done' (a desire for revenge) and a cold-blooded and planned killing (a considered desire for revenge). There is a good example of this in *Jewell* [2014] EWCA Crim 414 in which the defendant claimed to have lost control and shot a workmate when collecting him for work one morning. However, there was evidence of planning, such as the presence of the gun on a journey to work and the arrangements that the defendant had made to flee to Scotland after the attack, so the trial judge refused to put the defence to the jury. The Court of Appeal upheld the conviction, with Rafferty LJ stating that there was undisputed evidence to refute the defendant's assertion that he lost control as the killing 'bore every hallmark of a pre-planned, cold-blooded execution'.

Qualifying triggers

Under the old law, a person could raise a defence of provocation if they were provoked to kill by things said, things done or by a combination of things said and things done. The new defence of loss of control rejected this open approach in favour of stipulating two qualifying triggers. The defendant must be able to point to one or both of these as the cause of his loss of control in order to avail himself of the new defence.

KEY STATUTE

Coroners and Justice Act 2009, section 55

(1) This section applies for the purposes of s. 54.

(2) A loss of self-control had a qualifying trigger if s. (3), (4) or (5) applies.

(3) This subsection applies if D's loss of self-control was attributable to D's fear of serious violence from V against D or another identified person.

    (a) This subjection applies if D's loss of self-control was attributable to a thing or things done or said (or both) which –

    (b) constituted circumstances of an extremely grave character, and

    (c) caused D to have a justifiable sense of being seriously wronged.

(4) This subsection applies if D's loss of self-control was attributable to a combination of the matters mentioned in ss. (3) and (4).

Fear of serious violence

Section 55(3) covers situations in which the defendant lost control and killed as a result of being in fear of serious violence, emanating from the victim. The defendant may fear that the violence will be used against himself or against a third party. The reference to an identified person means that the defendant must fear that violence is going to be used against a specific person rather than that serious violence is going to be used against people in general.

According to the Explanatory Notes that accompany the Act, a subjective standard will be applied so the defendant will be able to raise a defence if they had a genuine fear of serious violence, even if the fear was not reasonable and other people in the same situation would not have been fearful.

□ REVISION NOTE

The creation of a defence to murder that applies if the defendant lost control and killed in response to their fear that the victim would use serious violence against them or another is similar to self-defence (which is covered in Chapter 17). It might help your preparation for a question dealing with these two defences if you took note of the ways in which the defences are similar (for example, both allow force to be used in a situation in which the defendant has an honestly-held mistaken belief that they are facing a threat) and how they differ (self-defence applies to any offence whereas loss of control applies only to murder). It is possible that loss of control will be useful for defendants who have used fatal force in a situation where it was not necessary to do so in the light of the threat that they faced, as this would preclude reliance on self-defence.

The relationship between self-defence and loss of control was explored by the Court of Appeal in *R* v *Dawes* [2013] EWCA Crim 322 in which the defendant stabbed a man who had an affair with his wife.

Justifiable sense of being seriously wronged

This qualifying trigger is closer in its scope to the old defence of provocation as it is open as to the nature of the circumstances that it covers. It does not stipulate what sorts of words or actions can give rise to a loss of control but the requirement is that they are of an 'extremely grave character'. It remains to be seen as case law emerges what sorts of situations will be accepted as circumstances of an extremely grave character. It has been stipulated by the Court of Appeal in *R* v *Hatter* [2013] EWCA Crim 322 that the break-up of a relationship will not normally suffice to establish circumstances of a grave character that give the defendant a justifiable sense of being seriously wronged – to find otherwise would extend a defence to everybody who killed a partner who ended a relationship – but that there may be circumstances in which a relationship ends that would be an exception to this general principle.

The Explanatory Notes stipulate that the inclusion of the word 'justifiable' is indicative of an objective test. This means that a defendant who lost control as a result of words and/or actions of an extremely grave character may be deprived of a defence of loss of control if the jury feel that the defendant's feeling that he was seriously wronged is not reasonable. This raises the possibility of problems arising from cases in which social or cultural differences could give rise to a disparity of views.

For example, in *Mohammed* [2005] EWCA Crim 1880, the defendant killed his daughter after catching her engaging in sexual intercourse. His plea of provocation (under the old law) was rejected as the court was not prepared to take his particular religious beliefs into account. This gives an example of a situation that could well cause difficulties in relation to this requirement that the defendant's sense that he has been seriously wronged is reasonable. If the new law had been in force, doubtless the defendant would have sought to argue that he lost control as a result of things done (his daughter's sexual activity) that caused him to feel seriously wronged (on the basis of her disregard for his principles, her abuse of his home and the tenets of their shared religion). Whether members of the jury who may not share the same religious beliefs would consider that his sense of being seriously wronged was justifiable is questionable.

Exclusions

One of the aims of the new defence was to ensure that it would not be available in certain situations in which the defendant had lost control and killed. These are outlined in section 55(6):

(a) D incited the things said or done that caused him to fear serious violence as an excuse to use violence.

(b) D incited the words/conduct that caused his sense of being seriously wronged as an excuse to use violence.

(c) The thing said or done that caused D to lose control was sexual infidelity.

The first two exclusions are not controversial as they simply preclude the defendant from relying on this defence if he created a situation in which he feared violence or felt seriously wronged so as to excuse his use of violence in response. This has been explored by the Court of Appeal in the conjoined appeals of *Dawes* and *Bowyer* [2013] EWCA Crim 322 where it was confirmed that 'the mere fact that in some general way the defendant was behaving badly and looking for and provoking trouble does not of itself lead to the disapplication of the qualifying triggers based on section 55(3),(4) and (5) unless his actions were intended to provide him with the excuse or opportunity to use violence' (Para. 58). In other words, the defendant will be deprived of a defence of loss of control only if he provoked the victim to attack him so as to have an excuse to use retaliatory violence.

The final exclusion – a loss of control arising from sexual infidelity – caused a great deal of controversy during the passage of the Act. Those who wanted to ensure that this provision was included argued that the old law of provocation gave a defence to jealous husbands who discovered that their wives were being unfaithful but there was little evidence to support this assertion. This position was considered by the Court of Appeal in its first interpretation of the loss of control legislation:

KEY CASE

R v *Clinton, Parker and Evans* [2012] EWCA Crim 2

Concerning: loss of control, sexual infidelity

Facts

Clinton killed his wife during an argument shortly after she had told him that she had been having an affair. He was convicted *inter alia* of murder and sentenced to 26 years' imprisonment. The jury considered the partial defence of diminished responsibility but the trial judge ruled that there was insufficient evidence of loss of control for the jury to consider it in the alternative.

Legal principle

The Court of Appeal considered whether or not sexual infidelity is wholly excluded from consideration as a permissible qualifying trigger within section 55. Judge CJ stated that:

The legislation was designed to prohibit the misuse of sexual infidelity as a potential trigger for loss of control in circumstances in which it was thought to have been misused in the former defence of provocation ... in short, sexual infidelity is not subject to a blanket exclusion when the loss of control is under consideration. Evidence of these matters may be deployed by the defendant and therefore the legislation proceeds on the basis that sexual infidelity is a permissible feature of the loss of control defence ... To compartmentalise sexual infidelity and exclude it when it is integral to the facts as a whole ... is unrealistic and carries with it the potential for injustice ... We have proceeded on the assumption that the legislation is not enacted with the intent or purpose that the criminal justice system should operate so as to create injustice.

The Court of Appeal allowed Clinton's appeal against conviction and ordered a retrial.

! Don't be tempted to . . .

Ignore the tricky potential contradiction between section 55(6)(c) (the exclusion of sexual infidelity) and section 55(4) loss of control arising from a sense of being seriously wronged. It seems reasonable to expect that a defendant who discovered that their spouse was unfaithful would experience a sense of being seriously wronged that could lead to a loss of control and yet the defence would not be available. In such circumstances, it is possible that lawyers will try to circumvent section 55(6)(c) by claiming that it was not the infidelity itself that led to the loss of control but rather it arose from feelings of rejection, humiliation or betrayal arising from the discovery or panic regarding the potential breakdown of the family unit. As Judge CJ said in *Clinton*, 'although express provision is made for the exclusion of some features of the defendant's situation, the fact that he/she has been sexually betrayed is not'.

Objective test

Just like the old defence of provocation, loss of control includes an objective element to ensure that defendants whose loss of control is unreasonable are not able to rely on the defence. Section 54(1)(c) specifies that the defence will succeed only if a person of the same age and sex as the defendant who has normal levels of tolerance and self-restraint might have responded by losing control and killing if they were in the same circumstances as the defendant.

Section 54(3) supplements section 54(1)(c) by explaining that the reference to the defendant's circumstances means all the circumstances surrounding and leading up to the killing except those factors that relate to the defendant's tolerance and his ability to exercise self-restraint. In this way, the test will not permit a defendant to rely on loss of control as a defence where the defendant is particularly short-tempered or prone to violent outbursts. A defendant is expected to have the same level of tolerance and self-restraint as is normal and acceptable in society, and those defendants who do not have these qualities will not be able to rely upon this defence. The impact of alcohol on the objective test was considered in *R* v *Asmelash* [2013] EWCA 157 where it was held that the question to be asked was whether a sober person with the expected level of tolerance and self-restraint would have behaved in the same way as the defendant if confronted by the same qualifying trigger. So, a defendant will not lose the defence because he was intoxicated, but he will be judged against the standards of control of a person who is not intoxicated.

! Don't be tempted to ...

Assume that the new law is better than the old law that it replaces or amends. There was a great deal of disagreement during the passage of the legislation about the correct scope and working of these two defences and there is plenty of academic commentary that draws attention to potential problems with the new law. You should also bear in mind that the Act implements only a part of the Law Commission's recommendations for the wholesale reform of homicide offences that would have created a tiered structure of offences of first and second degree murder to reflect different levels of culpability. These proposals are set out in full in Law Com. No. 304.

■ Putting it all together

Answer guidelines

See the essay question at the start of the chapter.

Approaching the question

This question invites a discussion of a quotation that expresses a particular opinion about the new defence of loss of control. It would be important to ensure that you follow the instructions and respond to the view expressed, rather than simply describing the old defence of provocation and comparing it with loss of control. This question does require a good knowledge of the old law as well as the new defence: it would not be possible to respond to the quotation if you were able to discuss only the new defence.

Important points to include

- A good starting point for answering this question would be to explain the view expressed in the quotation. This demonstrates to your marker that you have understood the central point of the question and it will give your essay a strong focus on the main issue from the start. Here, the quotation suggests that loss of control is very similar to the defence of provocation that it replaced and that any changes are only minor.

- You could start by providing a brief outline of the role of the Coroners and Justice Act 2009 in changing the partial defences to murder and note that it implemented some of the Law Commission's recommendations for the reform of the law of homicide. This sets the context for the main thrust of your answer.

- Rather than falling into the trap of having a paragraph that describes provocation and then another that describes loss of control, try to make your essay more dynamic and focused by dealing with the two side by side. A good way to do this would be to start by noting one of the key similarities of the two defences: the two-stage structure that has a subjective and an objective limb. Remember to link your answer to the question by saying that the similarities in structure support the view that there is little difference between the defences.

- Loss of control has two manifestations, one of which – the justifiable sense of being wronged – bears a greater resemblance to provocation than the other, so it makes sense to look at this similarity first as it also supports the view expressed in the quotation. Look for similarities – the idea of things said and/or done that have caused the defendant to lose control and kill – as well as the differences – the inclusion of a requirement that it is justifiable for the defendant to feel as he does.

- The qualifying trigger concerning fear of serious violence is a more significant difference so it would be possible to use this to disagree with the view expressed in the quotation.

- Although it is true that both defences had an objective limb, be sure to explain that one of the key objectives of the new defence was to overcome some of the uncertainty that had arisen about the correct scope of the objective limb of provocation due to conflicting case law.

Make your answer stand out

One way in which you could add strength to your essay would be to use case law decided under the old law to illustrate your points. For example, if you wanted to highlight the impact of the fear of serious violence qualifying trigger, you could make reference to case law in which battered women who killed their abusers struggled to satisfy the requirements of provocation. You can use the facts to demonstrate that such cases would now fit within the new defence.

Try to find a way to work in references to academic commentary that you have read in preparation for a question of this nature. Is there a point from an article, perhaps about the exclusion of sexual infidelity, that you could make? It would also be useful to be able to refer to specific points raised in Law Com. No. 304.

READ TO IMPRESS

Gibson, M. (2011) Intoxicants and Diminished Responsibility: The Impact of the Coroners and Justice Act 2009. *Criminal Law Review*, 909.

Miles, J. (2009) The Coroners and Justice Act 2009: a 'Dog's Breakfast' of Homicide Reform. *Archbold News*, 10: 6.

Withey, C. (2011) Loss of Control, Loss of Opportunity? *Criminal Law Review*.

www.pearsoned.co.uk/lawexpress

 Go online to access more revision support, including quizzes to test your knowledge, sample questions with answer guidelines, podcasts you can download and more!

Involuntary manslaughter

8

Revision checklist

Essential points you should know:

☐ The relationship between murder and involuntary manslaughter

☐ The distinction between voluntary and involuntary manslaughter

☐ The elements of unlawful dangerous act (constructive) manslaughter

☐ The operation of gross negligence manslaughter and corporate manslaughter

☐ The weaknesses in the law and proposals for reform

Topic map

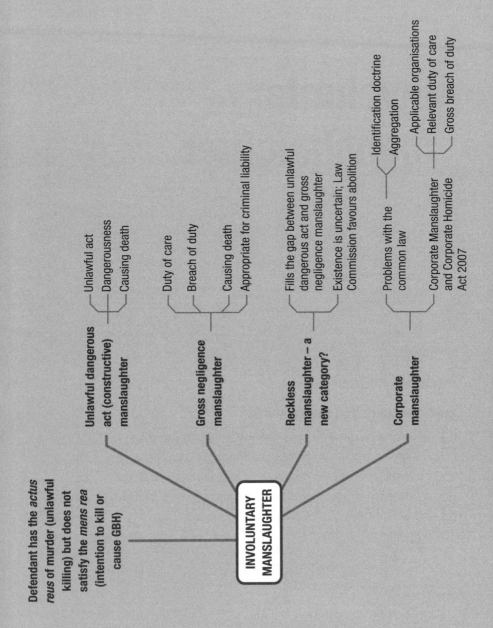

Defendant has the *actus reus* of murder (unlawful killing) but does not satisfy the *mens rea* (intention to kill or cause GBH)

INVOLUNTARY MANSLAUGHTER

Unlawful dangerous act (constructive) manslaughter
- Unlawful act
- Dangerousness
- Causing death

Gross negligence manslaughter
- Duty of care
- Breach of duty
- Causing death
- Appropriate for criminal liability

Reckless manslaughter – a new category?
- Fills the gap between unlawful dangerous act and gross negligence manslaughter
- Existence is uncertain; Law Commission favours abolition

Corporate manslaughter
- Problems with the common law
  - Identification doctrine
  - Aggregation
- Corporate Manslaughter and Corporate Homicide Act 2007
  - Applicable organisations
  - Relevant duty of care
  - Gross breach of duty

A printable version of this topic map is available from **www.pearsoned.co.uk/lawexpress**

▮ Introduction

Involuntary manslaughter covers situations in which the defendant has caused death but does not satisfy the *mens rea* requirements of murder; it is a less culpable form of homicide.

This makes it a key revision topic as questions may test your ability to distinguish between levels of culpability in homicide offences, i.e. it requires an understanding of the relationship between murder and involuntary manslaughter.

There are two well-established categories of involuntary manslaughter (unlawful dangerous act manslaughter – sometimes referred to as constructive manslaughter – and gross negligence manslaughter) that largely require understanding of recognised legal principles. The existence of the third category – reckless manslaughter – is more controversial and requires a deeper grasp of policy issues. Reckless manslaughter is more speculative; there is some debate about whether it actually exists as a separate category at all. Awareness of the gaps in the law is essential as is an ability to comment upon proposals for reform.

Corporate manslaughter is a more recent statutory development.

ASSESSMENT ADVICE

Essay questions

Essay questions on involuntary manslaughter are not common but could easily arise so it would be sensible to be prepared. It would be advisable to ensure that you have a clear understanding of the relationship between murder and involuntary manslaughter as well as a strong grasp of the way that the different manifestations of involuntary manslaughter relate to each other. Armed with this knowledge, you should be able to tackle essays about the effectiveness of the current law and any need for reform. Essay questions that focus on corporate manslaughter are quite common and require an ability to explain and evaluate the statutory framework for imposing liability for causing death upon an organisation.

Problem questions

Problem questions involving death should start with a discussion of liability for murder (the most serious homicide offence). If the *mens rea* of murder cannot be established, the focus should shift to involuntary manslaughter. The clues that should alert you to the two well-established categories of involuntary manslaughter are the commission of some other offence that led to death (constructive manslaughter) or the existence of a duty of care between the defendant and the victim (gross negligence manslaughter).

Sample question

Could you answer this question? Below is a typical essay question that could arise on this topic. Guidelines on answering the question are included at the end of this chapter, whilst a sample problem question and guidance on tackling it can be found on the companion website.

ESSAY QUESTION

'Involuntary manslaughter is an offence of ill-defined boundaries covering the middle ground between murder and accidental death.'

Critically evaluate the accuracy of this statement.

Unlawful dangerous act (constructive) manslaughter

Unlawful dangerous act manslaughter (also known as UDA manslaughter or constructive manslaughter) is a common law offence so its elements are found in case law. It builds (constructs) liability on some other (non-homicide) offence that has caused the victim's death and has three elements:

- Was the defendant's act unlawful?
- Was the unlawful act dangerous?
- Did the unlawful and dangerous act cause death?

Unlawful act

As its name suggests, UDA manslaughter requires an unlawful act. This must be a complete criminal offence: the *actus reus* and *mens rea* of an offence must be established. Civil liability will not suffice.

KEY CASE

R v Lamb [1967] 2 QB 981 (CA)

Concerning: UDA manslaughter, unlawful act

Facts

The defendant pointed a gun at his friend as a joke. He knew that it contained bullets but that these were not in the 'fire' position. He pulled the trigger as a joke. The mechanism of the gun rotated the chamber so that the gun fired. The victim died of injuries sustained. The defendant's conviction for involuntary manslaughter was quashed on the basis that the defendant's actions did not amount to a criminal offence, not even common assault.

Legal principle

UDA manslaughter requires a criminally unlawful act. In the absence of the *actus reus* and *mens rea* of common assault being established, there was no unlawful act upon which liability for UDA manslaughter could be constructed.

✎ EXAM TIP

The requirement of a criminal offence as the basis of UDA manslaughter means that the starting point for any discussion of liability is to identify the *actus reus* and *mens rea* of an appropriate offence.

When looking for an offence upon which to base liability, there are a few important points to bear in mind, as follows.

Act not omission

UDA manslaughter can only be based on a positive act. Even if the defendant fails to act when he has a duty to do so (Chapter 2) and this causes death, there can be no liability for UDA manslaughter.

KEY CASE

R v Lowe [1973] QB 702 (CA)

Concerning: UDA manslaughter, unlawful act

Facts

The defendant failed to call a doctor to attend to his ailing nine-week-old baby and she died soon after. His conviction for manslaughter was quashed.

Legal principle

UDA manslaughter requires a positive act. An omission, even a deliberate omission, will not suffice.

Variable *mens rea*

The *mens rea* of UDA manslaughter corresponds with the *mens rea* of the unlawful act upon which liability is based. This means that it differs from case to case:

■ Dan throws a brick through the window of a moving train, killing the driver. The basis of liability is criminal damage; the *mens rea* is intention or recklessness as to the damage/destruction of another's property.

■ Dave slaps Victoria around the face during an argument. She falls, hits her head on the kerb and dies as a result. Liability is based upon battery; the *mens rea* is intention to apply unlawful force to the body of another (or recklessness thereto).

These examples illustrate the variability of the *mens rea* requirement. They also demonstrate the way that liability for UDA manslaughter is based upon some other offence, even if death is an entirely unforeseeable consequence.

✎ EXAM TIP

If death arises from an attack, base liability on battery, this is the most straightforward non-fatal offence. UDA manslaughter can be based upon any unlawful act, however trivial, so do not complicate matters by trying to establish one of the more serious offences. Never base liability on section 18 of the Offences Against the Person Act 1861 (see Chapter 9). If the ulterior intent for this offence exists (intention to cause GBH) and the victim has died, the appropriate offence is murder not involuntary manslaughter.

Dangerousness

The unlawful act must also be dangerous. The test of dangerousness in UDA manslaughter is outlined in *Church*.

KEY CASE

R v Church [1966] 1 QB 59 (CA)

Concerning: UDA manslaughter, dangerousness

Facts

The defendant knocked the victim unconscious. Believing her to be dead, he pushed her body in the river where she drowned.

Legal principle

It is not enough that an unlawful act caused death. The unlawful act must be one that 'all sober and reasonable people would inevitably recognise must subject the other person to . . . the risk of some (albeit not serious) harm'.

In *Newbury and Jones,* the court considered whether the defendant must realise that his act is dangerous.

KEY CASE

R v Newbury and Jones [1977] AC 500 (HL)

Concerning: UDA manslaughter, dangerousness

Facts

The defendants threw a slab from a bridge onto a train, killing the guard. They appealed against their convictions for manslaughter on the basis that they did not appreciate that their conduct carried a risk of harm.

Legal principle

Provided that the defendant intentionally does an act that is both unlawful and dangerous, he need not recognise its dangerousness; there is no requirement that the defendant foresees a risk of harm to others arising from his unlawful act.

✎ EXAM TIP

Look out for an unlawful act that a sober and reasonable person would realise carried a risk of harm to others, even if the defendant is oblivious to the risk. Remember, in *Attorney-General's Reference (No. 3 of 1994)* [1998] AC 245 (HL), Lord Hope stated 'dangerousness in this context is not a high standard. All it requires is an act likely to injure the other person.'

Causation

The unlawful and dangerous act must satisfy the ordinary rules of causation (see Chapter 2); it must be both a factual and legal cause of death.

■ Gross negligence manslaughter

This is based not on criminal wrongdoing but on negligence, a concept usually associated with civil law. The offence is established if the defendant has been so negligent that criminal liability is appropriate.

- Does the defendant have a duty towards the victim?
- Is the defendant in breach of duty?
- Did the breach of duty cause death?
- Should the conduct be characterised as criminal?

Duty of care

The first step in establishing liability for gross negligence manslaughter is to identify a duty that exists between the defendant and the victim. There are two ways that this can arise:

- *Duty of care:* based on 'ordinary principles' of negligence (*Adomako*). Established readily in relation to professional and contractual relationships and in relation to road users.
- *Duty to act:* a person is liable for failure to act only if he has a duty to do so (see Chapter 2).

Breach of duty

Breach of duty differs depending upon whether the defendant had a duty of care or a duty to act:

- Duty of care: breached by poor performance of the duty. Evaluate what the defendant did and whether this fell short of what was expected of him (*Adomako*).
- Duty to act: breached by failure to act. Establish that the defendant has a duty to act and that he failed to do so.

KEY CASE

R v *Adomako* [1995] 1 AC 171 (HL)

Concerning: breach of duty

Facts

The defendant, an anaesthetist, failed to notice the patient's oxygen supply had become disconnected during an operation. The patient died from lack of oxygen.

Legal principle

The defendant's conduct must have 'departed from the proper standard of care incumbent upon him'. Where a person holds themselves out as possessing some special skill or knowledge, then their conduct will be judged against the reasonably competent professional in the field.

✎ EXAM TIP

When dealing with breach of duty, make a realistic argument about the expectations of *reasonably competent professionals* in the relevant field on the basis of the facts provided. You will not be expected to comment with authority on the standards and practices of doctors, for example, only to draw attention to facts that suggest that the defendant has fallen below a reasonable standard of competence.

Causing death

The ordinary principles of causation apply (see Chapter 2); the defendant's breach of duty must be the factual and legal cause of death. Note that this may differ from the way in which causation is established in relation to murder.

Murder	Gross negligence manslaughter
Dave is a qualified gas fitter employed to service Vanessa's boiler. He rushes the job and reconnects the circuits incorrectly. This causes pressure in the boiler and it explodes during the night. Vanessa is killed in the ensuing fire.	
Vanessa would not have died 'but for' Dave's failure to wire the circuits correctly (factual causation). There are no other causes of her death so legal causation is established. Dave has caused Vanessa's death, satisfying the *actus reus* of murder (although probably not the *mens rea*).	As a qualified gas fitter contracted to service the boiler, Dave owes a duty of care to Vanessa. By failing to wire the boiler correctly, he has not performed his duties to the standard expected of a reasonably competent gas fitter, thus is in breach of duty of care. As this breach has caused the explosion of the boiler that started the fire in which Vanessa died, Dave's breach of duty has caused Vanessa's death. (You could break this down into factual and legal causation if this had not been addressed earlier in the question.)
Establishing causation for the purposes of murder requires only that the defendant's conduct, taken as a whole, has caused death.	For the purposes of gross negligence manslaughter, the discussion of causation needs to be more specific and phrased in terms of duty and breach of duty.

> ✎ **EXAM TIP**
>
> The illustration above, in relation to causation, may seem like an insignificant point but it is just the sort of detail that demonstrates a comprehensive awareness of the requirements of the two offences and, as such, will really help your answer to stand out and impress the examiners.

Appropriate for the imposition of criminal liability

It is this fourth element that distinguishes civil negligence for causing death and gross negligence manslaughter. If the three preceding stages are satisfied, the defendant will still not attract criminal liability unless his conduct is 'so bad' that this is appropriate. This is a question of fact for the jury and it can take any factors into account in reaching a decision.

Students often work through the first three stages then fail to apply the facts in relation to the fourth, so careful attention to this stage could attract a lot of credit.

■ Reckless manslaughter – a separate category?

UDA manslaughter and gross negligence manslaughter may not cover all culpable killings. UDA manslaughter requires the *actus reus* and *mens rea* of an offence and gross negligence manslaughter requires breach of duty. If neither of these things exist, the killing cannot fall within these categories of manslaughter.

This gap in the law could be filled by a new category of manslaughter based upon subjective recklessness; that is, reckless manslaughter. It could be established if the defendant had caused death without awareness that his conduct caused a subjective risk of causing death or serious harm provided that the level of the risk that was foreseen was less than a virtual certainty (otherwise the defendant would be liable for murder on the basis of oblique intention: see Chapters 3 and 6). Although reckless manslaughter seems to have been recognised in case law – *Lidar* (2000) 4 *Archbold News* 40 – it is more speculative than UDA manslaughter and gross negligence manslaughter. Indeed, there is some academic debate about whether this form of involuntary manslaughter actually exists at all and the Law Commission has recommended the abolition of this category of manslaughter within its overall programme of recommendations for reform of homicide offences.

 Make your answer stand out

Elliot's (2001) article provides a good outline of the reasoning in *Lidar* and considers the implications for this area of law if an offence of reckless manslaughter were recognised. You could also consider whether reckless manslaughter would solve the difficulties faced by the courts in imposing liability for murder on drug-dealers whose 'customers' die from an overdose. Heaton's (2003) article outlines the way in which such situations have been dealt with by case law. Reference to relevant academic commentary will always strengthen your answers.

Reckless manslaughter is based upon foresight of a risk of death or serious harm. In this respect, it is similar to oblique intention, although that requires foresight of a risk that death/serious injury is a virtually certain consequence.

You might find it useful to revisit the text on *mens rea* (see Chapter 3) to ensure that you can recognise the difference between oblique intention (giving rise to liability for murder) and subjective recklessness (the basis for involuntary manslaughter).

■ Corporate manslaughter

An additional form of manslaughter is corporate manslaughter. Since a corporation has a legal personality, it can be criminally liable in the same way that a natural person can. At common law, this required the elements of gross negligence manslaughter to be established.

Problems with the common law

Identification doctrine

In *Bolton* v *Graham* [1957] 1 QB 159 (CA), Lord Denning drew an analogy between a person and a corporation: the directors and managers of the corporation are like the human body's brain and nerve centre, since they control what the corporation actually does. The directors and managers, once identified, are the directing mind and will of the company and it is their state of mind that is treated as the mental state of the corporation. This is known as the identification doctrine.

The courts have, however, encountered difficulties in determining who might be identified as the directing mind and will of the company (see, for example, *Tesco* v *Nattrass* [1972] AC 153 (HL)).

Aggregation

Whilst a corporation cannot be liable for murder (since it cannot serve a prison sentence), it was established in *Re Attorney-General's Reference (No. 2 of 1999)* [2000] QB 796 (CA) that a corporation could be liable for manslaughter, but only if an identified human individual was liable for the same crime and that individual was part of the controlling mind and will of the company. An aggregation of multiple minor failures by company officers that led to a gross breach by the company overall is not sufficient.

The practical consequence of this was that convictions for corporate manslaughter were rare, leading to increasing public concern that corporations that had caused death were not being held liable for the consequences of their actions. This followed a series of large-scale disasters in which convictions did not follow: such as the Paddington rail crash, the Herald of Free Enterprise ferry capsize, and the King's Cross underground fire.

As a result, the Corporate Manslaughter and Corporate Homicide Act 2007 came into force in April 2008, providing a new statutory offence of corporate manslaughter:

KEY STATUTE

Corporate Manslaughter and Corporate Homicide Act 2007, section 1

(1) An organisation to which this section applies is guilty of an offence if the way in which its activities are managed or organised –

    (a) causes a person's death, and

    (b) amounts to a gross breach of a relevant duty of care owed by the organisation to the deceased.

. . .

(3) An organisation is guilty of an offence under this section only if the way in which its activities are managed or organised by its senior management is a substantial element in the breach referred to in subsection (1).

This offence has several elements: the organisation must be one to which the Act applies; there must be a relevant duty of care; there must have been a gross breach of that duty; the senior management's management or organisation of the organisation's business must be a substantial element of the gross breach of duty.

Applicable organisations

The organisations that are covered by the offence are:

- corporations;
- police forces;
- partnerships, trade unions or employers' associations (which are employers themselves);
- most government departments (listed in Schedule 1 to the Act).

Relevant duty of care

The relevant duties of care of a corporation are provided in section 2 of the Act and comprise various duties owed under the law of negligence:

- the duty to its employees or other workers working for it or providing services;
- the duty as an occupier of premises;

- the duties in connection with the supply of goods or services; any construction or main-tenance operations; any other commercial activity; or its use of any plant, vehicle or other thing; and
- the duties owed to persons in custody.

Various government policy decisions, policing, emergency service, military, probation and child protection activities are excluded (sections 3–7 of the Act).

Section 2(5) provides – highly unusually – that the existence of a duty of care is a matter of law, but the judge must make any findings of fact to decide the question. At common law, the existence of the duty was left to the jury to decide (*R* v *Evans (Gemma)* [2009] EWCA Crim 650).

Gross breach of duty

A breach of duty of care by an organisation is a gross breach if the conduct alleged to amount to a breach of the duty of care falls far below what can reasonably be expected of the organisation in the circumstances (section 1(4)(b)).

Section 8 of the Act provides that the jury *must* consider whether there is any evidence to show that the organisation failed to comply with any health and safety legislation that related to the alleged breach and, if so:

- how serious that failure was; and
- how much of a risk of death it posed.

The jury *may*:

- consider the extent to which the evidence shows that there were attitudes, policies, systems or accepted practices within the organisation that were likely to have encouraged a failure to comply with health and safety legislation or to have produced tolerance of such failure;
- have regard to any health and safety guidance that related to the alleged breach;
- have regard to any other matters it considers to be relevant.

Senior management

The senior management of the organisation is defined in section 1(4)(c) as the persons who play significant roles in the making of decisions about how the whole or a substantial part of its activities are to be managed or organised, or the actual managing or organising of the whole of a substantial part of those activities. This is broader than the common law position of 'directing mind or will'.

Failure to comply with health and safety guidance can give rise to potential criminal liability for both the organisation and its individual directors, officers and managers. In *R* v *Geotechnical Holding Ltd* [2011] EWCA Crim 1338, charges included corporate manslaughter (and breach of health and safety legislation) against the company together with breach of the Health and Safety at Work Act 1974 against the (sole) director of the company.

Subsequent successful prosecutions have all been against smaller organisations owned by their directors so it has been straightforward to attribute the failings that led to death to those in a senior management position. The law has yet to be tested against a larger, more complex organisation.

■ Putting it all together

Answer guidelines

See the essay question at the start of the chapter. A diagram illustrating how to structure your answer is available on the companion website.

Approaching the question

This is a typical question dealing with the relationship between the different types of involuntary manslaughter. In order to tackle such a question, you would need a good grasp of the scope of the two main categories of involuntary manslaughter and be able to give examples of the sorts of killings that they cover. To do well, you should also be able to comment upon the possibility of the existence of a third category of involuntary manslaughter (reckless manslaughter) and comment upon its relationship with the two other offences.

Important points to include

- ■ The starting point for the essay should be to establish the context for the discussion by explaining the role of involuntary manslaughter in homicide offences and establishing how this category of offences occupies the 'middle ground' between murder and accidental death that is mentioned in the question.

- ■ Although it is never a good idea to provide too much descriptive detail, it is important to ensure that there is sufficient description to support the analysis. In relation to this question, it would be a good idea to provide a clear and concise explanation of each type of manslaughter by reference to its composite elements. This should not be too lengthy but it should capture the essence of each offence.

- ■ If the question makes reference to 'ill-defined boundaries', you would need to consider what the boundaries are that need to be discussed. There are three different boundaries that could be considered here:

  - ☐ The boundary between murder and involuntary manslaughter. You would need to explain that the offences share a common *actus reus,* thus the difference lies with the *mens rea* requirement: a defendant who lacks the *mens rea* for murder can only be convicted of involuntary manslaughter.

☐ The boundary between involuntary manslaughter and accidental death. The obvious focus here would be gross negligence manslaughter as it is a very close relative of civil negligence. Make sure that you can pinpoint the distinguishing factor, giving examples to aid clarity, and that you can comment upon whether the offence is defined with sufficient precision so that the boundary between criminal law and civil law is clear.

☐ The boundary between the two main types of involuntary manslaughter. How clear is the distinction between constructive manslaughter and gross negligence manslaughter? Is there any conduct that you can think of that falls into both categories? Alternatively, is there an unacceptable gap between the two offences?

 ### Make your answer stand out

The law on reckless manslaughter is uncertain. This factor causes many students to overlook it entirely but it could play an important role in filling the gap between constructive manslaughter and gross negligence manslaughter. This makes it an important element of your revision for an essay question on involuntary manslaughter as your essay will stand out from the rest if you are able to provide some discussion on such a tricky issue.

Remember that involuntary manslaughter is a common law offence, thus it is defined by case law. It is particularly important that you can make effective use of case law to explain the scope of the offences and illustrate any arguments that you raise in the course of the essay.

READ TO IMPRESS

Elliot, C. (2001) What Direction for Gross Negligence Manslaughter? *Journal of Criminal Law,* 65: 145.

Gobert, J. (2008) The Corporate Manslaughter and Corporate Homicide Act 2007 – Thirteen Years in the Making but Was it Worth the Wait? *Modern Law Review,* 71: 413.

Heaton, R. (2003) Dealing in Death. *Criminal Law Review,* 497.

Herring, J. and Palsar, E. (2007) The duty of care in gross negligence manslaughter. *Criminal Law Review,* 24.

Ormerod, D. and Taylor, R. (2008) The Corporate Manslaughter and Corporate Homicide Act 2007. *Criminal Law Review,* 589.

Virgo, G. (1995) Reconstructing Manslaughter on Defective Foundations. *Cambridge Law Journal,* 54: 14.

www.pearsoned.co.uk/lawexpress

Go online to access more revision support, including quizzes to test your knowledge, sample questions with answer guidelines, podcasts you can download and more!

Non-fatal offences

Revision checklist

Essential points you should know:

☐ The *actus reus* and *mens rea* of the five offences covered in this chapter: assault, battery, section 47, section 20 and section 18 of the Offences Against the Person Act 1861

☐ The distinction between common assault and battery and their relationship with assault occasioning actual bodily harm (section 47)

☐ The meaning of 'bodily harm' (actual/grievous) in relation to both physical and psychological injury

☐ The issues surrounding the *mens rea* of the statutory offences: 'half *mens rea*' (section 47), the Mowatt gloss (section 20) and the ulterior intent requirement (section 18)

☐ The availability of consent as a defence to non-fatal offences

Topic map

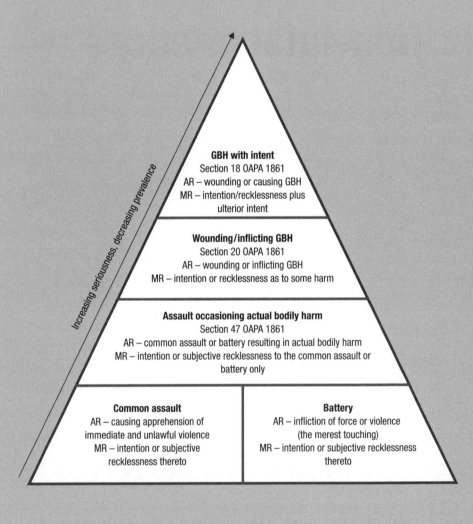

◼ Introduction

Non-fatal offences against the person are a collection of common law and statutory offences that do not fit together very well.

The offences found in the Offences Against the Person Act 1861 (OAPA) originally came from a variety of other sources but were collected together in a single consolidating statute whilst the less serious offences of assault and battery are common law offences. The result is that there is some inconsistency in terminology and a fair degree of overlap between the offences as well as some gaps in their coverage. This can be a confusing area of law to study but the best approach is to accept that there is some inconsistency arising as a result of the different sources of the offences and over 140 years of judicial interpretation.

ASSESSMENT ADVICE

Essay questions

Essay questions dealing with non-fatal offences are common due to the number of complexities associated with this area of law. They might be broad questions that require an ability to see the way that offences relate to each other or more narrowly focused questions dealing with specific issues. Topics such as the expansion of the law to cover psychiatric injury and the transmission of sexually transmitted diseases are a popular basis for an essay as is the issue of when consent can provide a defence to non-fatal offences.

Problem questions

Problem questions involving non-fatal offences are popular with examiners. They could appear on their own, combine with other offences, involve multiple parties (accessories: see Chapter 5) or appear in conjunction with any of the defences. Their flexibility makes them an important revision topic. It is essential that you are able to provide a correct statement of the *actus reus* and *mens rea* of each of the offences as your answer will be flawed from the outset without an accurate legal framework.

■ Sample question

Could you answer this question? Below is a typical problem question that could arise on this topic. Guidelines for answering this question are included at the end of this chapter. Another sample question and guidance on tackling it can be found on the companion website.

PROBLEM QUESTION

Danielle (13) asks David (14) to pierce her navel with a needle. She lies down and closes her eyes. David thinks that it will be difficult to get the needle through her navel so he pierces her ear instead. Danielle is furious because her parents have prohibited her from having her ears pierced. She threatens to punch David so he runs downstairs. He trips on the stairs in his haste, falls and breaks his arm. Derek, Danielle's stepfather, finds out what has happened and beats Danielle severely with a belt causing bruising to her buttocks. Danielle's mother, Daisy, is so distressed by the bad relationship between her husband and daughter that she has to be treated for depression.

Discuss the criminal liability of the parties.

■ Common assault

Common assault is a low-level offence that is based upon causing another to expect an attack. It does not involve any physical contact between defendant and victim.

KEY DEFINITION: Common assault

An assault is an act which causes another person to apprehend the infliction of immediate unlawful force on his person.

Collins v *Wilcock* [1984] 1 WLR 1172 at 1177

Three *actus reus* elements	Two alternative *mens rea* elements
An act	Intention to cause apprehension of immediate violence
Apprehension	or
Immediate violence	Subjective recklessness as to whether such apprehension is caused

Actus reus elements

There are three elements that make up the *actus reus* of common assault – the act, apprehension and immediate violence – each of which must be established in turn.

The act

Assault requires a positive act so cannot be committed by omission (Chapter 2). It used to be thought that this positive act was limited to conduct and did not include words but this view was dismissed by the House of Lords in *Ireland* (below). This is an important case that raises several important issues relating to non-fatal offences that will be discussed at various points in this chapter.

KEY CASE

R v *Ireland* [1998] AC 147 (HL)

Concerning: assault by words/silence

Facts

The defendant made a series of silent calls causing the recipients to suffer anxiety, depression and stress. One of the issues considered by the House of Lords was whether (1) words and (2) silence were an act that could be the basis of liability for common assault.

Legal principle

The House of Lords dismissed the long-standing principle that words could not amount to an assault as 'unrealistic and indefensible' stating that 'a thing said is a thing done'. In other words, words are actions.

Silent calls could be characterised as an omission (failure to speak) which would not provide a basis for assault. However, the House of Lords held that silent calls were a form of positive communication as the defendant intended his silence to communicate a threat. As such, silence in this context would amount to a positive act.

✎ EXAM TIP

Problem questions frequently involve words as an assault so *Ireland* is an important case. Remember that the other requirements of the offence must also be satisfied.

A trickier situation involves silence: the defendant does not reply when asked, 'You're not going to hurt me, are you?' Remember, that *Ireland* distinguishes silent telephone calls (a positive form of communicating) and silence in person (which may still constitute an omission and thus cannot be the basis of assault).

Apprehension

The act must cause apprehension of violence. Apprehension, in this sense, does not mean fear; it means expectation. It is a common mistake (made by lecturers and judges as well as students) to use 'apprehension' and 'fear' interchangeably. The differences are shown in Figure 9.1.

Figure 9.1

FEAR	APPREHENSION
Darren drives past Vernon and shouts abuse and threats at him. Vernon is afraid as he knows Darren has a reputation for violence.	Vernon shouts abuse as Darren drives past. Darren is so angry that he stops the car and runs towards Vernon, waving his fists. Vernon is eager for a fight and races to confront Darren.
Vernon is fearful as he knows Darren is violent but he does not apprehend (anticipate) violence as Darren has driven away. Words can only constitute an assault if they cause an apprehension of immediate unlawful violence. Causing a general state of fearfulness will not suffice; there must be an expectation of an imminent attack.	Darren is waving his fists so Vernon is expecting violence to be imminent. He is not afraid; he is eager to fight. This will nonetheless amount to common assault as Vernon apprehends (anticipates) violence from Darren. The fact that he is not afraid is irrelevant.

The example in Figure 9.1 illustrates an important distinction in the meaning of the two words:

- a person may apprehend violence without being fearful (common assault);
- a person may fear violence without expecting that it is imminent (no offence).

Immediate violence

The immediacy requirement of common assault is consistent with the overall purpose of the offence, which is to prohibit causing an expectation of imminent attack.

KEY CASE

R v Ireland **[1998] AC 147 (HL)**

Concerning: common assault, immediacy

Facts

Facts as above.

Legal principle

The House of Lords confirmed that only apprehension of *immediate* violence would suffice for assault. This was satisfied in relation to silent calls: 'What, if not the possibility of imminent personal violence, was the victim terrified about?'

KEY CASE

R v *Constanza* [1997] 2 Cr App R 492 (CA)

Concerning: assault; immediate apprehension of unlawful violence

Facts

As part of a stalking campaign, the defendant sent over 800 letters to the victim within eight months. The final letter was hand-delivered, giving rise to a charge of assault.

Legal principle

The Court of Appeal addressed the immediacy requirement by holding that the letter caused an apprehension of violence at *some time not excluding the immediate future.*

Again, there is an important distinction here:

- apprehension of immediate violence (common assault);
- immediate apprehension of deferred violence (no offence).

Mens rea of assault

The three elements of the *actus reus* can be complicated but the *mens rea* of assault is reassuringly straightforward, requiring either:

- intention to cause apprehension of immediate unlawful violence (deliberately causing the *actus reus*); or
- subjective recklessness thereto (the defendant must foresee a risk that the victim will apprehend immediate unlawful violence).

📖 REVISION NOTE

Refresh your memory on subjective *Cunningham* recklessness (see Chapter 3). Remember it is based upon what the defendant actually foresaw rather than what he ought to have foreseen.

■ Battery

Battery is the least serious of the non-fatal offences that involves physical violence.

> **KEY DEFINITION: Battery**
>
> A battery is the actual infliction of unlawful force on another person.
>
> *Collins* v *Wilcock* [1984] 1 WLR 1172 at 1177

Three *actus reus* elements	Two alternative *mens rea* elements
Direct or indirect	Intention to make direct/indirect non-consensual physical contact with another
Non-consensual	or
Physical contact	Subjective recklessness thereto

Actus reus elements

The *actus reus* of battery is comprised of three elements, all of which must be satisfied.

Direct or indirect

Battery is based upon physical contact, whether direct (one person touching another) or indirect (as in *Haystead* [2000] 3 All ER 890 (DC), where the defendant hit a woman causing her to drop the baby she was holding: he was convicted of battery on the baby, even though he did not touch it).

Non-consensual

Battery requires non-consensual touching. Consent may either be express (the victim agrees to contact) or implied (from the inevitable contact arising from participation in everyday life). Examples of implied consent were given in *Collins* v *Wilcox* [1984] 1 WLR 1172 (DC) as:

- jostling on the underground;
- having one's hand seized in friendship;
- amicable back-slapping.

Physical contact

There must be some physical contact with the victim. Even minor contact will suffice and it includes touching a person's clothing whilst they are wearing it: *Thomas* (1985) 81 Cr App R 331 (CA).

It is misleading to describe battery as 'violence' as it includes very minor physical contact and often results in no injury or very minor injuries. It is only the level of injury that distinguishes battery from section 47 OAPA as demonstrated by the CPS Charging Standards for the two offences:

Battery	Actual bodily harm
Scratches/grazes	Temporary loss of sensory functions
Minor bruising	Extensive or multiple bruising
Superficial cuts	Minor cuts requiring stitching
Black eyes	Minor fractures

✎ **EXAM TIP**

Focusing on the level of harm caused is a useful means of deciding what offence is appropriate in a problem question. The line between battery and section 47 is particularly important if consent is involved.

Mens rea of battery

As with common assault, the *mens rea* of battery is satisfied either by intention to make physical contact with the victim or by subjective recklessness as to such contact.

❗ Don't be tempted to . . .

Think about the everyday use of the words 'assault' and 'battery'. Students often struggle to grasp the non-physical nature of common assault. In normal conversation 'he assaulted me' generally means that there has been physical contact but this would be a battery in law and not a common assault. Try to remember the following key points to help you to avoid this common error (and see Figure 9.2).

☐ Common assault and battery are two separate offences but they usually occur in swift succession, i.e. a common assault is followed by a battery, so they are often part of the same incident.

☐ Common assault never involves physical contact. It is the apprehension of physical contact.

☐ Battery involves physical contact. If the parties have touched, the defendant has committed a battery. Ask yourself whether the victim realised that this was going to happen to determine whether there is also liability for common assault.

Figure 9.2

Timing of events →	
COMMON ASSAULT	**BATTERY**

Definition	
The defendant causes the victim to apprehend immediate unlawful violence	The defendant applies non-consensual physical contact to the victim's body

In other words	
The victim sees that an attack is imminent	The attack on the victim takes place

For example	
Vincent sees Derek running towards him with an axe	Derek hits Vincent over the head with the axe

■ Consent

Consent can be a defence to non-fatal offences as it negates the unlawfulness of the force used. All non-fatal offences except common assault require unlawful force. Why would someone consent to force? It is important to remember that battery involves a very minor level of force as mere touching will suffice: a hug would be a battery if consent were not a defence. Equally, more serious physical harm such as surgery or ear-piercing would fall within section 18 OAPA if it were not possible for the victim to consent.

However, the law does not allow consent to operate as a defence to all instances of non-fatal violence. It strives to achieve a balance between *personal autonomy* (the right of individuals to control what happens to them) and *prevention of harm* (to individuals and to society). This raises two questions that have been addressed by the courts:

1. Where should the line be drawn between offences to which individuals should be able to consent to freely and those where consent is not generally permitted?

2. Once the line is drawn and a category of offences is established where an individual is not generally permitted to consent, what exceptions exist where consent should be recognised?

The boundaries of consent

In *Brown,* the House of Lords considered where the line was to be drawn between offences to which a person could give consent and those where consent would be recognised only in exceptional circumstances.

R v Brown [1994] 1 AC 212 (HL)

Concerning: consent, bodily harm

Facts

The defendants were sado-masochistic homosexuals charged with battery and offences under section 47 and section 20 OAPA as a result of injuries caused during consensual sexual activity. They argued that the victims had consented to the activities and to the infliction of injuries.

Legal principle

The House of Lords ruled that consent was only a defence to conduct that did not result in bodily harm (battery). In relation to offences resulting in bodily harm, there was a range of exceptions where consent was a defence such as surgery and sports but this was justified on the basis of public interest. The House of Lords refused to enlarge that category to include consensual sexual activities, stating that it was not in the public interest for people to cause each other bodily harm for no good reason.

This gives rise to a clear division between offences to which there are no limitations to the use of consent and offences to which consent is available only in limited circumstances, as Figure 9.3 illustrates.

Figure 9.3

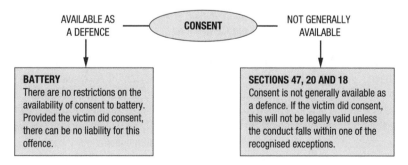

Exceptional circumstances

According to *Brown,* the general rule is that consent is not available to offences that result in bodily harm (ss. 47, 20 and 18). This is because 'it is not in the public interest that people should ... cause each other actual bodily harm for no good reason': *Re Attorney-General's Reference (No. 6 of 1980)* [1981] 1 QB 715 (CA). Following on from that, it is accepted that there are circumstances in which consent is permitted to injuries that would fall within ss. 47, 20 and 18 on the public policy basis that there is a 'good reason' to allow a defence. The following are the categories of conduct in which it is accepted that consent will be permitted as a defence:

- *Lawful surgery:* this includes cosmetic surgery as well as necessary medical intervention.
- *Ear-piercing and tattooing:* regarded by the House of Lords in *Brown* as a matter of personal choice and the exercise of autonomy.
- *Properly conducted sporting activities:* in *Barnes* [2005] 1 WLR 910 (CA), the Court of Appeal held the defendant was criminally liable for injury caused by a tackle in football on the basis that it was so far outside of the 'rules of the game' that criminal liability was appropriate.
- *Manly horseplay:* for example, *Aitken* [1992] 1 WLR 1006 (CA) where defendants who set light to an RAF colleague covered in white spirit as part of a prank were permitted a defence of consent.

In *Brown,* the House of Lords refused to accept that there was 'good reason' to allow a defence of consent in relation to sado-masochistic homosexual activities. This attracted some criticism from those who felt that the decision was influenced by moral considerations and distaste for the defendants' activities. The principle has been refined and clarified in subsequent case law, as illustrated in Figure 9.4.

 Make your answer stand out

You should consider the further complication that arises in relation to consent if the defendant has practised some kind of deception in order to obtain consent. This may invalidate the consent so that the defence is not available to the defendant, but that depends upon the nature of the deception. For example, the defendant in *Richardson* [1999] QB 444 (CA) did not inform her patients that her licence to practise dentistry had been revoked but that was not a deception that invalidated their consent as the nature and quality of the act was unchanged. By contrast, consent was invalidated in *Tabassum* [2000] Cr App R 328 (CA) as the defendant misrepresented to victims that he was a doctor undertaking breast examinations. Williams's (2008) article discusses these cases and deceptive consent in other areas of criminal law and provides a comprehensive grounding to the issues raised that might help you to prepare for an essay on the topic.

Figure 9.4

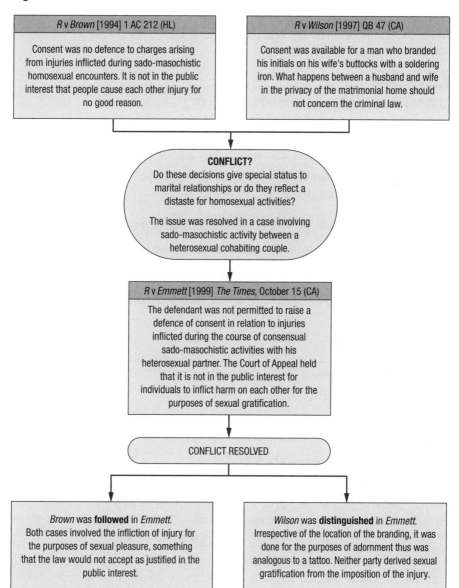

R v Brown [1994] 1 AC 212 (HL)

Consent was no defence to charges arising from injuries inflicted during sado-masochistic homosexual encounters. It is not in the public interest that people cause each other injury for no good reason.

R v Wilson [1997] QB 47 (CA)

Consent was available for a man who branded his initials on his wife's buttocks with a soldering iron. What happens between a husband and wife in the privacy of the matrimonial home should not concern the criminal law.

CONFLICT?
Do these decisions give special status to marital relationships or do they reflect a distaste for homosexual activities?

The issue was resolved in a case involving sado-masochistic activity between a heterosexual cohabiting couple.

R v Emmett [1999] The Times, October 15 (CA)

The defendant was not permitted to raise a defence of consent in relation to injuries inflicted during the course of consensual sado-masochistic activities with his heterosexual partner. The Court of Appeal held that it is not in the public interest for individuals to inflict harm on each other for the purposes of sexual gratification.

CONFLICT RESOLVED

Brown was **followed** in *Emmett*. Both cases involved the infliction of injury for the purposes of sexual pleasure, something that the law would not accept as justified in the public interest.

Wilson was **distinguished** in *Emmett*. Irrespective of the location of the branding, it was done for the purposes of adornment thus was analogous to a tattoo. Neither party derived sexual gratification from the imposition of the injury.

Assault occasioning actual bodily harm

This is the least serious of the non-fatal offences found in the Offences Against the Person Act 1861.

Offences Against the Person Act 1861, section 47

Whosoever shall be convicted on indictment of any assault occasioning actual bodily harm shall be liable ... to imprisonment for any term not exceeding five years.

Section 47 states the penalty rather than defining the offence. Elaboration on the elements of the offence can be found in case law.

Two *actus reus* elements	Two alternative *mens rea* elements
The *actus reus* of common assault	The *mens rea* of common assault
or	or
The *actus reus* of battery	The *mens rea* of battery
plus	
Actual bodily harm	

Actus reus elements

In essence, section 47 is a common assault or battery that results in actual bodily harm. As such, there are two different ways in which the *actus reus* of the offence can be satisfied:

- assault resulting in actual bodily harm (ABH);
- battery resulting in ABH.

The only difference between section 47 and assault/battery is the level of harm that occurs. For this reason, it is sometimes called 'aggravated assault' with the aggravating feature being the severity of the harm arising from the common assault or battery.

! Don't be tempted to ...

Confuse terminology. Both the offences are called 'assault occasioning ABH'; there is no separate offence of battery occasioning ABH. This is because the word 'assault' in section 47 actually means 'common assault or battery'. Make sure that you take care to use terminology correctly.

Actual bodily harm

The common law definition of ABH is vague. *Donovan* [1934] 2 KB 498 (CA) described it as harm that is 'more than merely transient or trifling'. There is a table under the recent heading 'Physical contact' showing how the CPS decides whether an injury should be charged as battery or under section 47, which demonstrates the sorts of injuries that are regarded as 'more than merely transient or trifling'.

Occasioning

The common assault or battery must *occasion* (cause) the injury. This is straightforward in relation to battery: injuries are caused by physical contact. Common assault leading to injury is harder to understand – 'sticks and stones may break my bones but words will never hurt me'. There are two ways that threatening words/conduct can cause injury:

- injuries sustained whilst escaping;
- psychological injuries.

Escape cases

The courts have held that the defendant retains responsibility for injuries sustained whilst escaping from threatened (common assault) or actual (battery) violence.

Assault: *R* v *Lewis* [1970] Crim LR 647 (CA)	Battery: *R* v *Roberts* [1972] 56 Cr App R 95 (CA)
The victim locked herself in the bedroom. Her husband started to break down the door so she jumped out of the window to escape. His common assault (breaking down the door caused her to apprehend immediate unlawful violence) was held to be the cause of the injuries sustained in the fall.	The victim was a passenger in a car driven by the defendant. He committed a battery by interfering with the victim's clothing. She jumped out of the moving vehicle to avoid his attentions. It was held that the defendant's battery caused the injuries sustained by the victim in the fall.

✎ EXAM TIP

If the defendant is not the *direct* cause of the victim's injuries, look for injuries caused *indirectly,* particularly following common assault. Even though the victim chose to escape, injuries will be attributed to the defendant unless the victim's conduct was 'so daft' as to be unforeseeable (*Roberts*) (see Chapter 2 for more detail on causation).

Psychiatric injury

The expansion of the law on non-fatal offences to include psychiatric injury is a relatively recent development, as the cases in Figure 9.5 demonstrate.

Figure 9.5

R v *Miller* [1954] 2 QB 282 (CA)
Injury to the victim's state of mind 'for the time being' amounted to 'bodily harm'.

R v *Chan Fook* [1994] 1 WLR 689 (CA)
Held that 'body' is not limited to flesh, skin and bones but includes organs, nervous system and brain. Mere emotions such as fear, distress and panic are excluded.

R v *Ireland* [1998] AC 147 (HL)
House of Lords confirmed *Chan Fook* and held that psychological injury could amount to actual bodily harm but that psychological injury should be a matter of expert evidence.

R v *Burstow* [1998] AC 147 (HL)
House of Lords held that a sufficiently serious psychological injury could amount to grievous bodily harm.

R v *Morris* [1998] 1 Cr App R 386 (CA)
In relation to psychological injury, expert evidence must be given by a psychiatrist, not a general practitioner.

KEY CASES

R v *Ireland; R* v *Burstow* **[1998] AC 147 (HL)**

Concerning: psychiatric injury

Facts

Ireland: see above. *Burstow*: a stalking case in which the defendant bombarded an acquaintance with unwanted attention for three years. The issue in both cases was whether the depressive symptoms suffered by the victims could amount to 'bodily harm' as previously this had been limited to physical injuries.

Legal principle

The House of Lords agreed that the draftsman of the OAPA would not have contemplated the inclusion of psychiatric injury within 'bodily harm'. However, the statute was of the 'always speaking' kind that expanded to accommodate new developments such as greater understanding of the link between mind and body. Harm to a person's mind that amounts to a recognised medical condition falls within 'bodily harm'.

In problem questions, look out for mention of depression, anxiety or sleeplessness resulting from the defendant's conduct, as this suggests psychiatric injury. Remember that the House of Lords held that this can amount to ABH (*Ireland*) or GBH (*Burstow*), depending on its severity.

Mens rea elements

There are two parts to the *actus reus* of section 47: (1) assault or battery and (2) ABH. The *mens rea* relates only to the first of these. This means that the *mens rea* of section 47 is identical to the *mens rea* of either assault or battery (whichever caused the ABH). This is why it is called an offence of half *mens rea* (see Figure 9.6).

Figure 9.6

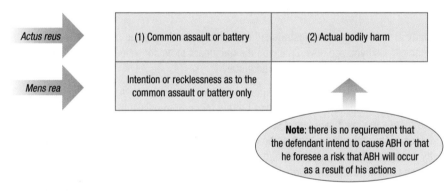

Actus reus	(1) Common assault or battery	(2) Actual bodily harm
Mens rea	Intention or recklessness as to the common assault or battery only	

Note: there is no requirement that the defendant intend to cause ABH or that he foresee a risk that ABH will occur as a result of his actions

KEY CASE

R v *Savage* [1992] 1 AC 699 (HL)

Concerning: half mens rea

Facts

The defendant poured her drink over the victim (battery). The glass slipped out of her hand, smashed and cut the victim. Her conviction under section 47 related to this injury. Her appeal against conviction was based on lack of *mens rea*: she argued that she neither intended injury nor foresaw that injury would be caused (see Figure 9.7).

Legal principle

The House of Lords dismissed the appeal, holding that the *mens rea* of section 47 required intention or subjective recklessness in relation to the common assault or battery only. There was no requirement of intention or foresight in respect of the injury caused by the assault or battery.

Figure 9.7

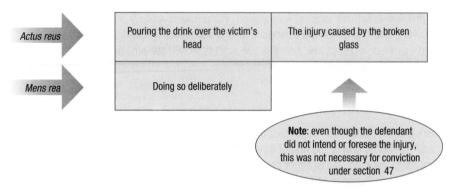

Many answers fail to demonstrate sufficient understanding of the *half mens* rea principle. Can you see how it allowed the defendant to be convicted when a full *mens rea* requirement would have led to acquittal?

Half *mens rea* makes it easier to establish liability for section 47. A defendant who has the *actus reus* and *mens rea* for a battery (or common assault) will be liable for the more serious offence under section 47 if the harm is greater than he planned or foresaw. This is justified because he has crossed the threshold into criminal behaviour by committing common assault/battery so will be liable for the consequences of his actions. The half *mens rea* principle is also a recognition that it is difficult to control the level of harm inflicted, so a person who intends only battery cannot escape liability for a more serious offence if he inadvertently causes more serious harm.

Stone (1992) provides some excellent analysis of the impact of Savage (and the joined appeal in *Parmenter,* which relates to the *mens rea* of section 20) that would be useful reading in preparation for an essay question.

■ Wounding or inflicting grievous bodily harm

KEY STATUTE

Offences Against the Person Act 1861, section 20

Whosoever shall unlawfully and maliciously wound or inflict any grievous bodily harm upon any other person, either with or without a weapon or instrument, shall be ... liable to ... five years' imprisonment.

Two alternative *actus reus* elements	Two alternative *mens rea* elements
Wounding	Intention
or	or
Inflicting grievous bodily harm	Recklessness as to the wound or the infliction of GBH

The combination of *actus reus* and *mens rea* elements gives rise to four different ways that section 20 may be satisfied:

1. *Intentional wounding:* the defendant uses a razor blade to slice open his girlfriend's face as revenge for her infidelity – he intends to inflict the wound.

2. *Intentional infliction of GBH:* the defendant kicks the victim in the head until he is unconscious, causing massive brain damage – he has deliberately brought about serious harm.

3. *Reckless wounding:* the defendant pushes the victim over during an argument, anticipating only that the victim will suffer bruising but she falls on broken glass and receives a cut on the hand – the defendant foresaw the risk of some harm and caused a wound.

4. *Reckless infliction of GBH:* the defendant pushes in jest, expecting that it will cause nothing more than bruising but the victim stumbles into the road where she is struck by a passing car and sustains serious injuries – the defendant foresaw the risk of some harm and caused serious bodily harm.

Actus reus elements

There are two alternative forms of *actus reus* for this offence: (1) wounding and (2) inflicting GBH.

Wounding and grievous bodily harm

KEY DEFINITION: Grievous bodily harm and wound

Grievous bodily harm (GBH) is a general term meaning 'really serious harm'.

DPP v *Smith* [1961] AC 290 (HL)

A wound is a break in the continuity of both layers of the skin.

C v *Eisenhower* [1984] QB 331 (DC)

These two forms of *actus reus* cover a wide range of harm. They will often overlap, i.e. an injury will amount to both a **wound** and GBH, but this is not always the case: not all wounds are serious and not all serious injuries involve a break in the continuity of the skin.

Students tend to get confused on this point, often treating 'wound' and 'GBH' as interchangeable terms. The table below demonstrates the distinction between the terms:

Wound only	Wound and GBH	GBH only
Minor cuts	Deep repeated cuts	Broken bones that do not pierce the skin
Syringe puncture	Broken bones piercing the skin	Psychiatric injury

Infliction

It was always thought that the requirement that GBH be *inflicted* on the victim meant something different from the requirement under section 18 that GBH was caused to the victim. However:

■ In *Burstow* (above), it was held that there is no distinction between 'cause' and 'inflict' in relation to psychiatric injury.

■ In *Dica* [2004] QB 1257 (CA), it was held that this also applied in relation to physical harm (this concerned the infliction of GBH by transmission of HIV during intercourse).

 Make your answer stand out

One of the more recent developments in relation to this offence concerns the transmission of HIV following intercourse between a defendant who is aware that he has the infection and a victim who lacks knowledge of this. *Dica* (above) and *Konzani* [2005] 2 Cr App R 198 (CA) deal with this issue and provide that a defence of consent will be available only if the victim gave informed consent, i.e. in the knowledge of the defendant's HIV status. Ryan (2006) provides an excellent analysis of these cases and their implications that would help you to prepare to tackle this tricky issue in an essay.

Mens rea of section 20

Section 20 refers to *malicious* wounding or infliction of GBH. 'Maliciously' denotes two alternative *mens rea* states: (1) intention and (2) subjective recklessness. The test of recklessness applicable to section 20 is a modified form of *Cunningham* recklessness. This is called the *Mowatt* gloss and was approved by the House of Lords in *Parmenter*.

KEY CASE

DPP v *Parmenter* [1992] 1 AC 699 (HL)

Concerning: recklessness, Mowatt gloss

Facts

The defendant's rough handling of his child caused broken bones. It was accepted that he had not intended to cause injury nor had he realised that there was a risk of injury. The trial judge directed the jury in terms of what the defendant *should have foreseen* would result from his actions.

Legal principle

The House of Lords upheld the ruling of the Court of Appeal that this was a misdirection.

- The standard of recklessness is subjective based upon what the defendant actually foresaw not what he ought to have foreseen.
- Foresight of the consequences was required but not foresight of their magnitude. This confirms the *Mowatt* gloss that foresight of some harm will suffice.

This means that it is easier to establish recklessness in relation to section 20 than it would be if a pure form of *Cunningham* recklessness was applied, as Figure 9.8 illustrates.

Figure 9.8

Pure *Cunningham* recklessness	Modified *Cunningham* recklessness
Requires that the defendant foresees a risk that his conduct will cause the prohibited consequence (*actus reus*).	The *Mowatt* gloss on *Cunningham* recklessness catches defendants who foresee that their actions will cause some harm but who do not expect it to be so serious that it amounts to GBH.
In relation to section 20, this would require that the defendant foresaw a risk that his conduct would wound or result in the infliction of GBH.	**The test of recklessness required for s. 20 is therefore foresight of a risk of *some* harm, albeit not harm of the severity that actually occurred.**
Foresight of the risk of harm less than GBH would not suffice.	

■ Grievous bodily harm with intent

The most serious non-fatal offence against the person is found in section 18, OAPA.

Offences Against the Person Act 1861, section 18

Whosoever shall unlawfully and maliciously ... wound or cause any grievous bodily harm ... with intent ... to do some grievous bodily harm to any person or with intent to resist or prevent the lawful apprehension or detainer of any person shall [be liable] to imprisonment for life.

Two alternative *actus reus* elements	Two cumulative *mens rea* elements
Wounding	Maliciousness (regarding wound/GBH)
or	and
Causing grievous bodily harm	Ulterior intent (to cause GBH or resist/prevent lawful detention)

This combination of *actus reus* and *mens rea* requirements means that there are four different manifestations of section 18 (see Figure 9.9).

Figure 9.9

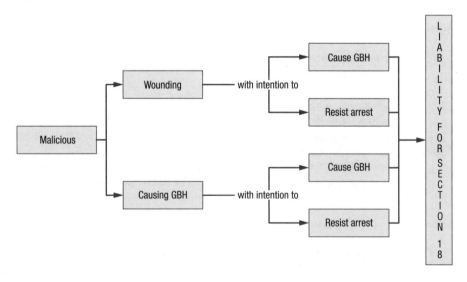

Actus reus elements

Like section 20, there are two different ways that the *actus reus* of section 18 can be satisfied: (1) unlawful wounding or (2) causing GBH.

Wounding/causing GBH

There is little distinction remaining between 'cause' and 'inflict', thus the *actus reus* of section 18 is the same as section 20, *except* that section 18 covers GBH caused by omission. Section 20 requires that GBH be inflicted by a positive act.

✎ EXAM TIP

Impress the examiner with this frequently overlooked point. There is credit to be gained by explaining (concisely) why a particular offence is not relevant. For example, 'The defendant's failure to act caused serious injury to the victim. *As liability for section 20 cannot be based on omission,* the defendant may be liable under section 18' will gain greater credit than 'The defendant has caused serious injury to the victim so may be liable under section 18'.

Mens rea elements

Section 18 has two *mens rea* requirements, both of which must be satisfied (see Figure 9.10).

Figure 9.10

STAGE 1 – MALICE
Was the wound or GBH caused intentionally or recklessly?
Remember that recklessness in this sense is subjective (as discussed in relation to section 20 above) so requires that the defendant was aware of the risk of some harm arising from his conduct.

STAGE 2 – ULTERIOR INTENT
Did the defendant possess ulterior intent?
Was he acting with the intention of: (a) causing GBH; or   (b) resisting or preventing lawful arrest?

Malice

Intention or modified subjective recklessness as to causing of GBH or wound (as under section 20).

Ulterior intent

This refers to the defendant's purpose in acting as he did:

- The defendant must intend to cause GBH rather than have a general intention to cause harm.

- An intention to wound will not suffice. Wounding only satisfied section 18 if it was caused with an intention to cause GBH or resist/prevent arrest.
- Intention to resist/prevent arrest covers the arrest of the defendant or a third party.
- There must be awareness of the arrest. A defendant who mistakenly thinks he (or another) is being attacked is not acting to resist/prevent arrest.
- The arrest must be lawful. Resisting an unlawful arrest is not sufficient to establish ulterior intent. However, resisting a lawful arrest in the mistaken belief that it is unlawful will satisfy the ulterior intent.

The requirements of sections 20 and 18 can cause confusion. The flow chart in Figure 9.11 should help you to work through problem questions in a methodical manner:

Figure 9.11

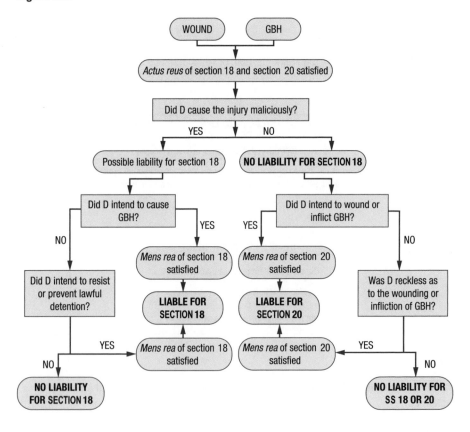

■ Proposals for reform

As you will have seen, the law relating to non-fatal offences is complex! In 2011, the Law Commission published its latest proposals for reform, stating that:

OFFENCES AGAINST THE PERSON

2.61 The Offences Against the Person Act 1861 is widely recognised as being outdated. It uses archaic language and follows a Victorian approach of listing separate offences for individual factual scenarios, many of which are no longer necessary (see for example the section 17 offence of impeding a person endeavouring to save himself from a shipwreck).

2.62 The structure of the Act is also unsatisfactory as there is no clear hierarchy of offences and the differences between sections 18, 20 and 47 are not clearly spelt out in the Act. Section 20 (maliciously wounding or inflicting grievous bodily harm) is seen as more serious than section 47 (assault occasioning actual bodily harm) but the maximum penalty (five years) is the same. Furthermore the *actus reus* for sections 18 (intentionally wounding or causing grievous bodily harm) and 20 appear to be the same apart from the distinction between 'causing' and 'inflicting', which is notoriously difficult to draw.

2.63 This project will therefore aim to restructure the law on offences against the person, probably by creating a structured hierarchy of offences, as well as modernising and simplifying the language by which these offences are defined. A further possibility would be to tie this new hierarchy of offences to mode of trial in order to clear up some of the procedural discrepancies.

The proposals for reform were set out in Consultation Paper No. 217 in April 2014 and can be found here: www.lawcom.gov.uk/wp-content/uploads/2015/06/cp217_offences_against_the_person.pdf

■ Putting it all together

Answer guidelines

See the problem question at the start of the chapter. A diagram illustrating how to structure your answer is available on the companion website.

Approaching the question

This is a typical problem question covering a range of non-fatal offences. It involves a number of parties and several different events that could give rise to liability. The ▶

trick to dealing with such a question effectively is to spend time at the beginning in untangling the facts to ensure that you are clear 'who has done what to whom'. A well-organised answer is more likely to cover all the issues.

Important points to include

- David has pierced Danielle's ear. Think about what sort of injury this is likely to involve. Although it is not particularly serious, it will fall within section 18 or section 20 as the continuity of the skin is broken by the puncture so it amounts to a wound. If an issue raises the possibility of liability for more than one offence, start with the most serious offence and work your way downwards until you reach a definite finding of liability. Applying the *mens rea* of section 18, David has intentionally caused a wound but he lacks the ulterior intention to cause GBH or prevent/resist arrest so liability is not established. The *mens rea* of section 20 is more easily satisfied so *prima facie* liability is established.

- Danielle chases David. He runs away so it is reasonable to assume that he apprehends immediate unlawful violence thus establishing the *actus reus* of assault. Did she intend to cause this or was she reckless as to whether he would apprehend such violence? If the answer is 'yes' then liability for common assault is established. As David fell and broke his arm when running away from Danielle, it is possible (applying the escape cases) that she is liable for a more serious offence. Explain how liability for section 47 would be established and then consider whether liability under section 20 is possible.

- Derek has beaten Danielle, causing serious bruising. Select an appropriate offence by deciding what severity of harm is involved. Serious bruising could fall within actual bodily harm as an injury which is 'more than merely transient and trifling', so consider liability for section 47. It is not difficult to establish a battery and it is clear that this was deliberate, as Derek's purpose was to punish Danielle.

- Daisy has suffered depression following this series of events so this should trigger a discussion of liability for psychiatric injury. The tricky issue here comes in selecting a defendant: would you establish liability in relation to Danielle or Derek or both parties? If you select one party rather than the other, you will need to explain your reasoning. Explain that psychiatric injury falls within the meaning of 'bodily harm' and consider what level of harm has been caused (grievous or actual). Once you have identified a relevant offence, consider whether its elements can be established.

Make your answer stand out

There are a couple of tricky issues of consent to be addressed here: did Danielle consent to the piercing or the beating? Consider whether each situation is one in which the law allows the victim to give consent. Both involve more serious offences than battery so consent will be valid only if it falls within one of the recognised exceptions. Piercing is one of these but probably only when carried out by a licensed individual which David (aged 14) is not and, in any case, Danielle consented to having her navel pierced, not her ear, so it is unlikely that consent will operate as a defence here. Although it is unlikely that she consented to a beating from her stepfather, this will fall within reasonable chastisement provided that the punishment imposed was reasonable.

The psychiatric injury issue is also complicated and requires careful handling. You would need to demonstrate an ability to deal with the relevant case law but also to recognise their limitations – neither *Ireland* nor *Burstow* had to deal with the complex matter of causation of psychiatric injury as both defendants entered guilty pleas. It would be easy to deal with Daisy's psychiatric injury without acknowledging the causation issue but stronger answers will tackle it, even though it makes reaching a conclusion about liability much harder. Remember that it is not always necessary (or even possible) to reach a definite conclusion about liability – all that you can do is to raise and explore the issues.

READ TO IMPRESS

Fafinski, S. (2005) Consent and the Rules of the Game: The Interplay of Civil and Criminal Liability for Sporting Injuries. *Journal of Criminal Law,* 69: 414.

Ryan, S. (2006) Reckless Transmission of HIV: Knowledge and Culpability. *Criminal Law Review,* 981.

Stone, R. (1992) Reckless Assaults After *Savage* and *Parmenter. Oxford Journal of Legal Studies,* 12: 578.

Williams, R. (2008) Deception, Mistake and the Vitiation of the Victim's Consent. *Law Quarterly Review,* 124: 132.

www.pearsoned.co.uk/lawexpress

Go online to access more revision support, including quizzes to test your knowledge, sample questions with answer guidelines, podcasts you can download and more!

10

Sexual offences

Revision checklist

Essential points you should know:

☐ The *actus reus* and *mens rea* of the various sexual offences

☐ The key distinctions between the Sexual Offences Act 2003 and the previous law

☐ The role of consent, including the operation of conclusive and evidential presumptions

☐ The relationship between the sexual offences

Topic map

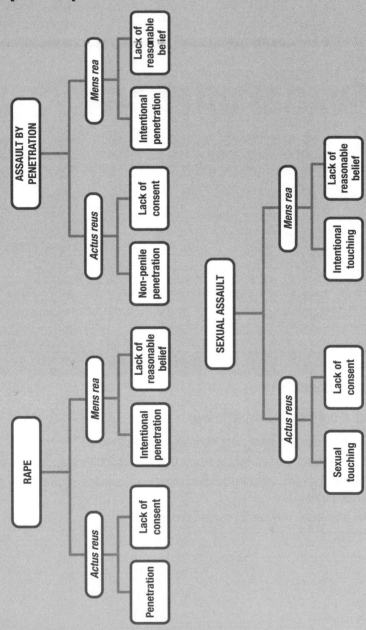

A printable version of this topic map is available from **www.pearsoned.co.uk/lawexpress**

■ Introduction

The law governing sexual offences was codified by the Sexual Offences Act 2003.

The Sexual Offences Act 2003 (SOA 2003) reformed the law on sexual offences by consolidation of the pre-existing statute and common law. It abolished some former criminal offences (repealing most of the Sexual Offences Acts 1956 and 1967 and the Indecency with Children Act 1960), and created a new law on rape and sexual assault as well as a host of other new offences, including offences committed against vulnerable people. This chapter focuses on four key areas: rape, assault by penetration, sexual assault and child sex offences.

ASSESSMENT ADVICE

Essay questions

Essay questions could focus on sexual offences following the changes in the law. An essay could focus on the changes made to a particular offence, e.g. rape, or ask more generally whether the law is effective. The scope of a general essay should be determined by reference to your course content, so be sure that you are familiar with the sexual offences on your syllabus. You should check to see how much detail you are expected to know on the old law and the extent to which it is covered on your course. This chapter will focus largely on the current law, although there will be some references to the old law.

Problem questions

Problem questions could cover a range of different offences within one question, thus requiring an understanding of how the offences relate to each other. Alternatively, there may be a single sexual offence in combination with other offences such as non-fatal offences or theft. You should be alert for the possibility of a question in which the rape victim attacks the rapist, raising the possibility of liability for a fatal or non-fatal offence and reliance on self-defence.

■ Sample question

Could you answer this question? Below is a typical problem question that could arise on this topic. Guidelines on answering the question are included at the end of this chapter, whilst a sample essay question and guidance on tackling it can be found on the companion website.

PROBLEM QUESTION

John is a cleaner at the university. He gets talking to Kelly in the coffee shop. They get on well and move on to the Student Union bar where they share a bottle of wine. Later, they are kissing in John's car when the door is pulled open and Kelly is pulled from the car by her father who is a professor of sociology. He shouts, 'How dare you, my daughter is only 13! I'll see that you are sacked for this.'

Despondent at the thought of losing his job, John goes to visit his friend, Penelope, hoping she will cheer him up. After a few drinks, they start to cuddle and Penelope undoes John's trousers and strokes his penis. He does not move but murmurs, 'I don't really think this is a good idea', but Penelope carries on. He pushes her away and, shortly afterwards, Penelope (who was very drunk) passes out. John feels upset and wants revenge, so he lifts her skirt and inserts a finger into her vagina.

Discuss any criminal liability that arises.

■ Rape

KEY STATUTE

Sexual Offences Act 2003, section 1(1)

A person (A) commits an offence if –

(a) he intentionally penetrates the vagina, anus or mouth of another person (B) with his penis,

(b) B does not consent to the penetration, and

(c) A does not reasonably believe that B consents.

Two *actus reus* elements	Two *mens rea* elements
Penile penetration by A of the vagina, anus or mouth of B	Intentional penetration
Absence of B's consent	A lacks a reasonable belief in B's consent

Penetration

The first aspect of the *actus reus* concerns the physical act. SOA 2003, section 79(2) defines penetration as a 'continuing act from entry to withdrawal'. This definition means that an initially lawful act becomes rape if consent is revoked during intercourse. This mirrors the position under the old law, except that the offence is widened to include penetration of or by surgically constructed body parts (in particular, through gender reassignment surgery) and oral penetration (anal penetration was formerly covered within the Criminal Justice and Public Order Act 1994).

Consent

There are two roles for consent in the offence of rape (see Figure 10.1).

Figure 10.1

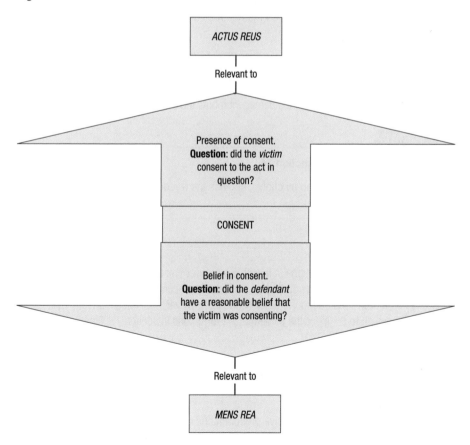

There is a difference between (a) whether the victim actually consents to penetration (*actus reus*) and (b) whether the defendant believes that she or he consents to penetration (*mens rea*). A good answer will demonstrate an understanding of the difference between the two by identifying facts from the problem that relate to each aspect of consent.

Scrutinise the facts of the question for evidence of both consent and belief in consent: for example, Veronica struggles with Denis during intercourse (lack of consent: *actus reus*) which he takes as evidence of her enthusiasm (belief in consent: *mens rea*).

Absence of consent

Lack of consent is part of the *actus reus* of rape. The old law offered little guidance on the meaning of consent, leaving it to the jury to decide on the basis of 'good sense, experience and knowledge of human nature and modern behaviour': *Olugboja* [1982] QB 320 (CA). The 2003 Act provides greater guidance by creating three different approaches to consent (see Figure 10.2).

This is quite complicated. In relation to sections 75 and 76, the prosecution have to establish one of the listed circumstances rather than having to prove that there was no consent. The definition of consent is found in section 74. This must be applied when there are no conclusive or evidential presumptions and where the defendant rebuts the evidential presumption of consent.

KEY STATUTE

Sexual Offences Act 2003, section 74

A person consents if he agreed by choice, and has the freedom and capacity to make that choice.

✎ EXAM TIP

When you apply the presumptions in a problem answer you should start by considering whether the absence of consent is to be conclusively presumed (section 76). If it is, then there is no point in considering the other sections. However, if it is not, explain why it is not, then move on to consider the evidential presumptions in section 75. Finally, if this fails, then consider section 74.

In an essay, you might start with the general rule under section 74 and then move on to consider the evidential and conclusive presumptions as exceptions to that rule.

The relationship between the conclusive presumptions under section 76 and the wider definition of consent in section 74 was considered by the Court of Appeal in *Jheeta*:

Figure 10.2

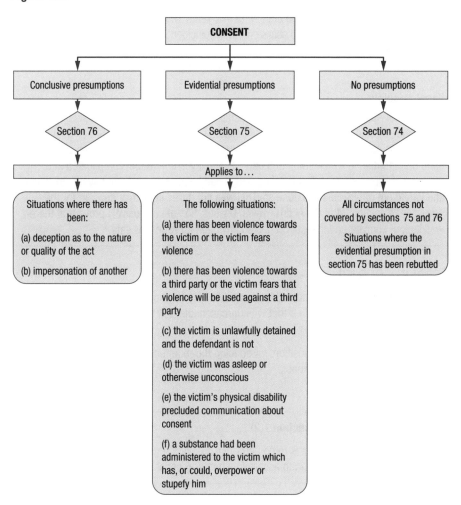

KEY CASE

R v *Jheeta* [2007] EWCA Crim 1699

Concerning: rape; consent; conclusive presumptions; purpose of act

Facts

The defendant (D) and victim (V) met at college and started a consensual sexual relationship. V began to receive anonymous threatening text messages. D (who, in fact, had sent the messages) reported the matter to the police on V's behalf. She subsequently received ▶

texts from 'PC Ken', 'PC Bob' and 'PC Martin' (ostensibly officers involved in her case, but actually sent from D) over a period of three or four years. During this time, V sought to end the relationship with D on several occasions. This coincided with texts from the 'police' to tell her that she should 'do her duty' and have intercourse with D and that she would be arrested and fined if she did not. D was charged with rape.

Legal principle

The Court of Appeal considered the relationship between section 76 (conclusive presumptions) and the wider definition of consent set out in section 74. Simon J. stated that '[V] was not deceived as to the nature or purpose of intercourse, but deceived as to the situation in which she found herself'. However, due to the 'complicated and unpleasant scheme' which D had fabricated, V had been pressured into having sex when she would not otherwise have done so. This was not a free choice, or consent for the purposes of section 74 of the Act. However, D's lies did not conclusively prove that there was lack of consent under section 76. D's conviction for rape was safe.

Belief in consent

Under the previous law, a defendant could avoid liability for rape if he had an honestly held mistaken belief in consent, even if that was unreasonable: *DPP* v *Morgan* [1976] AC 182 (HL) (often called 'the rapist's charter').

The current law reversed this position, introducing the requirement that the defendant's belief in consent must be reasonable.

KEY STATUTE

Sexual Offences Act 2003, section 1(2)

Whether a belief is reasonable is to be determined having regard to all the circumstances including any steps A has taken to ascertain whether B consents.

One particular problematic area concerns how consent is to be determined when the victim is extremely intoxicated. This relates not only to the *actus reus* of the offence – whether the victim was able to give consent – but also the *mens rea* of the offence: did the victim's intoxication impact on the defendant's belief in consent? The issues of the victim's capacity to give consent has been considered by the courts in *Bree* [2008] QB 131.

KEY CASE

R v *Bree* [2008] QB 131 (CA)

Concerning: rape; consent; intoxication

Facts

The appellant and the victim (M) had spent an evening together and had voluntarily consumed a considerable amount of alcohol before returning to M's flat and having sexual intercourse. The prosecution initially alleged that M had lacked the capacity to consent to the intercourse because she had been unconscious throughout most of the sexual activity but, following the evidence at trial, altered its position to maintain that, although her ability to resist B's sexual advances had been hampered by the effects of alcohol, she still had capacity to consent and that she had made clear, so far as she could, that she did not wish to have sexual intercourse.

Legal principle

The Court of Appeal held that the proper construction of section 74 was that if, through drink, or for any other reason, the complainant had temporarily lost her capacity to choose whether to have sexual intercourse on the relevant occasion, she was not consenting. However, where the complainant had voluntarily consumed substantial quantities of alcohol, but nevertheless remained capable of choosing whether to have intercourse, and agreed to do so, that would not be rape.

The court also commented that 'we should perhaps underline that, as a matter of practical reality, capacity to consent may well evaporate well before a complainant becomes unconscious'.

Intention

The defendant's penetration of the vagina, anus or mouth must be intentional. This is generally a straightforward requirement as it requires only that the sexual activity that took place was done deliberately.

■ Assault by penetration

This offence was introduced to bridge the gap between rape and sexual assault (previously indecent assault). Prior to its introduction, all non-consensual sexual attacks short of rape were covered by a single offence, thus giving little measure of relative seriousness. Assault by penetration elevates non-penile penetration to an equivalent seriousness with rape.

KEY STATUTE

Sexual Offences Act 2003, section 2(1)

A person (A) commits an offence if –

(a) he intentionally penetrates the vagina or anus of another person (B) with a part of his body or anything else,

(b) the penetration is sexual,

(c) B does not consent to the penetration, and

(d) A does not reasonably believe that B consents.

This replicates several features of rape but is both narrower in some respects (in that it covers only penetration of the anus and vagina but not of the mouth) and wider in others (it is not limited to penile penetration and, as a consequence, can be committed by both male and female defendants).

Two *actus reus* elements	Two *mens rea* elements
Non-penile sexual penetration of the vagina or anus	Intentional penetration
Absence of B's consent	A lacks a reasonable belief in B's consent

Sexual

The only unexplored element concerns the requirement that the penetration must be sexual in nature. This is presumed in relation to rape. 'Sexual' in relation to this (plus touching or other activity) is defined in section 78.

KEY STATUTE

Sexual Offences Act 2003, section 78

Penetration, touching or other activity is sexual if a reasonable person would consider that –

(a) whatever its circumstances or any person's purpose in relation to it, it is because of its nature sexual, or

(b) because of its nature it may be sexual and because of its circumstances or the purpose of any person in relation to it (or both) it is sexual.

This provision was considered in *H* [2005] 1 WLR 2005 (CA) in which the Court of Appeal provided a two-stage test when touching is not of its nature sexual. The questions to be addressed are:

- Would the jury, as 12 reasonable people, consider that the touching *could* be sexual?
- Would the jury, as 12 reasonable people and *in all the circumstances of the case,* consider that the purpose of the touching *had in fact* been sexual?

Examples of conduct which has been held to be sexual include:

- grabbing a pocket on V's tracksuit bottoms (*H* [2005] 1 WLR 2005 (CA));
- kissing V's face (*W* [2005] EWCA Crim 3138);
- D rubbing his penis on V's body (*Osmani* [2006] EWCA Crim 816);
- touching V's breasts (*Burns* [2006] EWCA Crim 1451).

◼ Sexual assault

This covers all non-penetrative sexual violation and is, therefore, an offence of immense scope.

KEY STATUTE

Sexual Offences Act 2003, section 3(1)

A person (A) commits an offence if –

(a)   he intentionally touches another person (B),

(b)   the touching is sexual,

(c)   B does not consent to the touching, and

(d)   A does not reasonably believe that B consents.

There is clear progression to the offences from non-consensual penile penetration (rape) to non-consensual non-penile penetration to the least serious offence involving non-consensual sexual touching. The consistency in language means that sexual assault breaks down into familiar elements:

Two *actus reus* elements	Two *mens rea* elements
Sexual touching	Intentional touching
Absence of B's consent	A lacks a reasonable belief in B's consent

As the meaning of 'sexual' has been considered in relation to assault by penetration, the only unfamiliar element in this offence is that of 'touching'. The breadth of the definition demonstrates the reach of this offence.

KEY STATUTE

Sexual Offences Act 2003, section 79(8)

Touching includes touching –

(a) with any part of the body,

(b) with anything else,

(c) through anything.

This makes it clear that no touching is excluded, however brief or transient. Remember that this is qualified by the requirement that the touching is sexual.

■ Child victims

The law makes a distinction between children under the age of 13 and children aged 13–16.

Sections 5, 6 and 7 of the SOA 2003 replicate sections 1, 2 and 3 in that they cover rape, assault by penetration and sexual assault, but in situations where the victim is a child aged under 13.

Section	Offence
5	Rape of a child under 13
6	Assault of a child under 13 by penetration
7	Sexual assault of a child under 13

The differences between the under-13 offences and those in sections 1–3 are that:

■ the child cannot give consent; any consent actually given is not legally recognised;

■ there can be no reasonable belief in consent;

■ the offence is one of strict liability in relation to age.

This means that the relevant offence is complete if intercourse, penetration or sexual touching occurs in relation to a person under the age of 13, irrespective of whether the person consented or even instigated the activity – *however old the person may look.*

In *R* v *G* [2009] 1 AC 92 (HL), the defendant, a 15-year-old boy, had sexual intercourse with a 12-year-old girl who had told him that she was 15 years of age. The complainant subsequently told friends that she had not consented to having sexual intercourse. The defendant was charged with rape of a child under 13, contrary to section 5 of the 2003 Act.

The complainant accepted that she had told the defendant that she was 15. The House of Lords held, in relation to the defendant's appeal against conviction, that proof of the intentional penile penetration of a child under 13 years of age was all that was required for a conviction under section 5. Moreover, the policy of the legislation was to protect children and there was nothing unjust or irrational about a law that provided that a male who so penetrated a young person who was in fact under 13 years of age had committed an offence, even though the complainant had misled the defendant into believing that she was older.

Sexual activity with a child

The 2003 Act also introduced the offence of sexual activity with a child.

KEY STATUTE

Sexual Offences Act 2003, section 9

A person aged 18 or over (A) commits an offence if –

(a)   he intentionally touches another person (B),

(b)   the touching is sexual, and

(c)   either –

  (i)   B is under 16 and A does not reasonably believe that B is 16 or over, or
  (ii)   B is under 13.

This offence makes a distinction between children under 13 and children over 13 but under 16. There is a defence where the complainant is under 16, but the defendant reasonably believes that they are 16 or over.

One *actus reus* element	Two *mens rea* elements
Sexual touching	Intentional touching
	If B is under 16: A lacks a reasonable belief that B is 16 or over
	If B is under 13: this *mens rea* element does not apply

■ Putting it all together

Answer guidelines

See the problem question at the start of this chapter. A diagram illustrating how to structure your answer is available on the companion website.

Approaching the question

This is an example of a standard problem question that has sexual offences as its main focus but that does also raise other areas of liability; for example, Kelly's father may incur liability for battery (pulling Kelly out of the car) and common assault (if his actions caused John to apprehend immediate unlawful violence). If you were answering this question in an examination, it would be important to include discussion of such offences as the question requires that you 'discuss any criminal liability that arises'. As such, you should consider whether each of the four people involved in the scenario have committed any offences. For the purposes of this chapter, the outline that follows will concentrate only on liability for sexual offences.

Important points to include

John kisses Kelly

Kelly is over 13, so the correct offence is for sexual activity with a child under section 9. We will assume that John is over 18, as he works at the university (if he was not, there is a corresponding offence under section 13 for defendants under 18).

- Is there touching?
- Is it sexual?
- Does John have a reasonable belief that Kelly is over 16?

John and Penelope cuddle

There is no intercourse or penetration at this point and we can assume that both parties are adults (assume this unless there is evidence to the contrary) so the only possible offence would be sexual assault (s. 3).

- Is there touching?
- Is it sexual?
- Is there consent?

Penelope strokes John's penis

Again, the only potential liability is for sexual assault. The issue here is that Penelope continued after John protested:

- Did John withdraw his consent?
- Did Penelope have a reasonable belief in his consent?
- What effect does her intoxication have on her liability?

John inserts his finger into Penelope's vagina

This cannot be rape as that covers only penetration with the penis so it must fall under section 2 – assault by penetration.

The issue here is that Penelope is asleep/unconscious so the evidential presumptions come into play to affect the two questions:

- Did Penelope consent?
- Did John have a reasonable belief in her consent?

 Make your answer stand out

To achieve a good mark, your answer must be methodical and cover all of the issues. This means that you should explore all potential areas of liability even if, on first reading, you are confident that no liability would arise. Remember that it is a valid finding to consider an issue and to conclude that it does not give rise to criminal liability – and that you will get marks for explaining why no liability arises. Simply omitting to discuss the issue will gather no marks at all. Here, it would be tempting to dismiss any possibility of liability arising from the cuddle as it seems to be consensual but it will take only a few sentences to explain this and your answer will be more comprehensive as a result.

Remember that consent plays a dual role in more sexual offences as it is part of the *actus reus* (did V consent?) and the *mens rea* (did D have a reasonable belief that V gave consent?). Demonstrate your knowledge and understanding by explaining this carefully and pulling out facts from the question that are relevant to establishing both actual consent and belief in consent. For example, when Penelope touches John's penis, he murmurs, 'I don't really think that this is a good idea'. We can use this statement as evidence that he did not consent to the touching (*actus reus*). We can then refer to the fact that he only murmured the words, rather than shouting, to argue that perhaps Penelope did not realise that he was communicating his lack of consent to the sexual touching. Of course, any ambiguity as to his meaning would have been clarified at the point that John pushed her away. Remember that thoughtful use of the facts is a really good way to demonstrate your understanding of the operation of the law.

READ TO IMPRESS

Ashworth, A. (2007) Rape, Consent and Intoxication. *Criminal Law Review,* 901.

Finch, E. and Munro, V. (2006) Breaking boundaries: sexual consent in the jury room. *Legal Studies,* 26: 303.

Rodwell, D.A.H. (2005) Problems with the Sexual Offences Act 2003. *Criminal Law Review,* 290.

Temkin, J. and Ashworth, A. (2004) Rape, Sexual Assault and the Problems of Consent. *Criminal Law Review,* 328.

Wolchover, D. and Heaton-Armstrong, A. (2008) Debunking Rape Myths. *New Law Journal,* 158: 117.

www.pearsoned.co.uk/lawexpress

 Go online to access more revision support, including quizzes to test your knowledge, sample questions with answer guidelines, podcasts you can download and more!

Criminal damage

Revision checklist

Essential points you should know:

☐ The *actus reus* and *mens rea* of each of the three offences

☐ The relationship between the basic and aggravated offences

☐ The scope of 'lawful excuse' and the role of 'consent' and 'protection of property'

☐ The test of recklessness and implications of *R* v *G* [2004] 1 AC 1034 (HL)

■ Topic map

CRIMINAL DAMAGE

Section 1(1) CDA 1971
AR: damage/destruction of property belonging to
another MR: intention or recklessness

AGGRAVATED CRIMINAL DAMAGE

Section 1(2) CDA 1971
With intention to endanger life or being
reckless whether life is endangered

ARSON

Section 1(3) CDA 1971
Damage/destruction caused by fire

A printable version of this topic map is available from **www.pearsoned.co.uk/lawexpress**

◼ Introduction

Criminal damage is a relatively straightforward offence involving damage or destruction of property.

The elements of the offence rarely cause problems for students but the 'defences' require more careful thought.

The basic offence is supplemented by two more serious variants: aggravated criminal damage and arson. These carry higher penalties due to the greater risk of harm to people: aggravated criminal damage involves volitional endangerment of life whilst the unpredictability of fire causes greater danger to life. Both offences have the basic offence at their core so can be regarded as criminal damage plus an additional element.

ASSESSMENT ADVICE

Essay questions

Essay questions on criminal damage are not common, probably because the offence is not particularly complicated. Recent developments in the recklessness requirement of the *mens rea* provide some scope for essay questions and the complicated components of 'lawful excuse' could be used as the basis for a challenging essay question.

Problem questions

Problem questions often involve criminal damage as a means of testing knowledge of omissions (Chapter 2) or the different tests of recklessness (Chapter 3). Criminal damage may also make an appearance as the 'unlawful act' in constructive manslaughter. Be alert for scenarios that raise the aggravated forms of the offence, as the aggravating features are often missed and the situation wrongly categorised as basic criminal damage.

◼ Sample question

Could you answer this question? Below is a typical problem question that could arise on this topic. Guidelines on answering the question are included at the end of this chapter, whilst a sample essay question and guidance on tackling it can be found on the companion website.

PROBLEM QUESTION

After an argument, Davy is burning his sister's collection of postcards in a small fire he started at the bottom of the garden. After he walks away from the smouldering embers, a spark from the fire sets light to the neighbour's wooden fence. Donald watches the fence burn but does nothing.

Discuss the criminal liability of Davy and Donald.

▉ Criminal damage

KEY STATUTE

Criminal Damage Act 1971, section 1(1)

A person who without lawful excuse destroys or damages any property belonging to another intending to destroy or damage any such property or being reckless as to whether any such property would be destroyed or damaged shall be guilty of an offence.

Four *actus reus* elements	Two alternative *mens rea* elements
Destruction/damage	Intention to damage/destroy property belonging to another
Property	or
Belonging to another	Recklessness thereto
Without lawful excuse	

Actus reus elements

Damage or destruction

Section 1(1) covers two types of harm to property:

- *damage*: material change affecting the value and/or utility of the property, i.e. ripping pages from a book; and
- *destruction*: total elimination of value/utility that renders the property wholly useless, i.e. putting a book through a shredder.

Although the damage or destruction of property usually results from a positive act, such as smashing a window, it can arise from a failure to act, such as dropping a cigarette and doing nothing to stop a fire from starting and destroying property. Revisit the text on *actus reus* (see Chapter 2) to refresh your memory on liability for omissions, particularly the duty to act arising from the creation of a dangerous situation.

Property

The definition of 'property' found in the Criminal Damage Act 1971 section 10 is similar to that used in theft (see Chapter 12) with two exceptions in that the criminal damage definition:

1. excludes intangible property such as credit balances; and
2. includes real property such as land and buildings. These cannot be stolen but are frequently the target of criminal damage.

Belonging to another

Criminal damage requires that property 'belongs to another'; it is not an offence to damage/destroy one's own property.

The aggravated offence does cover damage/destruction of one's own property; this is a key distinction between the two offences.

Lawful excuse

! Don't be tempted to . . .

Agonise over whether 'lawful excuse' is a defence or part of the *actus reus* of the offence. Different textbooks and, indeed, different judges have different views on this. This chapter is not the place to pursue this issue but, as different lecturers will have their own views, check your course materials to find which approach they advocate. The overall outcome in a problem question will be the same, irrespective of whether lawful excuse is treated as part of the offence or as a defence.

KEY STATUTE

Criminal Damage Act 1971, section 5(2)

(a) if at the time of the act[s] . . . he believed that the person[s] whom he believed to be entitled to consent to the destruction of or damage to the property . . . had so consented, or would have consented to it if he or they had known of the destruction or damage and its circumstances; or ▶

> (b) if he destroyed or damaged ... the property ... in order to protect property belonging to himself or another or a right or interest in property ... and at the time of the act or acts alleged to constitute the offence he believed –
>
>   (i) that the property, right or interest was in immediate need of protection; and
>   (ii) that the means of protection adopted ... were ... reasonable having regard to all the circumstances.

Section 5 is a detailed provision but its essence is that there are two situations in which the defendant will have a lawful excuse to damage or destroy property:

1. He believed the owner *consented* to the damage/destruction or would have done had they known of the circumstances.

2. He destroyed/damaged property believing this to be the most reasonable way to *protect property* from immediate threat.

Consent

The belief that the owner would consent to the damage/destruction of property must be honestly held but need not be reasonable. This can lead to seemingly anomalous conclusions.

! Don't be tempted to ...

Focus on the reasonableness of the defendant's behaviour. The issue here is the defendant's belief in consent, not whether or not he has acted in a reasonable way. The two situations outlined here may help you to understand the distinction:

(a) Delores breaks a window to enter Victoria's house, because she thinks that her missing child may be inside. Delores is afraid that Victoria will be furious about the broken window, suggesting that she believes Victoria would not have consented to the damage. Delores is unlikely to be able to rely on lawful excuse.

(b) Victor agrees to lend his golf clubs to Dennis and to leave his house keys 'in the usual place' so Dennis can collect them while he is out. Dennis cannot find the key so he smashes a window and leaves a note saying, 'Fancy forgetting to leave me the key. I'll help you sweep up the glass later.' The jokey tone of the note suggests that Dennis believes Victor will consent to the damage, therefore he may be able to rely on lawful excuse.

Most people would consider that Delores behaved more reasonably than Dennis but this is irrelevant to whether the defendant honestly believed the owner would consent to the damage. Focus on what the defendant believes rather than what you think about his behaviour and remember to take into account the following:

- An honestly held belief need not be reasonable.
- It does not matter if the belief is mistaken, i.e. Dennis would still be able to rely on lawful excuse even if Victor was furious about the damage.

Protection of property

This is more complicated than lawful excuse based on consent. There are three requirements that must be satisfied:

1. there must be an *immediate threat* to property;
2. the steps taken to protect the property must be *reasonable*; and
3. the property must be damaged or destroyed *in order to protect it.*

KEY CASE

R v *Hunt* (1978) 66 Cr App R 105 (CA)

Concerning: lawful excuse, protection of property

Facts

The defendant was worried about inadequate fire-safety precautions in sheltered accommodation but his concerns were dismissed by the management. He started a fire in order to draw attention to the inoperable fire alarms and inadequacy of the evacuation procedures.

Legal principle

Lawful excuse was not available as the defendant was motivated by a desire to draw attention to safety defects rather than to protect property. The issue of whether actions were undertaken 'in order to protect property' was an objective question to be determined by the court with no regard for the defendant's motive or intentions.

This was affirmed in *Hill and Hall* (1989) 89 Cr App R 74 (CA) which gave rise to a two-stage test based upon the statutory requirements (see Figure 11.1).

Figure 11.1

STAGE 1 – SUBJECTIVE
Did the defendant believe that the property was in immediate need of protection and that the means used to protect the property were reasonable?

STAGE 2 – OBJECTIVE
Was the defendant's act performed in order to protect property?

Mens rea elements

Intention

Intentional damage/destruction of property is usually straightforward as the defendant's aim will be evident.

There must be intention in relation to all aspects of the *actus reus* so the defendant must intend to damage/destroy property *belonging to another*: a person who intentionally damages property believing that it is his own is not liable.

Recklessness

For many years, criminal damage was based on objective **recklessness** but, since the House of Lords overruled *Caldwell* [1982] AC 341 (HL), the test has been subjective.

> **📖 REVISION NOTE**
>
> *R* v *G* is covered in the text on *mens rea* (see Chapter 3). It has profound implications on criminal damage, so make sure that you understand the new subjective *mens rea* test.
>
> Remember, all cases decided using *Caldwell* recklessness were based on the now obsolete objective test of recklessness.

> **KEY DEFINITION: Recklessness**
>
> A person acts recklessly . . . with respect to –
>
> (i)   a circumstance when he is aware of a risk that it exists or will exist;
>
> (ii) a result when he is aware of a risk that it will occur;
>
> and it is, in the circumstances known to him, unreasonable to take the risk *R* v *G* [2004] 1 AC 1034 (HL)

There are three points to note:

1. This test of recklessness is based on volitional risk-taking, therefore, the defendant must be aware that there is a risk that property belonging to another will be damaged.

2. It is irrelevant that the defendant thinks that the risk of damage is very small; it is awareness of a risk that is the basis of recklessness, not awareness of the magnitude of the risk.

3. *R* v *G* differs from other forms of subjective recklessness as it contains explicit references to 'reasonable' risk-taking.

! Don't be tempted to . . .

Neglect the circumstances surrounding the defendant's actions when assessing the reasonableness of his risk-taking.

R v *G* recklessness acknowledges that not all risk-taking is unreasonable and that liability only attaches to unreasonable risk-taking. This involves consideration of the:

■ probability of the harm occurring; and
■ social utility of the defendant's conduct.

For example, a person who swerves whilst driving and hits a wall will be viewed as reckless if he did so because his attention was distracted by his CD player. This has no social utility and is relatively high risk. However, if he swerved to avoid a child who had run into the road, the higher social utility is likely to render this a reasonable risk.

Look at the facts in a problem question for evidence of social utility and the level of probability of harm occurring in order to evaluate whether the defendant has taken an unreasonable risk, i.e. whether he has been reckless for the purposes of criminal damage. (Remember that *R* v *G* applies only to criminal damage.)

■ Aggravated criminal damage

KEY STATUTE

Criminal Damage Act 1971, section 1(2)

A person who without lawful excuse destroys or damages any property, whether belonging to himself or another –

(a) intending to destroy or damage any property or being reckless as to whether any property would be destroyed or damaged; and

(b) intending by the destruction or damage to endanger the life of another or being reckless as to whether the life of another would be thereby endangered is guilty of an offence.

Aggravated criminal damage differs in two ways from the basic offence: one relating to the *mens rea* and the other to the *actus reus* of the offence (see Figure 11.2).

Figure 11.2

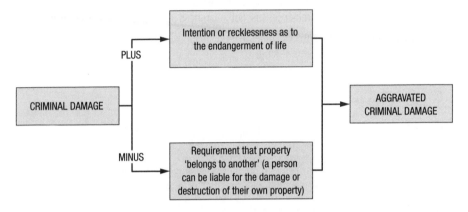

Actus reus elements

Belonging to another

In general, a person may do anything they wish with their own property, including destroying or damaging it; however, to do so in such a way that the lives of others are endangered attracts criminal liability.

Mens rea elements

Endangerment of life

The major distinction between the basic and aggravated offences lies with the requirement that the defendant intends or is reckless as to the endangerment of life:

- There is no need for life to be endangered. This is a *mens rea* element so concerns the defendant's state of mind not his actions.
- The defendant must intend that life is endangered by the damage/destruction of property (or be reckless thereto).

KEY CASE

R v *Steer* [1988] AC 111 (HL)

Concerning: endangerment of life

Facts

As a result of a grudge against his former business partner, the defendant fired a rifle at the windows of his house, causing damage. Nobody inside the house was injured. The defendant's conviction for criminal damage with intent to endanger life was quashed by the House of Lords.

Legal principle

It must be the damage to property that endangers life not the means by which the property is damaged. Therefore, the defendant must have intended to endanger life by smashing windows or foreseen a risk that life would be endangered by smashing windows. The means by which the windows were smashed – firing a rifle – and the life-endangering potential of this method of damaging property were irrelevant and could not be used as a basis for liability.

It is not enough that the defendant's act causes criminal damage and endangers life; the defendant must intend or foresee that the criminal damage caused by his act will endanger life.

 Make your answer stand out

The distinction that the courts have made between 'endangerment by criminal damage' and 'endangerment by the means used to cause criminal damage' has been criticised as a 'dismal distinction'. There is an excellent critical evaluation of the distinction and its implications in Elliot (1997) which you could read in preparation for an essay question on the topic.

Arson

This offence replicates criminal damage when the means used to damage/destroy property is fire.

KEY STATUTE

Criminal Damage Act 1971, section 1(3)

An offence committed under this section by destroying or damaging property by fire shall be charged as arson.

■ Putting it all together

Answer guidelines

See the problem question at the start of the chapter. A diagram illustrating how to structure your answer is available on the companion website.

Approaching the question

This is an example of a problem question on criminal damage. It looks deceptively simple and could give rise to a poor answer that does not deal with all the issues that are raised. It is always tempting for students to make an instinctive evaluation of the facts and reach a conclusion about liability without working through the elements of the offence in a methodical manner. You will see that this sample question only raises issues associated with criminal damage. It is quite unlikely that you would find a question that did this on an examination paper so you should expect that questions such as this would be part of a larger question that raised more issues.

Important points to include

■ It is important to work out how many issues there are in the problem scenario and ensure that you deal with each of these separately even if they involve the same offence or give rise to similar issues. Answers get very tangled and complicated if you try to combine different issues and this lack of clarity is likely to result in an answer that attracts a lower mark than a more structured and organised answer.

■ Davy has destroyed his sister's postcards. As he did so by fire, the charge will be arson under section 1(3) of the Criminal Damage Act 1971. Set out the *actus reus* and *mens rea* of criminal damage and establish each element of the offence in turn by picking up on specific facts from the problem. For example, he has destroyed (burnt) property (postcards) belonging to another (his sister) and he did so deliberately (intention). There is nothing in the facts to suggest he has lawful excuse: could you argue that he believed that she would have consented? As he is acting in anger, this seems unlikely.

■ The fire has spread to the neighbour's fence. The *actus reus* resembles the postcard situation but the *mens rea* differs because here Davy did not aim to set fire to the fence. As such, you would need to consider recklessness rather than intention. It is essential here that you select the correct test of recklessness (*R v G*), as an answer that applied the old *Caldwell* test would be likely to suffer a significant deduction in marks and might even fail outright if the examiner considered that a fundamental error had been made.

■ Donald has not done anything so it might seem that he has no criminal liability. However, the instructions that accompany the problem scenario stipulate that his criminal liability should be considered so it would be foolish not to do so. Is it possible that he could incur liability for criminal damage on the basis of his failure to act? This is possible only if he has a duty to act and no such duty is suggested by the facts. Even if you have to conclude that he has no liability, this must still be raised and explored, otherwise you will not have done what the question requires. Also, you should remember that an explanation of why liability cannot be imposed can be just as effective at demonstrating your knowledge as a discussion that concludes that a defendant has incurred liability.

 ## Make your answer stand out

The omissions argument provides greatest scope to impress your examiner. A weak answer would omit any discussion of Donald's liability on the assumption that he has done nothing so has no liability. A better answer would address Donald's position by explaining that a person can be liable for the consequences of an omission if they have a duty to act but would conclude that Donald does not fall within any of the categories of duty so has no liability. A strong answer would take this further by speculating about Donald's identity so as to contemplate situations in which he would have a duty to act. For example, if Donald is Davy's friend he may have helped to start the fire (duty arising from the creation of a dangerous situation) or he may be the gardener employed by the neighbours (possible contractual basis for a duty to act).

Make sure that you consider all elements of the offence, even if this is only to explain that they are not relevant. For example, it is likely that your conclusion with regard to Davy's liability will be that he is liable for criminal damage in relation to his sister's postcards, but did you reach this conclusion after considering lawful excuse? It takes only a couple of sentences to deal with these issues and it will add strength to your answer. For example, you could say, 'There is no suggestion that Davy was acting to protect property from damage by starting the fire and burning his sister's postcards so section 5(2)(b) will not apply.' That deals with the protection of property limb of lawful excuse in a concise manner. Equally, you could point out that Davy is burning the postcards after an argument with his sister, thus it is likely that this is an act of revenge rather than something that he is doing with her permission: section 5(2)(a).

READ TO IMPRESS

Elliot, D.W. (1997) Endangering Life by Destroying or Damaging Property. *Criminal Law Review*, 382.

Reed, A. (2003) Objective Recklessness and Criminal Damage. *Journal of Criminal Law*, 67: 109.

www.pearsoned.co.uk/lawexpress

 Go online to access more revision support, including quizzes to test your knowledge, sample questions with answer guidelines, podcasts you can download and more!

Theft

Revision checklist

Essential points you should know:

- [ ] The *actus reus* and *mens rea* of theft
- [ ] The difficulties associated with the ownership, possession and transfer of property
- [ ] The implications for theft of judicial interpretation of 'appropriation'
- [ ] The *Ghosh* test of dishonesty
- [ ] The 'thought rather than action' nature of intention permanently to deprive

■ Topic map

```
┌─────────────────────────────────────┐
│               THEFT                  │
│     Section 1(1) Theft Act 1968      │
└─────────────────────────────────────┘
```

```
┌──────────────────────────────┐   ┌──────────────────────────────────────┐
│          Actus reus          │   │              Mens rea                │
│                              │   │                                      │
│   Appropriation (Section 3)   │   │  Dishonesty (Section 2 and Ghosh test) │
│      Property (Section 4)      │   │ Intention permanently to deprive (Section 6) │
│  Belonging to another (Section 5) │   │                                      │
└──────────────────────────────┘   └──────────────────────────────────────┘
```

A printable version of this topic map is available from **www.pearsoned.co.uk/lawexpress**

■ Introduction

There is a surprising gap between the legal meaning of theft and the everyday understanding of the word.

This always causes problems for students who struggle to understand why situations that 'feel' like theft attract no liability under the Theft Act 1968 whilst other situations that they do not think of as theft, such as reclaiming one's own property, fall foul of the law. This mismatch leads many students astray as they apply their instinctive evaluation of theft and reach erroneous conclusions. The advice 'follow the legal rules and accept the conclusion they produce' is frequently ignored but is really the key to success in this area of law.

ASSESSMENT ADVICE

Essay questions

Essay questions on theft can take a variety of forms. They could require consideration of the offence as a whole, examine the overlap between theft and other offences or focus on a narrow issue such as appropriation. Make sure that you only tackle narrowly drawn essays if you have sufficient depth of knowledge: there is no point in answering a question on dishonesty if all you can do is state the *Ghosh* test.

Problem questions

Problem questions on theft, usually in conjunction with other offences, are popular. In a problem scenario, it is not likely that all the elements of the theft are problematic so you will need to demonstrate that you can identify all five elements, but devote more attention to the ones that raise complex issues. It is important to do this as, if you give equal weight to each element, you are not demonstrating to the examiner that you can distinguish between straightforward and complex issues.

■ Sample question

Could you answer this question? Below is a typical problem question that could arise on this topic. Guidelines on answering the question are included at the end of this chapter, whilst a sample essay question and guidance on tackling it can be found on the companion website.

PROBLEM QUESTION

Dan goes to his tutor's office to return a book he borrowed. The room is empty but the door is open, so Dan goes inside. He sees another copy of the same book and thinks that the tutor probably has several so decides not to return the copy he has been using. He also spots an exam paper on the desk and leans across to read the questions. Later, confident about his success in the coming exam, he tells his grandmother, who is easily confused, that he has already taken it and gained top marks, hoping that she will reward him with a laptop as she has promised. She gives him £500.

Discuss Dan's liability for theft.

■ Theft

KEY STATUTE

Theft Act 1968, section 1(1)

A person is guilty of theft if he dishonestly appropriates property belonging to another with the intention of permanently depriving the other of it.

Three *actus reus* elements	Two *mens rea* elements
Appropriation	Dishonesty
Property	Intention permanently to deprive
Belonging to another	

Actus reus elements

Property

KEY STATUTE

Theft Act 1968, section 4(1)

Property includes money and all other property, real or personal, including things in action and other intangible property.

Figure 12.1

Things that amount to property	Things that do not amount to property
• Money (coins, notes, currency) • Real property • Personal property (any tangible object that is not real property) • Things in action (something that cannot be seen but that can be enforced by legal action)	• Land: section 4(2) • Mushrooms, flowers, fruit and foliage growing wild: section 4(3) • Wild creatures, tamed or untamed: section 4(4) • Confidential information: *Oxford* v *Moss* (1979) 68 Cr App R 183 (DC) • Corpses: *R* v *Kelly* [1999] QB 621 (CA)

Some examples of things that do and do not amount to property are shown in Figure 12.1. Problems rarely arise with tangible property, i.e. things with physical presence that can be touched, although money always causes confusion. Intangible property, such as things in action, can also be troublesome.

! Don't be tempted to . . .

Confuse the way that different forms of payment operate when it comes to consumer transactions in problem questions. This is something that is often misunderstood so be careful to demonstrate your understanding of the way that the various forms of payment give rise to liability. Remember that all forms of payment are treated differently by the law from the way that they are understood in everyday society.

Money has value to people due to its purchasing capacity rather than its physical existence. If someone replaces your £50 note with five £10 notes, it is likely that you will not mind because they have the same value. The law, however, is concerned with this unauthorised substitution of one piece of property (1 × £50) with another (5 × £10) rather than its value (£50 irrespective of its composition). To understand money from a legal perspective, swap money for cars: if someone takes your VW Golf and returns a Ford Fiesta (both worth £1,000), you still have a car of the same value, but you will object to the unauthorised substitution of different property. This is how the law regards money, by its physical existence not its value.

Credit cards and cheques should also be regarded in terms of their physical presence as pieces of plastic and paper with no inherent value that can be stolen (theft of physical property). If they are used, the owner's account reduces accordingly and this may be theft of a thing in action (credit balance) but the two should not be confused. Their use will also give rise to liability for fraud by false representation (see Chapter 14) as the defendant represents that he is authorised to use the card.

Credit balances are things in action, which means that a person can sue his bank to recover his money if it were withheld (hence it is a 'thing' that the account holder can bring an 'action' to recover). The use of a stolen cheque or credit card reduces the ▶

account holder's balance, thus it is theft of a thing in action as the money that can be recovered from the bank by legal action is reduced or eliminated. Again, there is a potential overlap with fraud by false representation if the defendant has practised deception in order to obtain a transfer of funds.

Belonging to another

KEY STATUTE

Theft Act 1968, section 5(1)

Property shall be regarded as belonging to any person having possession or control of it, or having in it any proprietary right or interest.

This definition of 'belonging to another' includes situations short of outright ownership. So, for example, if Adam is in possession of a book belonging to Ben, then the book belongs to Adam (as he has possession and control) and Ben (as he has a proprietary interest). This can lead to some complicated situations, such as the conclusion that a defendant can be liable for theft of his own property as was the case in *Turner (No. 2)* [1971] 1 WLR 901 (CA) where the defendant was held to be guilty of theft for removing his car from outside a garage where it had undergone repair. This was because the garage was in possession of the car so it belonged to them for the purposes of theft.

Section 5 also covers two situations in which 'belonging to another' can be particularly complicated:

1. Property is given to the defendant for a particular purpose, e.g. a charity collection.
2. Property is passed to the defendant by mistake, e.g. an overpayment of wages.

Section 5(3) covers situations in which property is given to the defendant for a particular purpose but he has used it in a different way for some other purpose. In such cases, property generally is regarded as 'belonging to' the original owner, even though the defendant has been given possession and control of the property.

KEY STATUTE

Theft Act 1968, section 5(3)

Where a person has received property from or on account of another and is under an obligation to the other to retain and deal with that property or its proceeds in a particular way, the property or proceeds shall be regarded . . . as belonging to another.

! Don't be tempted to . . .

Overlook the problems that are created for the operation of section 5(3) in a problem question if there has not been a segregation of funds. Case law is not as clear as it could be on this point so the issue will need to be handled carefully to ensure that you apply the correct law based upon the facts of the problem.

In *Hall* [1973] QB 126 (CA), it was held that a travel agent who received payments from customers, but did not use this to purchase holidays on their behalf, could not be liable for theft because he had paid the money into his general trading account. This mingling of funds meant that there was no ascertainable property that had remained in the ownership of the customer. Money could fall within section 5(3) only if it was kept separately, as this denoted that it was received for a particular purpose.

This requirement was doubted in *Wain* [1995] 2 Cr App R 660 (CA) in which the defendant kept money donated to charity for himself and claimed he was not liable for theft as the donations had been mingled with his own money. The court held that the requirement for segregation of funds created a false distinction between a collector who received money in a collection box (who would be liable if he kept the money) and one who mingled it with his own money (who would not be liable). It was held that anyone who collects money for charity should be liable if he keeps it for his own use.

Wain could be seen as rejecting the need for segregation of funds entirely, in which case *Hall* would now be decided differently, or it could be limited in application to situations involving money collected for charity.

If a problem question raises section 5(3) in the context of charitable donations, *Wain* should be followed. In any other circumstances, both *Hall* and *Wain* should be applied with an explanation that the case law is unclear on this point and the result would depend on which line of authority was preferred by the courts in subsequent cases.

Next, consider property received by mistake.

KEY STATUTE

Theft Act 1968, section 5(4)

Where a person gets property by another's mistake and is under an obligation to make restoration . . . of the property or its proceeds . . . then [this] shall be regarded . . . as belonging to the person entitled to restoration and an intention not to make restoration shall be regarded accordingly as an intention to deprive that person of the property or proceeds.

Section 5(4) provides that property (again, usually money), which is passed to the defendant by mistake, is regarded as 'belonging to' the original owner. This means that failure to return the property once the mistake has been realised amounts to theft.

The failure must be deliberate so the defendant must be aware that he has received property by mistake. For example, in *Re Attorney-General's Reference (No. 1 of 1983)* [1985] QB 182 (CA), a computer error led to an overpayment of wages into the defendant's account, which she noticed but failed to return, giving rise to liability for theft. Had she failed to notice the overpayment, she would not have been liable.

An important point to remember here is that the mistake that triggers this section must be made by the person who has parted with the property. It is common for students to use this section when the defendant has made a mistake but that is not the correct way to use this section.

Appropriation

KEY STATUTE

Theft Act 1968, section 3(1)

Any assumption by a person of the rights of the owner amounts to an appropriation and this includes, where he has come by the property (innocently or not) without stealing it, any later assumption of a right to it by keeping it or dealing with it as owner.

This definition raises three questions:

- What are the rights of the owner?
- Do all of them have to be assumed for appropriation to take place?
- Is there still an appropriation if the owner consents to the appropriation of his rights?

Bundles of rights

The owner of property has the right to do anything with it. The owner of a book can read it, throw it away, write in it or destroy it. It is because property can be used in a whole range of ways that ownership carries a bundle of different rights over property (which includes unusual uses, e.g. the owner of a book could bury it in the garden).

Assumption of rights

It is because ownership conveys a bundle of rights that appropriation is satisfied by the assumption of *any* of the rights rather than *all* of the rights of ownership: *Morris* [1984] AC 320 (HL). A defendant who reads a book belonging to another, writes in it or destroys it has committed the *actus reus* of theft just as much as a defendant who has treated it in a way that is more consistent with everyday notions of theft, i.e. taken it out of the owner's possession.

Consent

There was conflict in case law as to whether the owner's consent to the property being taken negates appropriation which was settled in *Gomez* (see Figure 12.2).

Figure 12.2

Lawrence v *MPC* [1972] AC 626 (HL)
A foreign passenger who was unfamiliar with the currency handed his wallet to a taxi driver to enable him to take the fare. The driver removed money greatly in excess of the correct fare. He argued that this could not amount to an appropriation because the owner consented to the removal of his property.
The House of Lords rejected this argument and held that the question was whether the rights of the owner had been assumed and the issue of consent was irrelevant.

CONFLICT

R v *Morris* [1984] AC 320 (HL)
The defendant switched the labels on goods in a supermarket in order to pay a lower price for the goods. He was apprehended prior to making payment and leaving the shop. It was argued that there was no appropriation because the goods had been picked up and handled with the implied consent of the owner.
The House of Lords held that appropriation implied that there was an adverse usurpation of the owner's rights, therefore, it was something that only happened if the owner did not consent to that assumption of his rights.

DPP v *Gomez* [1993] AC 442 (HL)
The defendant was the assistant manager of an electrical goods shop who accepted worthless cheques. He told the manager that the cheques were valid so the manager authorised the release of property valued at £16,000. The defendant argued that he could not be liable for theft because the manager consented to the removal of the property.
The House of Lords addressed the conflict between the previous cases and chose to follow *Lawrence*, holding that consent is not relevant to the question of appropriation.

Note: *Morris* was overruled on this point but is still good law for the proposition that assumption of any one of the rights of the owner amounts to appropriation.

 Make your answer stand out

It is important to demonstrate that you understand how the legal definition of theft differs from the everyday understanding of the offence. As appropriation is the assumption of any of the rights of the owner, even if the owner consents to this assumption, the *actus reus* of theft is satisfied every time we do something with another person's property. In other words, we all fulfil the *actus reus* of theft all the time: picking up a book, borrowing a pen, taking a packet of biscuits off the shelf in a shop. ▶

This means that the only difference between theft and lawful behaviour rests in the *mens rea* and, of course, as *mens rea* refers to the mental state then it is difficult to see any difference between a lawful shopper holding a bottle of wine and a thief who holds a bottle intending to take it from the shop without paying.

These issues and associated points concerning the approach taken by the courts to appropriation are discussed by Shute (2002) who considers the difficulties that arise with the dishonest receipt of gifts in cases such as *Hinks* [2001] 2 AC 241 (HL). A consideration of these issues would be beneficial in an essay question on this topic.

KEY CASE

R v *Hinks* [2001] 2 AC 241 (HL)

Concerning: appropriation, gifts

Facts

The defendant encouraged the victim, a man of limited intelligence, to withdraw money from the building society and deposit it in her account. She contended that these were valid gifts but was, nonetheless, convicted of theft.

Legal principle

The House of Lords held that, following *Gomez,* receipt of a gift that amounted to a valid transfer of ownership at civil law could still amount to theft if it was dishonestly induced by the defendant.

Mens rea elements

Dishonesty

KEY STATUTE

Theft Act 1968, section 2(1)

A person's appropriation of property is not to be regarded as dishonest:

(a) if he appropriates property in the belief that he has in law the right to deprive the other of it, on behalf of himself or of a third party;

(b) if he appropriates property in the belief that he would have had the other's consent if the other knew of the appropriation and the circumstances of it; or

(c) if he appropriates property in the belief that the person to whom the property belongs cannot be discovered by taking reasonable steps.

This is not a definition of dishonesty but a statement of situations that are *not* dishonest. They are all subjective tests so are determined on the basis of what the defendant believed, irrespective of how others would interpret the situation. If none of these situations applies, the general test of dishonesty outlined in *Ghosh* (below) should be applied.

KEY CASE

R v *Ghosh* [1982] QB 1053 (CA)

Concerning: dishonesty

Facts

The defendant was a surgeon who claimed fees for operations that were carried out by other surgeons, which should have attracted no fee (because they were on NHS patients). He asserted that he believed he was entitled to the fees so was not dishonest.

Legal principle

The Court of Appeal held that, outside of section 2, dishonesty could not be assessed on a purely subjective standard and formulated a two-stage test:

(1) Was what was done dishonest according to the ordinary standards of reasonable and honest people?

(2) Did the defendant realise that reasonable and honest people regard what he did as dishonest?

If the answer to both questions is 'yes', the defendant is dishonest. If the answer to either question is 'no', the defendant is not dishonest.

✎ EXAM TIP

It is common for students to misstate the *Ghosh* test. As dishonesty is part of every theft problem as well as questions on other property offences (see Chapters 13 and 14), it is essential to be able to state the test correctly and apply it to the facts. Remember, though, to apply the negative definition from section 2 *before* the *Ghosh* test (see Figure 12.3) in relation to theft only.

Figure 12.3

STAGE 1 – NEGATIVE DEFINITION

Consider whether the defendant falls within any of the three situations contained in section 2. Look for evidence that he believed:

(a) he was legally (rather than morally) entitled to take the property;

(b) that the owner would agree to him taking the property if they knew;

(c) that the owner could not be found by taking reasonable steps.

Remember that these must be honestly held beliefs but they do not have to be accurate.

If any of the negative definitions are satisfied, the defendant is not dishonest and cannot be liable for theft. If none of the section 2 situations apply, go on to apply the *Ghosh* test.

STAGE 2 – GHOSH TEST

Provide an accurate statement of the *Ghosh* test and apply it to the facts to establish dishonesty.

(1) The first stage is objective so consider what 'reasonable and honest' people would think about the defendant's conduct. This is often a matter of making generalisations about social standards of honesty: most people view taking property from shops without paying is dishonest.

(2) The second stage is based upon what the defendant thinks about ordinary standards of honesty. Is he aware that 'reasonable and honest' people would consider his conduct to be dishonest even though he thinks that it is acceptable? Look for evidence of surreptitious behaviour in the facts: a defendant who sneaks out or hides goods cannot believe that ordinary people would believe that he was being honest.

Intention permanently to deprive

KEY STATUTE

Theft Act 1968, section 6(1)

A person . . . is regarded as having the intention of permanently depriving . . . if his intention is to treat the thing as his own to dispose of regardless of the other's rights . . . [B]orrowing or lending . . . may amount to so treating it if, but only if, the borrowing or lending is for a period and in circumstances making it equivalent to an outright taking or disposal.

Section 6(1) includes situations where the property is taken on a temporary basis (borrowing) so goes beyond what might ordinarily be thought of as permanent deprivation.

KEY CASE

R v Lloyd **[1985] QB 829 (CA)**

Concerning: borrowing, intention permanently to deprive

Facts

The defendant worked at a cinema and removed films so that pirate copies could be made. The copying process took a few hours, after which the films were returned. He appealed against his conviction for theft on the basis that he intended only temporary deprivation.

Legal principle

The Court of Appeal held that borrowing would amount to outright taking only where the property was returned in such a changed state that all its goodness and virtue were gone. The partial diminution of value represented by the copying of the films would not suffice, despite the reduction in revenue caused by the availability of pirate films.

One of the commonest mistakes is to focus on whether the property was actually taken on a permanent basis. This leads to inaccurate conclusions. Not only can borrowing satisfy the intention permanently to deprive but situations that involve only a transient interference with another's property can give rise to liability, i.e. picking up goods in a shop intending to steal them but having a change of heart and leaving without them. This is because intention permanently to deprive is concerned with the defendant's state of mind, not his actions. Consider what the defendant's intentions were at the time he appropriated the property: if it was to remove it permanently, then his liability is established irrespective of what he actually went on to do.

■ Putting it all together

Answer guidelines

See the problem question at the start of the chapter. A diagram illustrating how to structure your answer is available on the companion website.

Approaching the question

This is an example of a problem question that raises several issues that give rise to potential liability for theft. The instructions stipulate that it is Dan's liability for theft ▶

only that is to be considered, so there is no merit in discussing the other offences that are raised on the facts (potential liability for burglary and fraud by false representation). If you encounter a similar set of facts that have a more general instruction to 'discuss Dan's liability', then it would be important to look out for other offences that have been committed.

Important points to include

■ The starting point should be to identify the three separate issues that arise in the question to ensure that each of these is dealt with separately. It would be a great mistake to try to deal with all three at the same time, even though the potential basis for liability is the same in each instance, as this would lead to a confused answer that lacks clarity. For example, combining the issues would lead you to write something like: 'The property in question is the book, the information on the exam paper and the £500 that belonged to the lecturer and Dan's grandmother.' Not only will this make it hard for you to deal with these issues, it creates confusion in your answer, as it is not clear who owns which of the listed pieces of property.

■ The first issue for consideration is whether Dan is guilty of theft of his lecturer's book. State the *actus reus* of theft (appropriation of property belonging to another) and look to the facts to see if each of these is established. You might say: 'The book is personal property (section 4 of the Theft Act 1968), which presumably belonged to the lecturer, as he loaned it to Dan.' The tricky issue on appropriation here is that Dan already has the book in his possession and control but that is covered by section 3 of the Theft Act 1968, which stipulates that appropriation includes keeping something after coming into lawful possession of it. You would then need to deal with the two *mens rea* issues: Dan decides to keep the book so has an intention to permanently deprive, but is he dishonest? Determine the issue of dishonesty by consideration of section 2, if it seems appropriate, on the facts and application of the *Ghosh* test.

■ The next potential basis for theft concerns Dan's behaviour with the examination paper. It would be important here to remember that confidential information does not fall within the definition of property in section 4, according to *Oxford* v *Moss*. Dan cannot steal the information on the exam paper but has he stolen the paper itself? Apply the five elements of theft to determine his liability.

■ The final point raises the issue of deceptive receipt of a gift. Dan has lied to persuade his grandmother to give him property. He has taken possession of the money, so the *actus reus* of theft is satisfied (remember here to refer to appropriate case law to establish that assumption of the rights of the owner with the owner's consent is still an appropriation). He intends to keep the money so has an intention to permanently deprive, so his liability rests on whether dishonesty can be established. Apply any of the section 2 exceptions that seem relevant and the *Ghosh* test to reach a decision on this point.

Make your answer stand out

Ensure that your answer makes reference to relevant case law. There should be a discussion of *Gomez* in relation to consent in appropriation and *Hinks* in relation to the dishonest receipt of a gift.

The point about the exam paper may seem straightforward but will need close attention to the facts to resolve it accurately. Confidential information cannot be stolen (*Oxford* v *Moss*) so he can be liable only if he has stolen the paper itself. It would be easy to conclude that he has not stolen it, as it was not removed from the room, but that would be to fall into the trap of applying common-sense understandings of the offence rather than working through the elements of theft and reaching a conclusion. The exam paper is property that belongs to the lecturer (he is in possession and control, even if the paper is owned by the university), but has it been appropriated? The facts say that Dan leaned across the desk to read it, which suggests that it has not been touched (which would amount to an appropriation), but is reading it in these circumstances something that only the owner has the right to do? It is a tenuous argument that lacks authority to determine whether this would amount to an appropriation but there would be a great deal of credit available for dealing with this difficult issue effectively.

Make sure that you are able to deal with dishonesty effectively. There are two common errors that occur in relation to theft: (1) failure to consider the section 2 exceptions and (2) misstatement of the *Ghosh* test. As so many mistakes are made here, your examiner will be pleased if you deal with this important aspect of theft in the correct manner.

READ TO IMPRESS

Parsons, S. (2002) Dishonest Appropriation after *Gomez* and *Hinks*. *Journal of Criminal Law*, 68: 520.

Shute, S. (2002) Appropriation and the Law of Theft. *Criminal Law Review*, 445.

www.pearsoned.co.uk/lawexpress

 Go online to access more revision support, including quizzes to test your knowledge, sample questions with answer guidelines, podcasts you can download and more!

13

Theft-related offences

Revision checklist

Essential points you should know:

- [ ] The *actus reus* and *mens rea* of the offences
- [ ] The relationship between theft and burglary/robbery
- [ ] The 'continuing act' approach to appropriation in robbery
- [ ] The distinction between the two forms of burglary

■ Topic map

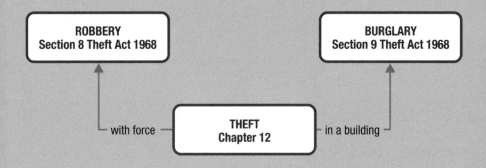

■ Introduction

Certain situations in which theft occurs are regarded as more serious so form the subject matter of separate offences.

Robbery involves the use of force to facilitate the theft, whereas burglary involves the intrusion into property, domestic or commercial, in order to steal. Burglary also has manifestations involving criminal damage and GBH, which often are overlooked.

The problems arising from these offences are similar to the problems associated with theft: robbery and burglary are terms used in everyday life, which bear only a passing resemblance to their legal meaning. It is essential that you disregard your preconceived understandings of these offences and focus instead on the legal definition of the elements of the robbery and burglary.

ASSESSMENT ADVICE

Essay questions

Essay questions on theft-related offences are uncommon but may arise either separately or in combination with theft. The important thing to remember is to focus on addressing the issue raised in the question rather than merely describing the elements of the offences.

Problem questions

Problem questions involving theft-related offences often combine theft with deception but can arise with any other offences and defences. Look for 'clues' in the question that trigger these offences: 'theft with force' (robbery) and 'theft in a building' (burglary) but also remember that burglary is not limited to theft but includes criminal damage and GBH.

■ Sample question

Could you answer this question? Below is a typical problem question that could arise on this topic. Guidelines on answering the question are included at the end of this chapter, whilst a sample essay question and guidance on tackling it can be found on the companion website.

PROBLEM QUESTION

Dan taps an elderly lady on the arm to attract her attention and asks directions to the town centre. Whilst she is pointing and her attention is distracted, he removes her purse from her bag without her noticing. Dan decides to steal a bottle of wine from the off-licence. He hides the wine under his coat, but is spotted by the shopkeeper who tries to stop him leaving, so Dan trips him over, causing the shopkeeper to break his leg.

Discuss Dan's liability.

Robbery

KEY STATUTE

Theft Act 1968, section 8(1)

A person is guilty of robbery if he steals, and immediately before or at the time of doing so, and in order to do so, he uses force on any person or puts or seeks to put any person in fear of being then and there subjected to force.

Actus reus elements	*Mens rea* elements
Actus reus of theft	*Mens rea* of theft
Force (or fear of force)	Intentional use of force
To any person	
At the time or immediately before the theft	

Actus reus elements

The *actus reus* elements can be encapsulated by answering four questions about robbery (see Figure 13.1).

Theft

As robbery is an aggravated form of theft, all the elements of theft must be present in order for robbery to be established (see Chapter 12).

Force/fear of force

There are four points to remember:

Figure 13.1

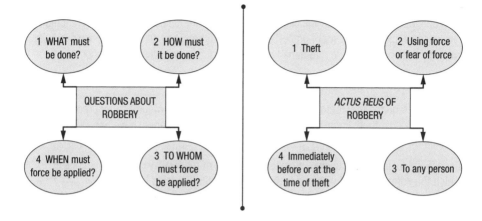

- The level of force may be minimal, e.g. pushing/jostling (*Dawson* (1977) 64 Cr App R 170 (CA)) as well as more serious violence.

- Force may be applied to the person or their property, e.g. grabbing a handbag without touching the owner: *Clouden* [1987] Crim LR 56 (CA). It is accepted that some physical contact will be too slight and transient to amount to force: for example, in *P* v *DPP* [2012] EWHC 165 (Admin), it was held that snatching a cigarette that the victim was holding would not amount to force.

- Fear of force will suffice. Look out for express ('give me that or else') or implied threats (menacing behaviour) that have induced fear in the victim.

- Force must be used to facilitate theft. The essence of robbery is that force is used to commit theft, so there must be a causal link between the theft and the force used.

✎ EXAM TIP

The fourth point can cause confusion, as students tend to take a mathematical approach:

FORCE + THEFT = ROBBERY

This can be a useful way to remember the requirements of robbery but it is not always strictly accurate. Imagine that the defendant knocks the victim to the ground, intending to rape her. She offers him money to leave her alone and he takes it. This would amount to theft and he has subjected her to force, but it would not amount to robbery. This is because he used force in order to rape *not* in order to steal.

As such, it is more useful to remember the offence as:

FORCE (used to commit) THEFT = ROBBERY

Any person

Often, force is used on the owner of the property but the reference to 'any person' in section 8 means that this need not be the case. Robbery would be too narrow if it was restricted to force used against the owner of property, as this would exclude, for example, bank robbery whereby the employees are threatened but clearly are not the owners of the money.

Immediately before or at the time

As robbery requires that force is used in order to steal, the use of force must precede or coincide with the theft. Force used after the theft is complete cannot have been instrumental in committing theft.

Despite the logic of this position, it limited the scope of robbery by placing situations in which the defendant used violence to get away after theft outside the offence.

KEY CASE

R v *Hale* (1978) 68 Cr App R 415 (CA)

Concerning: timing of force

Facts

The defendant's accomplice stole jewellery whilst the defendant remained downstairs with the owner of the house. He tied her to a chair and threatened to harm her child if she called the police after they left. He argued that the force occurred after the theft so he could not be liable for robbery.

Legal principle

Appropriation is a continuing act that commences with the first assumption of the owner's rights but which does not cease immediately (the duration of appropriation is a question of fact for the jury).

✎ EXAM TIP

Do not dismiss situations in which force is used *after* theft is complete without considering whether there is a continuing appropriation. If, after applying *Hale*, you conclude there is no robbery, the defendant may still be liable for theft and a non-fatal offence (Chapter 9).

Mens rea elements

This combines the *mens rea* of theft with an intention to use force in order to steal. In *R* v *Vinall* [2011] EWCA Crim 5252, the defendants punched the victim from his bicycle, took it and then left it 50 yards away. They were not liable for robbery since they did not have an intention permanently to deprive the victim of their property (and thus did not satisfy the *mens rea* of theft) at the time that force was used on the victim. (Incidentally, they could have been charged under section 12(5) Theft Act 1968 for taking a pedal cycle without consent or authority!)

◼ Burglary

KEY STATUTE

Theft Act 1968, section 9(1)

A person is guilty of burglary if –

(a) he enters any building or part of a building as a trespasser and with intent to commit any such offence as mentioned in subsection (2) below; or

(b) having entered any building or part of a building as a trespasser he steals or attempts to steal . . . inflicts or attempts to inflict on any person therein any grievous bodily harm.

Actus reus elements	*Mens rea* elements
Entry	Intention/recklessness as to trespass
Building (or part of)	Ulterior intent (s. 9(1)(a) only)
As a trespasser	
Actual offence (s. 9(1)(b) only)	

This creates two separate offences with some common elements (see Figure 13.2).

Common elements

Entry

In most cases, the defendant will enter the building in the ordinary sense of the word in that he will go right inside the building with his whole body in order to commit an offence, e.g. going into a house to steal the television. In such cases, the 'entry' element of burglary is straightforward. There are situations where there has been something less than complete entry into a building:

- ◼ Partial entry: if the defendant puts only part of his body into the building, this will suffice to satisfy the 'entry' element, e.g. the defendant puts his hand through an open window to remove a purse from inside the building: *Brown* [1985] Crim LR 212 (CA).

■ Use of an instrument or innocent agent: if the defendant remains wholly outside of the building but uses some other means to access the inside of the building, this may still amount to 'entry' for the purposes of burglary, e.g. the defendant sends a small child in through a cat flap to remove property or uses a long stick to lift property out through an open window.

Figure 13.2

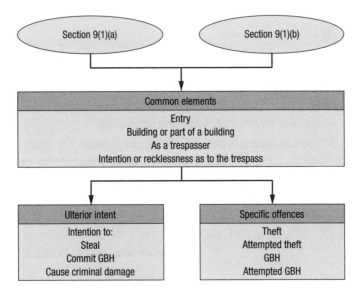

Building or part of a building

Buildings usually are straightforward but there are two tricky areas:

1. Non-typical structures. Section 9(4) specifies that inhabited vehicles and vessels are within the meaning of 'building'. Other structures are judged according to whether they are of sufficient size and permanence: *Stevens* v *Gourley* [1859] 7 CB (NS) 99 (DC).

2. Separate areas within a building, such as individual rooms in a multiple-occupancy house and 'staff only' areas in shops.

KEY CASE

R v *Walkington* **[1979] 1 WLR 1169 (CA)**

Concerning: part of a building

Facts

The defendant went behind a shop counter and interfered with the till. He argued that he was not liable for burglary as he had not formed the intention to steal before entering the shop and that the till area was not a separate 'part of a building'.

> **Legal principle**
>
> It was held that a part of a building was determined by the presence of a physical demarcation, such as separate rooms, notices restricting entry or some form of barrier, such as a counter.

As a trespasser

The defendant must enter the building or part of building as a trespasser, i.e. he must enter without the knowledge or permission of the owner or person otherwise entitled to grant permission. Case law has considered whether it is enough that he lacks permission or whether he must know that he has no permission to enter.

KEY CASE

R v *Collins* [1973] QB 100 (CA)

Concerning: trespass

Facts

The defendant, naked apart from his socks, climbed a ladder and looked through the victim's bedroom window. She assumed it was her boyfriend and beckoned him into the room. She realised her mistake during intercourse. He was charged with section 9(1)(a) burglary which, at the time, included intention to rape within the ulterior intent.

Legal principle

Trespass requires entry without permission so, if the defendant believed he had permission to enter prior to any part of his body crossing the threshold, then he would not be a trespasser and cannot be liable for burglary.

This highlights the dual aspects of trespass in burglary:

- entry into a building (or part of) without permission: *actus reus*;
- knowledge that there is no permission or awareness that there is a risk that there is no permission to enter: *mens rea.*

Permission to enter may be express or implied and may be limited to particular parts of the building or to entry for a specific purpose. For example, permission to enter a hotel may include the lounge, but will exclude the kitchens. A person who exceeds the extent of his permission may still be a trespasser.

KEY CASE

R v *Jones and Smith* **[1976] 1 WLR 672 (CA)**

Concerning: exceeding permission to enter

Facts

The defendant entered his father's house with a friend to steal two televisions. He had general permission to enter the house and argued that this meant that he was not a trespasser for the purposes of burglary.

Legal principle

It was held that a person who enters a building for an unlawful purpose will be a trespasser in that building, irrespective of any express or implied permission to enter that has been extended to him.

✎ EXAM TIP

This is an important case as it means that a person who does have permission to enter a building can be a trespasser and therefore liable for burglary if he acts in a way that is inconsistent with the permission that he has been granted. For example, a supermarket extends general permission to the public to enter in order to shop but not in order to steal.

It is important to remember that trespass is a tort (a civil wrong) and not a criminal offence. Students often forget this and reach a conclusion that includes reference to a defendant's liability for trespass, possibly due to the misleading and inaccurate signs that read 'trespassers will be prosecuted'. To find the defendant guilty of trespass when it does not exist as a criminal offence is a fundamental flaw that will seriously damage your answer. Trespass is one element of the offence of burglary so will not give rise to liability on its own as *Laing* [1995] Crim LR 395 (CA) demonstrates. Here, the defendant was found in the stockroom of a shop after closing time. He had not stolen anything nor had he attempted to do so, and there was no evidence that he had entered the shop or the stockroom with the intention to steal. He was undoubtedly a trespasser but he could not be found guilty of burglary as the other elements of the offence were absent.

Ulterior intent

In addition to these common elements, section 9(1)(a) requires an ulterior intent to commit theft, GBH or criminal damage *at the time that the defendant entered the building*. If the intent is not present upon entry, subsequent formation of ulterior intent will not amount to burglary.

> ✎ **EXAM TIP**
>
> Focus on what was in the defendant's mind at his point of entry into the building. Conditional intent will suffice: if the defendant intended to steal only if he could find something of value, this will satisfy the ulterior intent requirement: *Re Attorney-General's Reference (Nos 1 and 2 of 1979)* [1980] QB 180 (CA).
>
> This can be applied to the other offences:
>
> ■ Does the defendant intend to cause harm if a particular person is in the building?
>
> ■ Does the defendant intend to smash particular property if he can find it?
>
> Remember that there is no need for the defendant to *do* anything; it is his intention that is crucial to liability, not his actions.

Specific offences

Section 9(1)(b) requires actual or attempted offending once the defendant is within the building, so he must satisfy:

■ all five elements of theft (see Chapter 12);

■ the elements of the Offences Against the Person Act 1861, section 20 (see Chapter 9); or

■ the requirements for liability for attempting either offence (see Chapter 4).

> ✎ **EXAM TIP**
>
> Problem questions may give rise to liability for more than one offence of burglary in order to test your ability to distinguish between section 9(1)(a) and (b) offences. Spend some time untangling the facts and working through the elements of the offences to ensure you select the appropriate offences as the basis for liability.

■ Putting it all together

Answer guidelines

See the problem question at the start of the chapter. A diagram illustrating how to structure your answer is available on the companion website.

▶

Approaching the question

This is an example of a problem question that raises issues of both robbery and burglary. The clues that should lead you to recognise these offences from the facts are that a theft occurs within a building (wine from the shop) so burglary should be discussed and there are two instances in which there has been some combination of force and theft (tapping the lady's arm to steal her purse and breaking the shopkeeper's leg to escape with the wine), so there is potential liability for robbery. Remember that if liability for robbery cannot be established, there may still be potential for liability for theft and the use of force as separate offences.

Important points to include

- The starting point should be to identify the three separate issues that arise in the question to ensure that each of these is dealt with separately. It often helps to work through the facts sentence by sentence in order to ensure that no relevant details are omitted.

- The first issue here concerns Dan's actions in tapping the lady's arm and taking her purse. This could easily be the basis for two separate offences: battery and theft. However, as force (which can be only minimal as in this case) was used to distract her attention so that her purse can be stolen, it seems reasonable to say that this was done in order to steal, so Dan may be liable for robbery.

- The facts state that Dan decides to steal a bottle of wine. If this intention was formed prior to his entry into the shop, then he will have potential liability for section 9(1)(a) burglary, as he has entered the shop intending to steal. However, if he formed this intention only after he went into the shop for some other purpose – perhaps to hide or to spend the elderly lady's money – then he cannot be liable for this offence.

- As soon as Dan removes the wine from the shelf intending to take it without paying, he will be liable for theft and, consequently, for section 9(1)(b) burglary. Make sure that you are able to identify all five elements of theft (see Chapter 12).

- The final issue here is whether Dan is liable for robbery when he uses force on the shopkeeper in order to escape with the wine. Credit would be available for pointing out here that section 8 states that force must be used *in order to steal,* i.e. before or at the time of the theft, which suggests that Dan is not liable for robbery. However, reference should then be made to the notion of 'continuing appropriation' from *Hale* and an argument could be made that Dan pushed the shopkeeper in order to complete the appropriation, which would then be regarded as force used at the time of the theft. This is a tricky point.

Make your answer stand out

The shopkeeper's broken leg would be regarded as 'really serious harm', so could fall within section 20 of the Offences Against the Person Act 1861 (wounding or inflicting GBH). There would be no reason not to discuss this as a potential basis for liability, as the instructions do not limit you to a consideration of robbery and burglary. A really clever point would be to note that GBH is one of the specified offences that can give rise to liability for section 9(1)(b) burglary. Your examiner is likely to be impressed if you can spot non-typical manifestations of burglary.

Do not neglect the elements of the specified offences when establishing liability under section 9(1)(b). As theft, criminal damage and GBH form part of this offence, they should be included in your revision of burglary and appear in your answer. This demonstrates to your examiner that you have a good grasp of other areas of the course.

READ TO IMPRESS

Finch, E. (2008) Robbery: Threat of Force. *Journal of Criminal Law,* 72: 187.

www.pearsoned.co.uk/lawexpress

 Go online to access more revision support, including quizzes to test your knowledge, sample questions with answer guidelines, podcasts you can download and more!

Fraud

■ Topic map

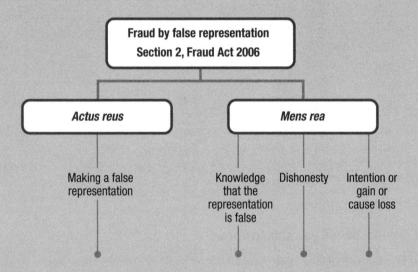

■ Introduction

The Fraud Act 2006 simplified the way that the law applied to deceptive behaviour.

Prior to this, the deception offences focused on the consequences of the defendant's behaviour, i.e. what he obtained as a consequence of his **deception**. If the defendant did not manage to deceive anyone or he did not obtain anything as a result of his deception, he would not incur criminal liability. The Fraud Act 2006 is based on the Law Commission Report on Fraud (Law Com. No. 276).

ASSESSMENT ADVICE

Essay questions

Essay questions often focus on developments in the law so, whilst it is obviously important that you are familiar with the Fraud Act 2006, you should also be able to explain how it differs from the old law and whether you think the new law is an improvement on the pre-existing position. The ability to support your evaluation by reference to academic writing on the topic should enable you to analyse the law critically, which will add strength to your essay.

Problem questions

Problem questions are unlikely to deal exclusively with fraud, so it is important that you understand how the new offence relates to other property offences, particularly theft. Finally, do not overlook the offence of making off without payment, which is the only offence from the Theft Act 1978 to have survived the enactment of the Fraud Act 2006.

■ Sample question

Could you answer this question? Below is a typical problem question that could arise on this topic. Guidelines on answering the question are included at the end of this chapter, whilst a sample essay question and guidance on tackling it can be found on the companion website.

PROBLEM QUESTION

Huw finds a wallet on the train on his way to a job interview. It contains £20 and a credit card, together with a scrap of paper with a four-digit number on it, which Huw thinks is the PIN for the card. Huw uses the cash to buy himself lunch. Huw then decides to buy an expensive watch from an exclusive jewellers, using the credit card. He selects a watch that costs £3,500 and hands the credit card to the sales assistant, but, before the card is put in the machine, Huw loses his nerve. He shouts, 'I've changed my mind – that watch doesn't suit me' and runs out of the shop, leaving the card behind. Unnerved by the experience, Huw is nervous during his job interview. He realises that the interview is going badly, so he decides to lie about his exam results to improve his chances of getting the job. Huw tells the interviewer that he has four A grades at A level and a first class degree in law. The interviewer does not believe him, as Huw had already completed an application form on which he stated (truthfully) that he had two Bs and a C, and a lower second class degree. Huw is not offered the job.

Discuss Huw's liability for property offences.

■ Elements of fraud

KEY STATUTE

Fraud Act 2006, section 1

(1) A person is guilty of fraud if he is in breach of any of the sections listed in subsection (2) (which provide for different ways of committing the offence).

(2) The sections are –

    (a) section 2 (fraud by false representation),

    (b) section 3 (fraud by failing to disclose information), and

    (c) section 4 (fraud by abuse of position).

In effect, section 1 of the Fraud Act 2006 states that there is a single offence of fraud that can be committed in three different ways:

1. by misrepresenting the truth (false representation);

2. by holding back information when there is a legal duty to disclose it (failing to disclose information);

3. by taking advantage of a position of authority that involves safeguarding the financial interests of another person (abuse of position).

As you will see, the offences committed by breaches of sections 3 and 4 are not of general application; these sections are relevant to particular people in particular situations so will not be covered in this chapter. The offence of fraud committed by false representation (a breach of section 2) is a more general offence that replaces the 'traditional' deception offences:

- obtaining property by deception (Theft Act 1968, s. 15);
- obtaining a money transfer by deception (Theft Act 1968, s. 15A);
- obtaining a pecuniary advantage by deception (Theft Act 1968, s. 16).

✎ EXAM TIP

Although these offences were repealed, it is important that you understand their elements and what sort of conduct they covered as well as the problems associated with them, as this will enable you to make a comparison between the old and the new law, if required.

KEY STATUTE

Fraud Act 2006, section 2(1)

A person is in breach of this section if he –

(a) dishonestly makes a false representation, and

(b) intends by making that representation –

to make a gain for himself or another, or

to cause loss to another or to expose another to a risk of loss.

Section 2(1) of the Fraud Act 2006 defines how the offence of fraud by false representation is committed. It can be broken down into its composite elements on the basis of the *actus reus* and *mens rea* of the offence.

One *actus reus* element	Three *mens rea* elements
Making a false representation	Dishonesty
	Knowing that the representation is false
	Intention to make a gain or cause a loss

The *actus reus* element

There is only one element to the *actus reus* of this offence and that is the making of a false representation. A representation is the communication or presentation of information to others. This may be by words, conduct or a combination of the two. For example, when you first encounter a new lecturer, he may make a spoken representation as to his identity by stating, 'I am your criminal law lecturer', as he enters the room, or may communicate this information by conduct. For example, if someone enters, mounts the platform in the lecture theatre and turns on a PowerPoint presentation with the title 'Criminal Law', it is likely that you will conclude from this conduct that the person concerned is your criminal law lecturer.

There are two elements to a false representation that you may need to take into account:

- It must be untrue or misleading.
- It can be express or implied.

Untrue or misleading

According to section 2(2)(a) of the Fraud Act 2006, a representation is false if it is untrue or misleading. In other words, a false representation involves creating an impression in the mind of another that something that is false is really true. Picking up on the example used above, if the person who states, 'I am your criminal law lecturer', is really a psychology lecturer, an IT technician or a student, the representation is false because it is untrue and gives a misleading impression as to the identity of the person before you.

Of course, it may be more difficult to establish that a representation by conduct is false. If, for example, the person who mounts the lecture platform and turns on the PowerPoint presentation is an IT technician who has come to check the equipment, you might have concluded that this was your criminal law lecturer, but the technician was not representing that this was the case. It is simply that you drew an incorrect conclusion from the facts.

✎ EXAM TIP

When dealing with the *actus reus* of fraud by false representation in a problem question, look at what the defendant has said and done and think about what impression that would have created in the mind of an observer. For example, if you saw a person enter a marquee past a sign that said 'wedding guests only', you would assume that this person had been invited to the wedding. The representation that is made is that the person has the authority to be in the marquee. If the person is an interloper intent on helping himself to the buffet food, then he has made a false representation. Remember that it is important to make reference to specific facts from the question to substantiate your conclusions on this point.

Express or implied

An express false representation is one in which the falsity is explicitly communicated to the target of the deception and it tends to involve a positive action. An implied representation tends to be more passive and, typically, will involve the defendant giving a false impression rather than making an explicit false statement.

The inclusion of implied false representation is an important one, as many of the deceptive acts that occur are based upon the impression that is given. For example, when you present a credit card to a cashier in the supermarket, you do not say, 'My name is Karen. This is my credit card. Look – here's my name on the front of the card', but your actions in presenting the card for payment imply that this is the case. Equally, you do not enter a restaurant and say to the waiter, 'I have the money to pay for the food that I order and I will make full payment before leaving the premises', but this is implicit in your actions in sitting at a table and ordering food.

The *mens rea* elements

As with many offences, the *mens rea* elements of this offence are the means by which a differentiation is made between lawful and unlawful conduct. In other words, the making of a false representation is not enough to give rise to liability unless it is done with the specified state of mind. This is because there are situations in which a false representation could be made in good faith, as the following examples demonstrate:

Inadvertent false impression	The technician who mounted the lecture platform and turned on the PowerPoint presentation did not mean to give the impression that he was a lecturer, as he was merely going about his work and checking the equipment in the lecture theatre.
Mistake of fact	If you are asked whether you have paid your university fees and you reply that you have, in the belief that your parents did so last week, you have made a false representation, if your parents forgot to send the cheque, but this was due to a mistaken belief in the accuracy of the statement.
Misunderstanding of the situation	If you are a guest in a hotel and enter a room with a sign that reads 'champagne reception for guests only' and are asked if you are a guest as you enter by a member of staff, you might say 'yes' on the basis that you believe he is asking whether you are a guest in the hotel, whereas he was actually asking whether you are a guest at the wedding that has arranged for the champagne reception to be held.

In each of these instances, at least one of the elements of the *mens rea* is missing. The *mens rea* of fraud by false representation requires:

- knowledge that the representation is false;
- dishonesty; and
- intention to make a gain or cause a loss.

For example, even if the IT technician is aware that the students in the lecture theatre think that he is a lecturer, he would not be liable for fraud by false representation as he is not dishonest and does not intend to make a gain or cause a loss by his representation.

All three elements must be established for liability to be complete. This means that not every deliberate falsehood or deception will fall within the scope of the offence. For example, if you were aware that the champagne reception was for wedding guests only and told a deliberate lie in order to gain admittance, you would have fulfilled the requirements of the *actus reus* (as you made a false representation that you were a guest at the wedding) and two elements of the *mens rea* (as you are aware that the representation is false and this is likely to fall within the test of dishonesty (discussed below) so your liability would depend upon your motivation for gaining admittance). If you made a false representation in order to help yourself to free champagne, then the final element of the *mens rea* would be established. However, if you wanted to get into the reception only in order to chat to someone, to see what the bride was wearing or for something to do to pass the time, then this would not amount to an intention to gain or cause loss (provided, of course, that you did not have any champagne whilst at the reception).

Each of the elements of the *mens rea* will now be discussed in more detail.

Knowledge that the representation is false

In general, the criminal law imposes liability only on those whose wrongful conduct is willed and volitional, thus it is only reasonable that liability for fraud cannot be established, unless the defendant knows that he has made a false representation. This excludes from the scope of liability those who are mistaken, confused or otherwise inaccurate in their statements. It follows that a defendant who believes he is telling the truth cannot be liable for this offence.

! Don't be tempted to . . .

Forget that the representation must be false at the time that it is made. This means that if a defendant makes a representation that is true, but then has a change of heart at a later date, he may not be liable for this offence. For example, if a person goes into a restaurant, sits down and orders a meal with every intention of paying for this at the end of the evening, he is not making a false representation. If, during the course of the meal, he decides to slip out without paying and gets up and leaves the restaurant, his subsequent change of heart cannot be 'backdated' to his original representation. It is for this reason that the offence of making off without payment has been retained from the Theft Act 1978, as it covers situations that are outside the reach of fraud by false representation by virtue of the time at which the dishonest or fraudulent intention was formed. It is important that you understand this point and that you are able to identify which offence to apply to factual situations on the basis of the point in time that the intention to act in a fraudulent manner is formed.

Dishonesty

In common with other property offences, there is a requirement that the defendant was dishonest. Dishonesty is established by reference to the two-stage *Ghosh* test derived from the Court of Appeal decision in *R* v *Ghosh* [1982] QB 1053 (CA) – see Figure 14.1.

Figure 14.1

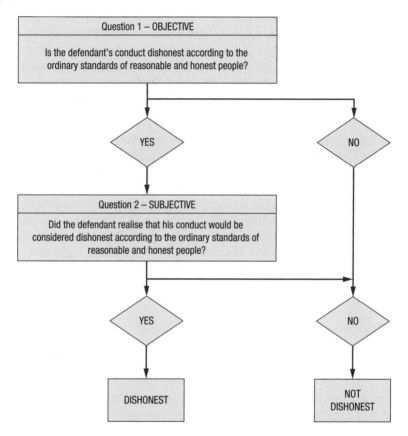

It is important to remember that the answer to both questions must be 'yes' or the defendant is not dishonest. The premise behind the test is that the conduct must be that which would be considered dishonest in ordinary society and the defendant must realise that this is the case. It is not open to the defendant to act according to his own standards of honesty.

1 The *Ghosh* test is often misstated as 'the standards of the ordinary man', 'the reasonable man must think the conduct is dishonest' or 'the honest standards of reasonable people'. All of these are along the right lines but are imprecise, so impress your examiner by getting it right and making reference to the key phrase: 'the ordinary standards of reasonable and honest people'.

2 Another way in which students lose marks in exams when dealing with the *Ghosh* test is by failing to apply the test to the facts. A good answer will make reference to specific facts from the problem to demonstrate that each element of the offence is established and the *Ghosh* test should not be left out of this process. The example below provides an illustration of the application of the *Ghosh* test in the context of fraud by false representation.

The reason that many students give for their failure to apply the *Ghosh* test to the facts is that this requires them to find evidence of (a) ordinary standards of honesty and (b) the defendant's beliefs about ordinary standards of honesty, and these may not be immediately obvious within the facts. This is a valid point, but remember that ordinary standards of honesty are those that are dominant in society, so reference can be made to acceptable honest behaviour within society rather than to the facts, whilst it may be the case that the defendant's behaviour is so manifestly contrary to those standards that he must realise that it would be viewed as dishonest. Alternatively, look for signs that the defendant has behaved surreptitiously, as this is good evidence that he is aware that his conduct would be considered dishonest by others.

Example

Warren is desperately short of money. He sneaks into his sister's bedroom, removes the gold necklace that was given to her for her 21st birthday and takes it to a shop that buys second-hand jewellery, hoping to sell it. Warren tells the jeweller that the necklace was left to him by his grandmother and agrees to wait whilst it is being valued. He grows nervous because he thinks that the jeweller is looking at him suspiciously, so he grabs the necklace and runs out of the shop.

All the elements of the offence of fraud by false representation are present. Warren has made a false representation by making out that the necklace was his to sell. He is aware that this is a false representation, as he knows that the necklace belongs to his sister and he intends to make a gain as he hopes to sell it. In terms of dishonesty, it is not difficult to conclude that selling property that does not belong to you without the knowledge and agreement of the owner would be considered dishonest, according to the ordinary standards of reasonable and honest people. Moreover, Warren must be aware that this is the case as he 'sneaks' into his sister's bedroom, lies about the neck-lace being a gift from his grandmother and runs out of the shop when he thinks that the jeweller is suspicious. These are the actions of a person who is aware that his actions would be considered dishonest by others.

Intention to make gain or cause loss

KEY STATUTE

Fraud Act 2006, section 5(2)

'Gain' and 'loss' –

(a) extend only to gain or loss in money or other property;

(b) include any such gain or loss whether temporary or permanent; and

(c) 'property' means any property whether real or personal (including things in action and intangible property).

Fraud Act 2006, section 5(3)

'Gain' includes a gain by keeping what one has, as well as a gain by getting what one does not have.

This provision makes it clear that 'gain' and 'loss' are interpreted broadly for the purposes of this offence. It would be usual to think of gain as getting something to keep that you did not have previously but section 5(2) makes it clear that temporary gain is included and section 5(3) goes further still by encompassing situations in which you retain possession of something that you already had (see Figure 14.2).

The most important point to note about this element of the offence is that it refers to what the defendant intended to do at the time that the false representation was made and not to what actually happened. This is because it is a *mens rea* element and not part of the *actus reus*. Provided the defendant intended to make a gain or cause a loss, this element of the offence is established, even if the defendant was unsuccessful. So, in the worked example above, in which Warren tries to sell his sister's necklace, he is liable for the section 2 offence, even though he left the shop without gaining any money for the necklace. This is because he intended to gain the money at the time that the false representation was made.

□ REVISION NOTE

The meaning of 'property' is the same as that applied to the offence of theft. You will find a detailed discussion of this definition of property in Chapter 12.

Figure 14.2

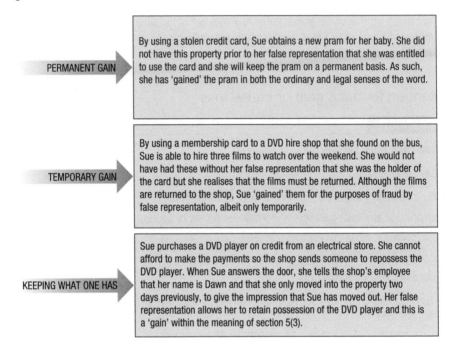

PERMANENT GAIN

By using a stolen credit card, Sue obtains a new pram for her baby. She did not have this property prior to her false representation that she was entitled to use the card and she will keep the pram on a permanent basis. As such, she has 'gained' the pram in both the ordinary and legal senses of the word.

TEMPORARY GAIN

By using a membership card to a DVD hire shop that she found on the bus, Sue is able to hire three films to watch over the weekend. She would not have had these without her false representation that she was the holder of the card but she realises that the films must be returned. Although the films are returned to the shop, Sue 'gained' them for the purposes of fraud by false representation, albeit only temporarily.

KEEPING WHAT ONE HAS

Sue purchases a DVD player on credit from an electrical store. She cannot afford to make the payments so the shop sends someone to repossess the DVD player. When Sue answers the door, she tells the shop's employee that her name is Dawn and that she only moved into the property two days previously, to give the impression that Sue has moved out. Her false representation allows her to retain possession of the DVD player and this is a 'gain' within the meaning of section 5(3).

◼ Shift of the point of liability

The central feature of the old law that was repealed by the Fraud Act 2006 is that something – property, a money transfer, a pecuniary advantage or services – would be obtained as a result of the defendant's deception (see Figure 14.3).

Figure 14.3

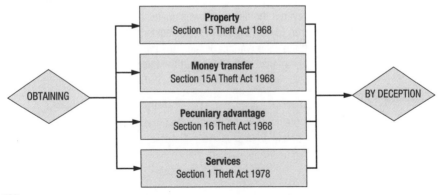

OBTAINING

Property
Section 15 Theft Act 1968

Money transfer
Section 15A Theft Act 1968

Pecuniary advantage
Section 16 Theft Act 1968

Services
Section 1 Theft Act 1978

BY DECEPTION

The key distinction between the old law and the new offence of fraud by false representation is that the old law focused on the acquisition of the property (money transfer, pecuniary advantage or services) so the offence would not be established if the defendant failed in his fraudulent endeavours (although he may be liable for attempting to obtain property by deception: see Chapter 4). The new offence switches the focus to the fraudulent behaviour as the central wrong – it is for this reason that the offence of fraud by false representation is established, even if the defendant does not deceive anyone or obtain the property that he was seeking to gain. This means that liability is incurred at an earlier point in the fraudulent process (see Figure 14.4).

Figure 14.4

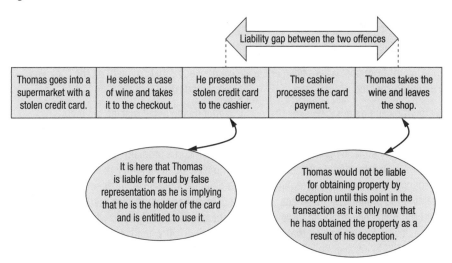

As liability under the old law arose at a later point in time, there was more scope for the defendant to avoid liability. He might have lost his nerve whilst waiting for the cashier to process the payment or he may have failed to deceive the cashier at all. Under the old law, it was an essential component of the offence that the deception was operative in obtaining the property; in other words, if the target of the deception was not actually deceived, the offence would not be established. The new law avoids these problems by imposing liability for making a false representation with a view to obtaining property, irrespective of whether this is successful.

 Make your answer stand out

If you were to attempt an essay question that focused on the effectiveness or impact of the new law, it would be important to be able to make a comparison with the old law. Professor Ormerod's (2007) excellent article on the Fraud Act 2006 reviews the problems with the old law and comments upon whether the new law has gone far enough in seeking to resolve these problems, so would provide valuable material for an essay on the topic.

Making off without payment

KEY STATUTE

Theft Act 1978, section 3

A person who, knowing that payment on the spot for any goods supplied or service done is required or expected from him, dishonestly makes off without having paid as required or expected and with intent to avoid payment of the amount due shall be guilty of an offence.

Three *actus reus* elements	Three *mens rea* elements
Goods supplied/services done	Dishonesty
Making off from spot where payment is required/expected	Knowledge that payment on the spot was required/expected
Without paying as required/expected	Intention to avoid making payment

The key to understanding this offence and identifying it in a problem scenario is to think about why it exists. It was originally introduced to fill a loophole left by the 'obtaining by deception' offences, as these required that the defendant practised a deception prior to obtaining the property. In instances where the defendant obtained property with a lawful intent but then decided to default on payment, there was no basis upon which to impose liability. It was for this reason that the offence of making off without payment was introduced and it tended to involve the initially lawful assumption of irretrievable property:

- petrol: mingles with the petrol already in the tank, thus is impossible to return;
- restaurant food: cannot be returned after consumption;
- services: cannot be given back after they have been performed.

Although the 'obtaining by deception' offences were repealed by the Fraud Act 2006, making off without payment survived because it still has a role to play. If someone used a self-service pump to fill his car with petrol in the knowledge that he did not have the means to pay and with the intention of driving away from the forecourt without paying, then clearly he has made a false representation, as it is implied in his conduct that he is an honest customer. This would give rise to liability under section 2 of the Fraud Act 2006. However, if the customer filled his car with petrol fully intending to pay for it but then had a change of heart and left without paying, he cannot be liable for fraud as there is no false representation; at the time that he represented by his conduct that he was an honest customer, this was not false because he intended to pay and so he was an honest customer. As this does not fall within fraud by false representation, the offence of making off without payment has survived to deal with this and similar situations.

The elements of making off without payment are not complicated:

- *Goods supplied/services provided:* property/services retain the same meaning.
- *Making off from the spot where payment is expected/required:* this is usually obvious. In *Aziz* [1993] Crim LR 708 (CA), this spot was held to be mobile in relation to taxi journeys rather than the defendant's stated or desired destination. Making off does not necessitate a dramatic exit or deliberate stealth; any departure will suffice (although speed or stealth may be evidence of a guilty state of mind).
- *Without paying as required/expected:* making off does not require a dramatic exit or deliberate stealth (although these are often evidence of wrongdoing). The defendant must make no offer of payment: an agreement to return later, even if not honest, defeats the offence (*Vincent* [2001] 1 WLR 1172 (CA)).
- *Dishonesty:* uses the *Ghosh* test.
- *Knowledge that payment on the spot was required/expected:* this is closely linked with dishonesty. A defendant who thought, for example, that a friend would be paying the bill does not know that payment is required/expected, thus may not be considered to be dishonest if he left without making payment.
- *Intention to avoid payment:* requires intention to avoid payment permanently. In *Allen* [1985] AC 1029 (HL), it was held that an intention to temporarily avoid payment will not suffice so a defendant who left a hotel owing a large bill which he genuinely hoped to be able to pay at a later date was not liable.

■ Putting it all together

Answer guidelines

See the problem question at the start of the chapter. A diagram illustrating how to structure your answer is available on the companion website.

Approaching the question

This problem question contains several issues that give rise to potential liability for fraud by false representation, although there is scope for liability for other offences as well. As there is only one defendant, the organisation of the answer should be quite straightforward, provided that only one issue is addressed at a time. It can be tempting to have an amalgamated discussion of issues that give rise to liability for the same offence, but this approach will make your answer muddled and is best avoided.

▶

Important points to include

- Huw finds the wallet on the train. This gives rise to potential liability for theft (see Chapter 12), as he has appropriated property belonging to another (*actus reus*) by picking up the wallet and his subsequent actions demonstrate that he has the intention to permanently deprive and the dishonesty required to satisfy the *mens rea.*

- Huw spends the money he finds in the wallet. This raises potential liability for theft (as above) but also for fraud by false representation (demonstrating the width of the offence), as he has implicitly represented that the money is his to spend by presenting it for payment; he knows this representation is untrue, it was done with a view to gain (the food) and it is likely that this would be dishonest if the *Ghosh* test were applied.

- Huw tries to buy an expensive watch. This issue is trickier than it might look and it would be easy to go wrong if an instinctive assessment is made about liability rather than applying the elements of the offence and accepting the conclusion that is reached. There has been a false representation (that Huw is entitled to use the card) and Huw knows that the representation is false. He makes this representation with a view to gaining the watch, and it is likely that it would be considered dishonest according to the ordinary standards of reasonable and honest people and that he is aware this is the case. As such, all of the elements of fraud by false representation are satisfied and liability is established.

- Huw lies about his qualifications. Again, it is important to apply the four elements of fraud rather than making an assessment of the situation:

  - ☐ there is a false representation (about the grades);
  - ☐ Huw knows that this is false (as he knows these are not his real grades);
  - ☐ it is done with a view to gain (the job and the salary that it brings);
  - ☐ it is likely that this would be considered to be dishonest.

 Make your answer stand out

When dealing with the attempt to buy the watch, it would be tempting to consider liability for attempted fraud on the basis that Huw has been unsuccessful and has left without the watch. This would be a mistake and would suggest to the marker that you have not grasped the key feature of the fraud offence, which is that there is no requirement that the defendant's deception is effective or believed. You could include a sentence explaining that his liability is attached to the making of the false representation, irrespective of whether it enables him to obtain the desired property, to emphasise your understanding of this point to your examiner.

Similarly, explain that fraud is concerned with the making of false statements rather than the consequences of doing so (unlike the old law) in relation to the exam grades. As such, it does not matter that the employer does not believe Huw. A strong answer would also explain that Huw's liability is not affected by his failure to get the job. The law requires that the false representation is made with a view to gain or cause loss, not that gain or loss actually occurs.

READ TO IMPRESS

Ormerod, D. (2007) The Fraud Act 2006 – Criminalising Lying. *Criminal Law Review,* 193.

Withey, C. (2007) The Fraud Act 2006 – Some Early Observations and Comparisons with the Former Law. *Journal of Criminal Law,* 71: 220.

www.pearsoned.co.uk/lawexpress

 Go online to access more revision support, including quizzes to test your knowledge, sample questions with answer guidelines, podcasts you can download and more!

Insanity and automatism

■ Topic map

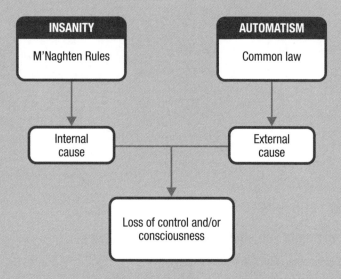

◼ Introduction

If a defendant is unable to control his movements or behaviour, his conduct is involuntary and should not lead to criminal liability.

Insanity and automatism both give rise to situations in which a person is unable to control his movement and/or behaviour. Insanity is caused by internal factors whilst automatism arises from external factors. Despite the obvious similarities between them, they have radically different outcomes for the defendant: automatism leads to acquittal whilst insanity results in a 'special verdict' of 'not guilty by reason of insanity'. For this reason, an ability to identify and distinguish between them is essential.

ASSESSMENT ADVICE

Essay questions

Essay questions on insanity tend to focus on its outdated nature and the need for reform, so be sure that you are able to identify weaknesses in the current law and comment upon ways that the law could be modernised and improved. Another common essay topic is the internal/external causes issue that distinguishes insanity and automatism. Make sure that you have a good grasp of case law in order to tackle such a question.

Problem questions

Problem questions involving insanity and/or automatism are quite common. Obviously, as these are defences, they are likely to arise in conjunction with one or more offences: liability must be established before it is necessary to discuss a defence. They could combine with any offence but are frequently combined with homicide and non-fatal offences. If there is any suggestion in the facts that the defendant suffered a lapse in consciousness or control, then a discussion of insanity (if the cause is internal) or automatism (external cause) is necessary.

▇ Sample question

Could you answer this question? Below is a typical essay question that could arise on this topic. Guidelines on answering the question are included at the end of this chapter, whilst a sample problem question and guidance on tackling it can be found on the companion website.

ESSAY QUESTION

Insanity has been described as a 'quagmire of law seldom entered into nowadays save by those in desperate need of some kind of defence'.

Explain and comment upon this view of insanity.

▇ Insanity

KEY DEFINITION: Insanity

At the time of committing the act, the defendant was labouring under such a defect of reason, arising from a defect of mind, that he did not know the nature and quality of his act or, if he did know this, that he did not know that what he was doing was wrong.

M'Naghten Rules [1843] 10 Cl & Fin 200 (see Figure 15.1)

✎ EXAM TIP

Apply the M'Naghten Rules to establish insanity. If the conclusion does not coincide with your perception of insanity (e.g. diabetes and epilepsy), accept this as a consequence of judicial interpretation. Insanity is a label applied to those who are not responsible for their actions when the offence was committed; it will not necessarily accord with medical or everyday ideas of insanity.

Figure 15.1

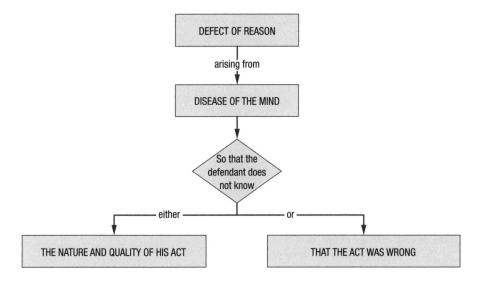

Defect of reason

A defect of reason arises when the defendant is incapable of exercising ordinary powers of reasoning.

KEY CASE

***R v Clarke* [1972] 1 All ER 219 (CA)**

Concerning: defect of reason

Facts

The defendant was charged with theft after putting groceries in her bag. She claimed she acted absent-mindedly whilst suffering from depression. The trial judge ruled that this amounted to a defect of reason and raised insanity.

Legal principle

It was held that 'defect of reason' required inability to exercise reason rather than a failure to do so at a time at which the exercise of reason was possible. The defendant in this case failed to exercise powers of reason but was not incapable of reasoning thus was not within the scope of insanity.

Defect of reason requires an *inability* to reason, not *failure* to reason. Look for evidence of:

- ability to reason: rational thinking, controlled behaviour;
- inability to reason: irrationality, strange or abnormal thoughts/behaviour.

Disease of the mind

Judicial interpretation of disease of the mind has moved the legal definition far away from the medical conception of insanity.

KEY CASE

R v *Sullivan* [1984] AC 156 (HL)

Concerning: disease of the mind

Facts

The defendant caused GBH during an epileptic fit.

Legal principle

The House of Lords held that the nature of the disease, physical or psychological, was irrelevant provided it affected the 'mental faculties of reason, memory and understanding' at the time of the offence.

This means that *any* disease that affects the way the mind reasons, remembers or comprehends is a 'disease of the mind' for the purposes of insanity and demonstrates a distinction between:

- disease of the mind (any disease that affects the functioning of the brain); and
- disease of the brain (more akin to mental illness).

! Don't be tempted to . . .

Assume that a 'disease of the mind' is automatically synonymous with order conceptions of mental illness. The approach that has been taken to 'disease of the mind' creates potential for everyday physical conditions to amount to insanity. This is a particular problem in relation to the divide between insanity (internal cause) and automatism (external cause) as physical conditions will always amount to an internal factor and give rise to insanity. You need to be careful not to confuse internal and external causes as they result in quite different outcomes, particularly for the defendant.

The implications of this are illustrated in relation to diabetes:

Internal cause: diabetics who fail to take medication (hyperglycaemia: high blood sugar) fall within insanity because the loss of consciousness/control arises from the disease itself: *Hennessy* [1989] 1 WLR 287 (CA).

External cause: diabetics who experience an adverse reaction to their medication (hypoglycaemia: low blood sugar) can rely on automatism as their inability to reason arises from an external cause, i.e. their medication: *Quick* [1973] QB 910 (CA). The exception to this occurs if the defendant was reckless in mismanaging his medication in which case his automatism is regarded as self-induced, thus cannot be relied upon to avoid liability: *Bailey* [1983] 1 WLR 760 (CA).

 Make your answer stand out

In an answer to an essay question in this area, you could consider the long-standing argument that a legal definition of insanity that encompasses ordinary medical conditions such as diabetes and epilepsy is unacceptable. It is likely that defendants suffering from such medical disorders refuse to rely on the defence due to the stigma attached to insanity. Mackay and Reuber (2007) consider a range of cases in which epilepsy has been used as the basis for a plea of insanity and present a persuasive argument in favour of a change in the law. Loughnan's (2007) article would also make excellent reading in preparation for an essay question as it covers a range of situations in which the insanity defence can be applied.

Nature and quality of the act

This requires lack of awareness of the *physical* nature and quality of the act (not its moral qualities). There must be a difference between the defendant's action and what he thinks he is doing:

- The *nature* of the act concerns its *characteristics,* e.g. the defendant put a baby on the fire believing it was a log.
- The *quality* of the act concerns its *consequences,* e.g. the defendant cut off the sleeping victim's head in order to watch him looking for it in the morning; he was aware of the nature of decapitation but not of its consequences.
- *Delusional motives* will not suffice, e.g. a defendant who battered his wife to death to prevent her abduction by aliens remains aware of the nature and quality of his act.

Knowledge that the act is wrong

If the defendant is aware of the nature and quality of his act, he may still raise insanity in his defence if he does not know that his actions are wrong (legally rather than morally).

KEY CASE

R v Windle [1952] 2 QB 826 (CA)

Concerning: knowledge that an act is legally wrong

Facts

The defendant was medically insane. He gave his suicidal wife an overdose. Upon arrest, he made reference to the likelihood that he would hang for his actions.

Legal principle

'Wrong' means 'contrary to law'. The defendant's comment showed awareness that his conduct was contrary to law so insanity was not established. It was irrelevant that he believed he was morally justified or that society in general would not condemn his actions.

 Make your answer stand out

A complex point on the operation of the M'Naghten Rules concerns whether they conflict with Article 5 of the European Convention on Human Rights which protects against the arbitrary deprivation of liberty, although it contains an exception in relation to 'unsound mind'. It was held in *Winterwerp* v *Netherland* [1979] 2 EHRR 387 (ECtHR) that a person should be detained on the basis of unsound mind only if three criteria were satisfied:

1 There is a strong correlation between legal and medical definitions of insanity.
2 The court's decision that the defendant is of unsound mind is based on objective medical evidence.
3 The court believes that the mental disorder is one that necessitates compulsory confinement.

Mackay and Gearty (2001) explore the compatibility of the M'Naghten Rules with Article 5 and consider ways in which the law could be altered to ensure that it did not interfere with Article 5. An ability to engage with this issue would greatly enhance an essay in this area.

■ Automatism

KEY DEFINITION: Automatism

An act which is done by the muscles without any control by the mind such as a spasm, a reflex action, or a convulsion; or an act done by a person who is not conscious of what he is doing such as an act done whilst suffering from concussion.

Bratty v *Attorney-General for NI* [1963] AC 386 (HL)

There are three requirements of automatism:

1. complete loss of control;
2. an external cause; and
3. automatism must not be self-induced.

Complete loss of control

As automatism is based on involuntary actions, the defendant must suffer complete loss of control and/or consciousness rather than an eroded ability to exercise control or partially impaired consciousness.

KEY CASE

Broome v *Perkins* **[1987] 85 Cr App R 321 (DC)**

Concerning: loss of control

Facts

The defendant sought to rely on automatism for charges arising from erratic driving whilst in hypoglycaemic shock.

Legal principle

Automatism requires a complete loss of control. The defendant maintained *some* control by steering and braking, thus his movements were not entirely involuntary and automatism would not be available.

External cause

The distinction between automatism and insanity is based upon external and internal causes of loss of control. External causes, such as blows to the head or the introduction of medication into the defendant's system, thus give rise to automatism.

Automatism must not be self-induced

Automatism leads to acquittal in recognition that the defendant's inability to control his actions renders him blameless for this behaviour. It follows that self-induced automatism cannot be used to avoid liability because the defendant was responsible for his lack of control:

■ In *Bailey* (above) failing to eat after taking insulin, despite awareness that this could lead to uncontrolled behaviour, amounted to self-induced automatism.

■ Disassociative states caused by consumption of alcohol or non-prescription drugs amount to self-induced automatism.

> **✎ EXAM TIP**
>
> Although cases on self-induced automatism have arisen only in relation to diabetes, the principle is generally applicable. Remember this, if you encounter a problem question where a defendant suffers an adverse reaction to taking too much medication or from combining alcohol and medication, for example, irrespective of the ailment for which the medication is prescribed. Adding a sentence that explains that this is analogous to the situation concerning the mismanagement of insulin by diabetics will really help your answer stand out.

■ Putting it all together

Answer guidelines

See the essay question at the start of the chapter. A diagram illustrating how to structure your answer is available on the companion website.

Approaching the question

This is a typical example of an essay question on insanity and its role in the criminal law today. The quotation suggests that the current law is a 'quagmire' and that a defendant would rely upon it only if desperate for a defence, so these are both issues that will need to be addressed in the essay.

Important points to include

■ Before deciding to tackle this question, you should make sure that you know enough about insanity to write a comprehensive essay that answers the question. It would not be enough to be able to state the test of insanity. To answer this question effectively, you must understand why it can be described as a quagmire (and make sure that you know what this word means, otherwise you are putting yourself at an immense disadvantage in trying to deal with the question) and why a defendant would need to be desperate to rely upon it. If you have no idea on either of these points, this question should not be tackled, even if you have a good general grasp of insanity, as you are limiting your prospects of success.

- The starting point for the essay would be to describe the current law of insanity, which requires an outline of the M'Naghten Rules and some elaboration on each of the elements of the defence.

- The quotation suggests that the law on insanity is a quagmire, so you would want to explain this and comment upon whether this is a reasonable comment. Try to identify some specific problems with insanity: e.g. the internal/external distinction, the departure from medical insanity. Make sure that you use examples from case law to explain these points.

- The second statement from the quotation that needs consideration is that a defendant would need to be desperate to rely on insanity. Identify some reasons why insanity is so infrequently used by defendants. There are examples in case law where a defendant, on being told that his line of defence raises insanity rather than automatism, has changed his plea to guilty rather than risk being found not guilty by reason of insanity. What is it about the defence that causes defendants to prefer conviction over a finding of insanity? Points to consider here are the social stigma attached to insanity and the disposal of the defendant after a finding of insanity, which used to be an indefinite stay in a mental institution.

- Make sure that you address both points raised by the quotation in your conclusion: is the law on insanity a quagmire and would a defendant need to be desperate to rely upon this defence? A powerful conclusion will be the last part of your essay that examiners read so make sure that they are left with a positive impression of both your legal knowledge and your ability to write an essay.

✓ Make your answer stand out

Can you identify the source of the quotation? If so, this will add real strength to your answer, as you will impress your examiner with your knowledge of this topic and, having realised that it is from *Quick,* you will appreciate that the criticism is directed towards the flaws of insanity arising from the internal/external distinction and the problems of labelling a medical disorder such as diabetes as insanity.

An ability to incorporate discussion of Article 5 of the European Convention on Human Rights (freedom from arbitrary deprivation of liberty) will add strength to ▶

your essay. Make sure that this is tied in with the issues raised by the question rather than merely added for the sake of it. In relation to this question, you could make the point that the European Court of Human Rights in *Winterwerp* outlined three criteria that must be satisfied before a person can be detained on the basis of 'unsound mind' and that these raise questions about the compatibility of domestic law with Article 5.

It would be important to note that judges now have discretion in disposal after a finding of not guilty by reason of insanity, so there is no longer a mandatory detention in a mental institution. However, although the consequences of a plea of insanity are less off-putting, the social stigma is as strong as ever, so it is likely that defendants will still avoid reliance on this defence. You might want to consider ways that this impediment could be overcome as a way to gain additional credit from your examiner.

READ TO IMPRESS

Loughnan, A. (2007) Manifest Madness: Towards a New Understanding of the Insanity Defence. *Modern Law Review,* 70: 379.

Mackay, R.D. and Gearty, C.A. (2001) On Being Insane in Jersey. *Criminal Law Review,* 560.

Mackay, R.D. and Reuber, M. (2007) Epilepsy and the Defence of Insanity: Time for Change? *Criminal Law Review,* 782.

www.pearsoned.co.uk/lawexpress

Go online to access more revision support, including quizzes to test your knowledge, sample questions with answer guidelines, podcasts you can download and more!

16

Intoxication

Revision checklist

Essential points you should know:

☐ The distinction between voluntary and involuntary intoxication

☐ The meaning of basic and specific intent and the relevance to intoxication

☐ The clash of policy and principle in relation to intoxication

■ Topic map

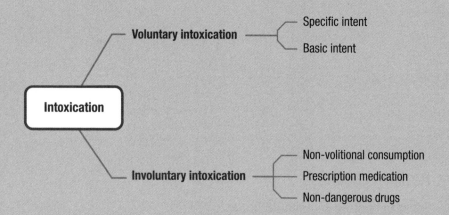

Intoxication

- Voluntary intoxication
  - Specific intent
  - Basic intent
- Involuntary intoxication
  - Non-volitional consumption
  - Prescription medication
  - Non-dangerous drugs

A printable version of this topic map is available from **www.pearsoned.co.uk/lawexpress**

■ Introduction

'I only did it because I was drunk' is a frequently expressed sentiment that is accepted as an excuse for all sorts of bad behaviour.

This is because it is well established that alcohol and drugs alter people's behaviour and attitudes. It is also true that a great deal of crime, particularly involving violence, is committed whilst the defendant is intoxicated. How, then, does the law view intoxication? It is essential that you understand the issues that have led to the development of a dual set of rules – voluntary and involuntary intoxication – as the courts attempt to reconcile principle and policy in relation to the intoxicated defendant.

ASSESSMENT ADVICE

Essay questions

Essay questions will either focus exclusively on intoxication, or include it within a question on states of mind more generally (Chapter 3) or its impact on the operation of other defences (such as self-defence, loss of control and duress). When tackling an essay involving intoxication, make sure that you situate your discussion within the context of the principle/policy debate, as this is a tricky point and one that is frequently overlooked.

Problem questions

Problem questions often involve intoxicated defendants. The level of detail required can vary enormously. It may be possible to deal with a simple issue of intoxication in a single sentence by explaining, for example, that voluntary intoxication is not a defence to crimes of basic intent whilst a more complex situation could combine with defences or raise issues of involuntary intoxication. The final complication is that intoxication could arise in combination with any offence, so it could pop up in absolutely any problem question. Look out for any mention of prescription drugs, alcohol or recreational (illegal) drugs by the defendant, as this should alert you to the need to consider the impact of intoxication on the defendant's liability.

◼ Sample question

Could you answer this question? Below is a typical problem question that could arise on this topic. Guidelines on answering the question are included at the end of this chapter, whilst a sample essay question and guidance on tackling it can be found on the companion website.

PROBLEM QUESTION

Douglas suspects that his wife, Valerie, is having an affair with Derek. After several hours of heavy drinking, he decides to confront her at Derek's house. Douglas storms into the house and finds Valerie lying naked on the floor. Enraged, he attacks her with a nearby poker, inflicting serious injuries. The noise rouses Derek from his drug-induced stupor. The effects of the hallucinogenic drugs that he has taken led him to conclude that Douglas is an alien, so he swings a knife at him, severing his hand. It later transpired that Valerie had given Derek the drugs earlier in the evening, telling him that they were headache tablets.

Discuss the criminal liability of Douglas and Derek.

◼ Types of intoxication

Intoxication may be voluntary or involuntary (see Figure 16.1):

Figure 16.1

VOLUNTARY INTOXICATION	INVOLUNTARY INTOXICATION
The defendant has knowingly ingested recreational drugs or alcohol, knowing their nature. This includes situations where the defendant has knowingly consumed alcohol but is mistaken as to its strength or where he has knowingly taken recreational drugs but is unclear about the effect they will have on him.	The defendant is unaware that he has ingested drugs or alcohol. It also covers intentional consumption of non-dangerous drugs (in accordance with instructions) or drugs such as valium that are known to have a soporific effect (provided the defendant was not reckless in taking them).
The defendant is to blame for his inability to control his behaviour so should not avoid liability for his actions unless he is so intoxicated that he is incapable of thought or reason.	The defendant is not to blame for his intoxication and so should not be held responsible for the consequences of it.

Voluntary intoxication

Although intoxication is viewed as something that affects behaviour, in law the emphasis is on its impact on the defendant's mind, specifically his ability to form *mens rea*. It is only if the defendant is so intoxicated that his ability to form *mens rea* is impaired that the law may take account of his voluntary intoxication. The extent to which it does so depends upon the nature of the offence he has committed as a distinction is made between crimes of **specific** and **basic intent**.

Specific and basic intent

The most straightforward way to distinguish crimes of specific and basic intent is based on the *mens rea* of the offence (see Figure 16.2).

Figure 16.2

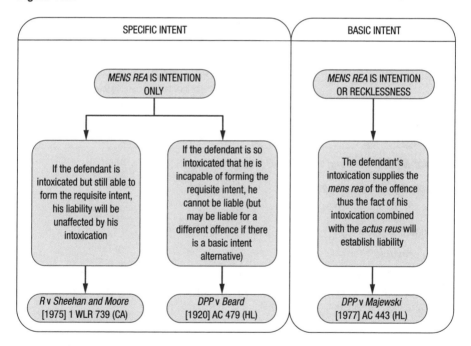

This illustrates that the level of the defendant's intoxication is central to determining how his liability will be affected.

The exception to this rule relates to *Dutch courage* situations, which are outlined in Figure 16.3.

Figure 16.3

CHAIN OF EVENTS	A-G for Northern Ireland v Gallagher [1963] AC 349 (HL)
The defendant forms the intention to commit a specific intent offence.	The defendant decides to kill his wife.
He consumes quantities of alcohol to give himself the courage to commit the *actus reus* of the offence.	He buys a knife and a bottle of whiskey, which he drinks to give himself the courage to go through with the killing.
He commits the *actus reus* whilst in a state of intoxication which is such that he lacks *mens rea*.	Whilst intoxicated, he cuts his wife's throat.
Should he be able to rely upon his intoxication to avoid liability?	He argued that he was so intoxicated that he was incapable of forming the intention to kill at the time he killed his wife.

KEY CASE

A-G for Northern Ireland v *Gallagher* [1963] AC 349 (HL)

Concerning: Dutch courage

Facts

See Figure 16.3.

Legal principle

It was held that a person who forms an intention to kill whilst sober and drinks to give himself Dutch courage to do the killing, and who then goes on to kill whilst intoxicated, cannot rely on intoxication to avoid liability.

 Make your answer stand out

One distinction that you could draw out in an essay on this topic arises from the fact that, according to general principles of criminal liability, *actus reus* and *mens rea* must coincide. However, applying this principle would result in acquittal in Dutch courage cases, as the defendant would not be able to form *mens rea* due to his intoxication.

Policy has prevailed here as a person who forms *mens rea* and negates that with intoxication in order to commit the offence is nonetheless held liable. As Lord Denning said: 'The wickedness of his mind before he got drunk is enough to condemn him, coupled with the act which he intended and did do.'

Basic intent

Policy considerations are evident in relation to voluntary intoxication and basic intent. A defendant cannot argue that he failed to recognise a risk of harm because he was intoxicated. The House of Lords in *Majewski* extended this further.

KEY CASE

DPP v *Majewski* **[1977] AC 443 (HL)**

Concerning: basic intent, intoxication

Facts

The defendant attacked a police officer whilst voluntarily intoxicated. He argued that he was so intoxicated that he could not form the requisite *mens rea*.

Legal principle

The effect of intoxication on the defendant's state of mind was only relevant to crimes of specific intent. In crimes of basic intent, the defendant's recklessness in taking drugs that rendered his behaviour uncontrolled and unpredictable was in itself sufficient to substitute for the *mens rea* of the offence.

In other words, if the *mens rea* of the offence includes recklessness, this is satisfied by the defendant's intoxication because it is reckless to render oneself into a state where behaviour cannot be controlled and crimes may be committed.

 Make your answer stand out

Majewski is open to criticism because it replaces the *mens rea* of an offence with abstract recklessness associated with becoming intoxicated. This means that all drunken people will be walking around with the *mens rea* for all basic intent offences and thus will be liable if they happen to commit the *actus reus* whilst drunk! Essays may invite a critical analysis of this position. Gardner's (1994) article provides an in-depth consideration of the implications of *Majewski* so would be excellent reading ▶

in preparation for an essay question. Virgo's (1993) article provides a useful summary of the Law Commission proposals for reform of the law of intoxication so would prepare you to suggest ways in which the law could be strengthened.

Involuntary intoxication

Involuntary intoxication falls into three categories, as shown in Figure 16.4.

Figure 16.4

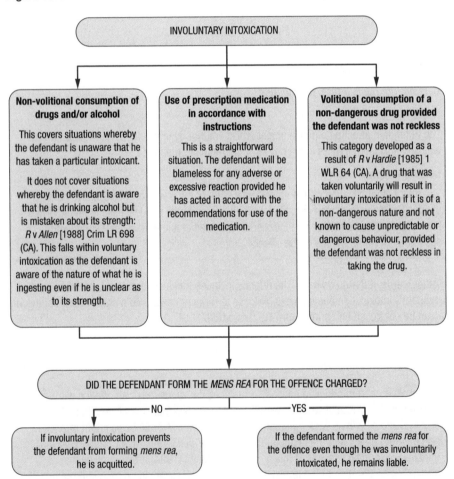

KEY CASE

R v *Hardie* [1985] 1 WLR 64 (CA)

Concerning: involuntary intoxication, non-dangerous drugs

Facts

The defendant took Valium, prescribed for his girlfriend, after an argument, believing it would calm him down. Under its influence, he started a fire that spread through the flat.

Legal principle

This did not fall within voluntary intoxication, thus the *Majewski* presumption of recklessness would not apply. Unlike recreational drugs and alcohol, which were known to cause unpredictable behaviour, Valium was known for its sedative effects. Consumption of non-dangerous drugs would amount to involuntary intoxication unless the consumption itself was reckless.

The way in which liability is determined in cases of involuntary intoxication is further demonstrated by *Kingston.*

KEY CASE

R v *Kingston* [1995] 2 AC 355 (HL)

Concerning: involuntary intoxication, mens rea

Facts

The defendant was drugged without his knowledge, by men who wished to blackmail him, and committed an act of indecency with a young boy who had also been drugged. He claimed that the drugs eroded his ability to resist the paedophilic urges that he managed to control whilst sober.

Legal principle

Although the defendant's will was weakened by drugs administered without his knowledge, he was still aware of his situation and knew his actions were wrong. As such, he had *mens rea* for the offence charged.

■ Putting it all together

Answer guidelines

See the problem question at the start of the chapter. A diagram illustrating how to structure your answer is available on the companion website.

Approaching the question

This is a typical example of a problem question that raises several different issues of intoxication. Even though it is clear that the focus of the essay is intoxication, remember that you need to establish *prima facie* liability before it becomes necessary to discuss intoxication, so deal with the offences suggested by the facts before tackling issues of intoxication. The issues of intoxication should be easy to spot due to the references to heavy drinking and the ingestion of hallucinogenic drugs.

Important points to include

- Start by planning your answer so that what you write is organised and well structured. There are two parties here so it makes sense to deal with each of them in turn. Look at the facts to assess what offences they have committed, categorise these as offences of either specific or basic intent and then determine whether the defendant's intoxication was voluntary or involuntary.

- Douglas has attacked Valerie with a poker, causing serious injuries. This is likely to give rise to liability under either section 18 or section 20 of the Offences Against the Person Act 1861. You will need to work through the elements of these offences to determine which is the most appropriate as a basis for liability. This makes an important difference to the question, as section 18 is an offence of specific intent and section 20 is an offence of basic intent. As Douglas has been drinking heavily, it appears that this is a case of voluntary intoxication. If liability under section 18 is established, you will need to consider whether Douglas is so intoxicated that he could not form *mens rea* for the offence. Even if this is the case, there is a basic intent alternative, so liability under section 20 should not be difficult to establish. Make sure that you explain and apply *Majewski.*

- Derek attacks Douglas with a knife, severing his hand. This is a serious injury that is again likely to fall under section 18 or section 20 of the Offences Against the Person Act 1861. Although Derek is under the influence of hallucinogenic drugs, he was told that they were headache tablets, hence involuntary intoxication needs to be considered. Are you able to work out which of the three categories of involuntary intoxication this would fall under? Look at Figure 16.4 for guidance. As Derek is not aware that he has taken recreational drugs, he will be able to rely on involuntary intoxication as a defence, provided that the drugs rendered him incapable of forming the *mens rea* of the offence. As he believes that Douglas is an alien, it seems unlikely that he is able to form the requisite *mens rea.*

 ## ✓ Make your answer stand out

Although it is clear that the main focus of the question is intoxication, a good answer will also provide clear and detailed coverage of the other issues raised by the question. In addition to the discussion of non-fatal offences that is needed to provide a basis for liability, there is also potential liability (Theft Act 1968) for section 9(1)(a) burglary (entering a building as a trespasser with the intent to cause serious harm) and section 9(1)(b) burglary (having entered a building as a trespasser, causing serious harm). These are straightforward issues that do not need to be discussed in any great detail but credit is available for spotting and addressing them.

Students may be tempted to consider Valerie's liability for pretending that the recreational drugs were harmless headache tablets. There are various offences that could be used here but these would be quite complex points that would attract no credit from the examiner as the instructions specify that it is Douglas and Derek's liability that must be considered.

Make sure that you have a clear grasp of the leading case law, as it is the source of the principles that need to be applied here. In particular, make sure that you can provide a clear and simple explanation of the *Majewski* principle.

READ TO IMPRESS

Gardner, S. (1994) The Importance of *Majewski. Oxford Journal of Legal Studies,* 14: 279.

Virgo, G. (1993) The Law Commission Consultation Paper on Intoxication and Criminal Liability: Reconciling Principle and Policy. *Criminal Law Review,* 415.

Williams, R. (2007) Voluntary Intoxication, Sexual Assault and the Future of *Majewski. Cambridge Law Journal,* 66: 260.

www.pearsoned.co.uk/lawexpress

 Go online to access more revision support, including quizzes to test your knowledge, sample questions with answer guidelines, podcasts you can download and more!

17

Self-defence

■ Topic map

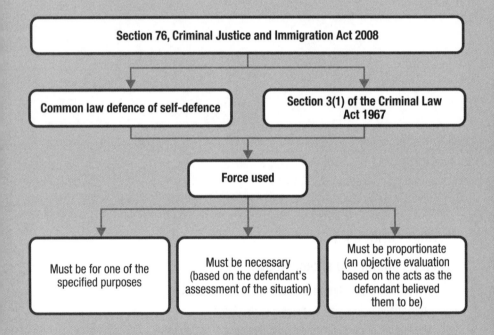

■ Introduction

There are circumstances in which the use of force, even fatal force, against another is justified and will not give rise to criminal liability.

A person can use force to protect themselves, their property and other people against threats of harm. Force may also be used to prevent the commission of a crime or to apprehend an offender.

The range of circumstances in which it is lawful to use force demonstrates the breadth of self-defence. Although usually described as a defence, self-defence is actually the absence of the unlawfulness element of the *actus reus* of fatal and non-fatal offences. As force used in self-defence is regarded as *lawful,* this unlawfulness requirement is not satisfied.

The operation of self-defence has been quite controversial so it is important to take account of principles in the area and the policy behind them in understanding this topic.

ASSESSMENT ADVICE

Essay questions

Essay questions on self-defence are quite common as this is a controversial area of law, particularly following the high-profile case of Tony Martin (*Martin* (*Anthony*) [2003] QB 1 (CA)) and the subsequent debate over the position of householders who attack intruders. It is possible that the recent codification of self-defence will prompt questions that consider whether this was a missed opportunity to alter or strengthen the law in this area.

Problem questions

Problem questions dealing with liability for fatal and non-fatal offences against the person often raise issues of self-defence, although it is important to remember that the defence is of general application so could be used, for example, in relation to pre-vention of an offence against property. Look out for facts that suggest that a defendant who has used force did so in order to protect himself or someone else from attack or in order to prevent an offence from taking place, as this should trigger a discussion of self-defence.

■ Sample question

Could you answer this question? Below is a typical problem question that could arise on this topic. Guidelines on answering the question are included at the end of this chapter, whilst a sample essay question and guidance on tackling it can be found on the companion website.

PROBLEM QUESTION

Vernon makes sexual advances to Davina at a party. Undeterred by her refusal, he follows her into a bedroom and pushes her onto the bed. Afraid he is going to rape her, Davina pushes him hard, causing him to fall off the bed and he breaks his arm. Davina rushes towards the door, but then returns and kicks Vernon hard in the groin, causing bruising.

Davina tells Donald what has happened. He sees a man with a broken arm who he thinks is Vernon (but who is actually Victor), so he tackles him to the ground, shouting 'he's a rapist, call the police'.

Discuss Davina's and Donald's liability.

■ Statutory basis of self-defence

Section 76 of the Criminal Justice and Immigration Act 2008 provides a statutory basis for self-defence but otherwise leaves the operation of the law unaltered. In essence, this provision enacts the law as it existed at common law but, in doing so, it has added much needed clarity to the law concerning the operation of the defence.

Section 76(2) stipulates that the defences in question are the common law defence of self-defence and the statutory defence found in section 3(1) of the Criminal Law Act 1967. The scope of these two defences and the relationship between them is outlined in the section that follows.

■ Scope of self-defence

Self-defence is convenient shorthand for two separate (but similar) situations that negate the unlawfulness of otherwise unlawful acts, as demonstrated by Figure 17.1.

Both self-defence and the use of defence in the prevention of crime are now covered by section 76 of the Criminal Justice and Immigration Act 2008, but the principles that guide

Figure 17.1

Self-defence	Prevention of crime
'It is both good law and good sense that a man who is attacked may defend himself. It is both good law and good sense that he may do, but only do, what is reasonably necessary': *Palmer* v *R* [1971] AC 814 (PC)	'A person may use such force as is reasonable in the circumstances in the prevention of crime, or in effecting or assisting in the lawful arrest of offenders or suspected offenders or of persons unlawfully at large' (s. 3(1) Criminal Law Act 1967)

POTENTIAL OVERLAP
A man who shoots a person who is attacking him both acts to defend himself and to prevent a crime.

the operation of the defence were developed at common law and justified the use of force in the following situations (detailed in section 76(10) of the Criminal Justice and Immigration Act 2008):

- *Protection of oneself:* Dawn runs towards Mark waving a samurai sword. Mark throws a rock at Dawn to stop her charge, which hits Dawn on the head and kills her. This may fall within self-defence, as Mark has used force in order to protect himself.

- *Protection of another:* Dawn sees Mark holding down a woman and thinks that Mark is about to commit rape. Dawn smashes her umbrella over Mark's head, knocking him unconscious and fracturing his skull. This may fall within self-defence, as Dawn acted to protect the other woman.

- *Protection of property:* Dawn sees Mark pick up a rock and walk towards her car. She thinks he is about to smash the window, so she rugby-tackles him to the ground, breaking his leg. Here, Dawn has used force to protect her property from harm.

- *Prevention of crime:* The three examples above demonstrate the overlap explained earlier in this section, as they all involve the prevention of crime as well as the protection of self, another or property.

- *Apprehension of a person unlawfully at large:* Dawn is sitting at a table outside a coffee shop when she sees Mark walking along the street. She knows that he has recently escaped from prison, so she trips him over as he walks past and sits on him to detain him until the police arrive.

Elements of self-defence

The situations outlined above justify the use of force but there are limitations to the level of force that may be used. Self-defence must involve 'reasonable force': section 76(1)(b) of the Criminal Justice and Immigration Act 2008. This has two elements (see Figure 17.2):

Figure 17.2

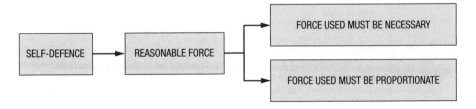

- the force used must be necessary; and
- the force used must be proportionate.

Necessity of force

Self-defence justifies the use of force that otherwise would be unlawful. In order to be justified, it must be necessary for the defendant to have used force. The necessity to use force is judged from the defendant's perspective, so the key question to ask is 'did the defendant think he needed to use force to protect himself, someone else or property or to prevent a crime or apprehend someone unlawfully at large?' If the answer to this question is 'yes', then this element of the defence is satisfied, even if other people would not have thought it necessary to use force, or if the defendant was incorrect and it was not actually necessary to use force. This issue of a mistaken belief in the need to use force is considered in the section that follows.

Mistaken belief

A defendant who is mistaken about the need to use force has, effectively, attacked an innocent person. However, this does not mean that the defence will not be available, as it was held in *Williams (Gladstone)* (below) that a person who honestly believes that he needs to use force will still have the defence available to him.

KEY CASE

R v Williams (Gladstone) [1987] 3 All ER 411 (CA)

Concerning: mistaken belief

Facts

The defendant observed one man attack another. He intervened and punched the attacker in order to protect the victim. However, the attacker had been trying to detain a man who had just committed a robbery, so the defendant was charged as a result of his actions and sought to rely on self-defence.

Legal principle

The reasonableness of the defendant's actions must be judged on the facts as he believed them to be. If the defendant's perception of events had been correct, self-defence would have been available and he should not be deprived of a defence because he was mistaken. Provided the mistaken belief was honestly held, it is immaterial that the mistake was not reasonable.

This principle is reinforced by section 76(3) and (4) of the Criminal Justice and Immigration Act 2008.

KEY STATUTE

Criminal Justice and Immigration Act 2008, section 76(3)

The question whether the degree of force used by the defendant was reasonable in the circumstances is to be decided by reference to the circumstances as the defendant believed them to be.

This confirms that the question of whether it is necessary to use force is determined by reference to the defendant's impression of the situation rather than the actual facts of the situation. In other words, if the defendant thinks he is about to be attacked, he is entitled to use force to protect himself. If it turns out that he was wrong and he was not about to be attacked, this does not change the fact that the defendant thought it was necessary to use force and so this element of the defence will be established. Section 76(4)(b) makes it clear that, if the defendant genuinely believes it was necessary to use force, then this limb of the defence is satisfied, even if the defendant was mistaken about the need to use force and this was an unreasonable mistake to make.

✎ EXAM TIP

This point often causes confusion, perhaps because it seems illogical to place such reliance on the defendant's impression of events. Remember that the question to be asked in relation to mistake is:

If the facts were as the defendant believed them to be, was the use of force necessary?

If the answer is 'yes' then the defendant may rely on self-defence, even though it was not actually necessary, even if the mistake was not one that others would have made.

The law accommodates mistaken belief in self-defence as an acknowledgement that instant decisions made in stressful situations may be inaccurate. However, case law has limited the availability of self-defence when the mistake about the need to use force was based on:

- *Mental illness:* In *Martin (Anthony)* [2003] QB 1 (CA), the defendant was not permitted to rely on self-defence following a mistake about the need to defend himself that was induced by his mental illness, which caused him to dramatically misinterpret events.

- *Consumption of drugs or alcohol:* In *O'Grady* [1987] QB 995 (CA), the defendant was not entitled to rely on an intoxicated mistake about the need to use force to defend himself, following the consumption of alcohol and hallucinogenic drugs. This limitation on the availability of self-defence is reinforced by section 76(5) of the Criminal Justice and Immigration Act 2008 which prohibits reliance on a mistaken belief induced by voluntary intoxication.

Duty to retreat

A further issue for consideration when determining the availability of self-defence is whether a defendant is entitled to argue that it was necessary for him to use force if he had an opportunity to retreat but did not take it. In *Bird* [1985] 1 WLR 816 (CA), it was said that an attempt to retreat demonstrated that a defendant was unwilling to fight so may negate any suggestion of retaliation or revenge.

> **✎ EXAM TIP**
>
> If the defendant had the opportunity to retreat but did not do so, it is not fatal to reliance on self-defence, but you will need to use the facts available to demonstrate that the defendant was not eager for a fight or that it was reasonable in the circumstances for him to stand his ground.

Section 76 of the Criminal Justice and Immigration Act 2008 was amended by section 148 of the Legal Aid, Sentencing and Punishment of Offenders Act 2012 to clarify *inter alia* the position regarding the possibility of retreat. A new section 76(6A) was inserted, which provides that:

> In deciding the question mentioned in subsection (3) [the question of whether the force used was reasonable in the circumstances] a possibility that D could have retreated is to be considered (so far as relevant) as a factor to be taken into account, rather than as giving rise to a duty to retreat.

Pre-emptive force

When determining whether it was necessary for the defendant to use force, it is also important to take into account the use of force to prevent an attack that is feared but has not yet taken place. Is it necessary to use force when you are not yet under attack but fear it is imminent? This issue was addressed by the Privy Council in *Beckford*.

Not only may a person resort to force in order to prevent an anticipated attack, it has been held that he may arm himself in order to do so. This has included making and storing fire bombs to protect property against attack from rioters: *Re Attorney-General's Reference (No. 2 of 1983)* [1984] QB 456 (CA).

KEY CASE

Beckford v *R* [1988] AC 130 (PC)

Concerning: pre-emptive attack

Facts

The defendant, a police officer, shot and killed an armed man who had been threatening others with a gun.

Legal principle

Lord Griffiths stated that 'a man about to be attacked does not have to wait for his assailant to strike the first blow or fire the first shot; circumstances may justify a pre-emptive strike'.

Level of force

Once it is established that the use of force was necessary, the next issue is to determine whether the level of force used was reasonable.

The general rule is that the force used must be *no more than necessary*: it must be proportionate to the threat. This means that the reasonableness of the force will depend upon the circumstances (see Figure 17.3).

Figure 17.3

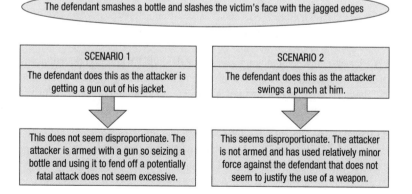

Although it is the defendant who determines whether the use of force is necessary, the reasonableness of the level of force is determined objectively, i.e. by the jury (see Figure 17.4).

Two factors must be taken into account:

- The level of force must be reasonable in response to the facts as the defendant believed them to be: *Owino* [1996] 2 Cr App R 128 (CA).
- Extreme situations can create pressure that distorts judgement: 'a person defending himself cannot weigh to a nicety the exact measure of his necessary defensive actions': *Palmer* [1971] AC 814 (PC).

In *Oye (Seun)* [2013] EWCA Crim 1725, the Court of Appeal considered whether a defendant's insanely held delusion that he was being attacked or threatened, which caused him to respond violently, entitled him to an acquittal on the basis of reasonable self-defence. In doing so, the court considered the meaning and effect of section 76. It considered that if self-defence was available where the defendant had a genuine, but insanely deluded, belief, then the 'potential implications for other cases are most disconcerting' before concluding that 'an insane person cannot set the standards of reasonableness as to the degree of force used by reference to his own insanity. In truth, it makes as little sense to talk of the reasonable lunatic as it did, in the context of cases on provocation, to talk of the reasonable glue-sniffer.'

■ Effect of self-defence

Self-defence justifies the force used so results in an outright acquittal if used successfully. There is no 'half-way measure' if, for example, the use of force was necessary but the level of force used was excessive: *Clegg* [1995] 1 AC 482 (HL) (see Figure 17.4).

 Make your answer stand out

There is a tension between the emphasis on the defendant's interpretation of events in relation to the necessity to resort to force and the objective evaluation of the level of force. However, an objective element is a necessary safeguard against the use of excessive force in society.

For an excellent exposition of the issues in relation to force used against intruders, see Jefferson (2005). This detailed article explains some complex points with clarity and would enable you to incorporate academic commentary into an essay on the topic.

Figure 17.4

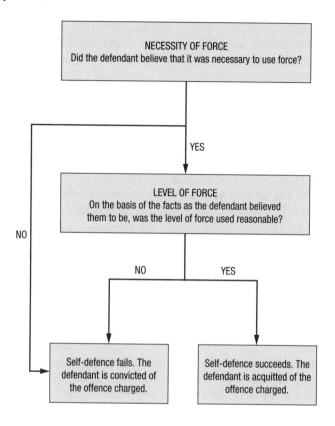

■ Putting it all together

Answer guidelines

See the problem question at the start of the chapter. A diagram illustrating how to structure your answer is available on the companion website.

Approaching the question

This is a problem question dealing with non-fatal offences against the person and self-defence. As self-defence is a defence, it comes into play only once *prima facie* liability for some offence has been established, so make sure that you can deal ▶

with both the offence and defence raised by the facts before deciding to answer the question. Remember, you would produce a very weak answer to this question if you were able to deal only with self-defence and not the basis of liability itself. Note that there is no need to consider Vernon's liability for attempted rape as the question specifies that you should consider only Davina's and Donald's liability.

Important points to include

- The starting point here is to identify the first offence and establish *prima facie* liability. Davina pushes Vernon, causing him to fall off the bed and break his arm. As this is a serious injury, it is likely that Davina is liable under section 20 of the Offences Against the Person Act 1861 (Chapter 9), although it may be that she did not foresee the possibility that her push would cause him any harm, in which case she is liable under section 47 for assault, occasioning actual bodily harm.

- Davina may be able to rely on self-defence. The first question is whether it was necessary for her to use force. Davina honestly believed that Vernon was going to rape her so, even if this belief is mistaken (*Williams* (*Gladstone*)), she is entitled to use force to defend herself. The next question to consider is how much force she is entitled to use and the answer is that she is entitled to use reasonable force to respond to the threat that she believed existed (*Owino*). The level of force she has used does not seem disproportionate to the threat, so it is likely that self-defence will be available.

- Davina returns to the room and kicks Vernon in the groin. Bruising is a relatively low level of harm, so the appropriate offence here is likely to be battery (Chapter 9). It is difficult to see any way for Davina to rely on self-defence here as Vernon does not seem to pose an ongoing threat to her and her return seems to be motivated by a desire for revenge. You could mention here that she has an opportunity to retreat that she has not taken (*Bird*).

- Donald tackles Victor to the ground in the mistaken belief that he is Vernon. Victor suffers serious bruising. This will give rise to liability for battery or section 47 of the Offences Against the Person Act 1861, depending on the severity of the bruises. He may be able to rely on self-defence in that he was acting to apprehend an offender. His mistake is an honest one (necessity) and it does not seem as if the level of force used is excessive (proportionality) if the facts were as he believed them to be.

 Make your answer stand out

It is common for students to focus on the protection of the person aspect of self-defence but to overlook the prevention of crime and apprehension of offenders elements, so make sure that you look out for these less common manifestations of the defence and deal with them appropriately. For instance, you could try to argue that Davina is acting to prevent an offender from escaping by kicking Vernon in the groin to incapacitate him.

A mistaken belief in the need to use force is a common area of confusion, so make sure that you have a clear grasp of the issue and that you are able to apply *Williams (Gladstone)* in order to reach a reasoned conclusion about the availability of the defence.

READ TO IMPRESS

Dingwall, G. (2007) Intoxicated Mistakes About the Need for Self-Defence. *Modern Law Review*, 70: 127.

Jefferson, M. (2005) Householders and the Use of Force Against Intruders. *Journal of Criminal Law*, 69: 405.

O'Sullivan, C. (2007) The Burglar and the Burglarised: Self-Defence, Home Defence and Barnes. *Irish Criminal Law Journal*, 17: 10.

www.pearsoned.co.uk/lawexpress

 Go online to access more revision support, including quizzes to test your knowledge, sample questions with answer guidelines, podcasts you can download and more!

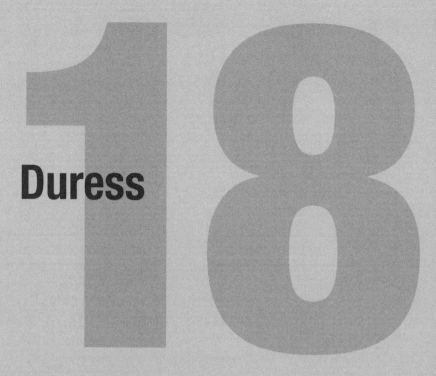

Duress

Revision checklist

Essential points you should know:

☐ The operation of duress by threats and duress of circumstances

☐ The availability of the defences and the rationale for their operation

☐ The types of threat that suffice to establish duress

☐ The circumstances that remove the defence of duress from the defendant

■ Topic map

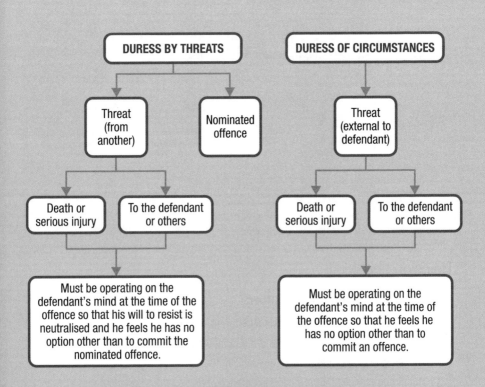

A printable version of this topic map is available from **www.pearsoned.co.uk/lawexpress**

■ Introduction

Traditionally, duress could be described as a 'he made me do it' defence.

It was this aspect of compulsion that led to offences committed under duress being regarded as 'morally involuntary', as the defendant acts out of fear rather than choice. Duress of circumstances evolved as a second species of duress (with the former becoming known as 'duress by threats') because there was a broader range of situations in which the defendant seemed to act, as he had no choice, but that fell outside of duress by threats. This resulted in two closely related defences with many similar elements.

ASSESSMENT ADVICE

Essay questions

Essay questions dealing with duress are not particularly common, but may arise, so the topic should not be neglected as an area for revision. Duress has attracted a fair amount of criticism based on its existence as a defence and its operation, so it has plenty of potential to appear as an essay question.

Problem questions

Problem questions often include duress as an issue, but remember that any defence can arise only if *prima facie* liability has been established, so duress will appear only in a question with at least one other issue. Any reference in the facts to the defendant being threatened if he does not commit an offence should trigger a discussion of duress by threats, whilst offences committed not because the defendant was threatened but because he felt that he had no choice could raise an issue of duress of circumstances. Keep a look out for any mention of gang membership or association with criminals, as this can render the defence unavailable.

■ Sample question

Could you answer this question? Below is a typical problem question that could arise on this topic. Guidelines on answering the question are included at the end of this chapter, whilst a sample essay question and guidance on tackling it can be found on the companion website.

■ Duress by threats

Duress is an absolute defence that leads to an acquittal. It is based on the notion that the defendant's will was overpowered by threats of harm to himself or others so that he had no choice other than to offend.

Nature of threat

Only threats of death or serious physical injury to the defendant (or certain others) will suffice. Threats of lesser harm, to damage property or reveal unpleasant or personal information, will not provide a basis for duress (even if they had an overwhelming influence on the defendant).

Immediacy

The requirement that the threat be immediate, related to the notion that duress provided an inescapable pressure to offend, but this has been broadened by judicial interpretation.

KEY CASE

R v Hudson and Taylor [1971] 2 QB 202 (CA)

Concerning: immediacy of threat

Facts

The defendants refused to give evidence at a trial because they had been threatened with violence if they did so by someone who was present in the courtroom. They gave false evidence, which led to the acquittal of the accused and sought to rely on duress at their own trial for perjury. They were initially unsuccessful as it was held that the threats could not be carried out immediately.

Legal principle

The issue was not whether the threats could be carried out immediately but whether they were operating on the defendants at the time of the threat. The Court of Appeal recognised that threats were no less powerful because they were not immediately effective.

✎ EXAM TIP

A threat that cannot be carried out at the time suggests an opportunity to avoid the threat, which would negate any claim of duress. Following *Hudson and Taylor*, it is important to consider whether the threat was operating on the defendant's mind at the time that he committed the offence, notwithstanding the fact that the threat could not be carried out immediately.

Causal nexus

There must be a link between the threat made and the offence committed. Effectively, the person issuing the threat must nominate a particular offence to be committed.

KEY CASE

R v *Cole* [1994] Crim LR 582 (CA)

Concerning: nexus between threat and offence

Facts

The defendant was threatened with violence if he did not repay money that he owed. In desperation, he committed two armed robberies to make the repayments.

Legal principle

Duress was not available as those making the threats had not told the defendant to commit robbery. The decision to offend was the result of free choice by the defendant which was inconsistent with the defence of duress.

This is an important limitation on the availability of duress. In Cole, the lenders knew the defendant had exhausted all lawful means of obtaining money so must have realised that their threats would compel him to offend, but their failure to specify an offence meant duress was not available.

This means that duress requires '*do this or else*' rather than '*do something or else*'.

Test for duress

KEY CASE

R v *Howe* [1987] 1 AC 417 (HL)

Concerning: two-stage test

Facts

The defendant sought to rely on duress as a defence to murder on the basis that he believed that he would be killed if he did not kill the victim as instructed.

Legal principle

The House of Lords upheld the two-stage test outlined in *Graham* [1982] 1 WLR 294 (CA).

This two-stage test (see Figure 18.1) requires not only that the defendant *was* overwhelmed by threats but also that a sober person of reasonable firmness *would have been* compelled to offend. An objective angle limits the availability of duress by establishing a standard of fortitude expected of members of society. In other words, if an ordinary person in the defendant's position would have resisted the threats, the defendant's defence of duress will fail.

Figure 18.1

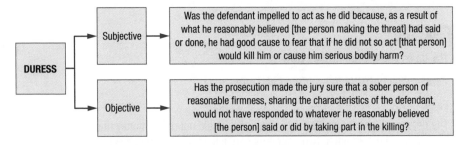

The Court of Appeal in *Bowen* [1997] 1 WLR 372 (CA) outlined three principles relevant to the attribution of the characteristics of the defendant to the reasonable man (see Figure 18.2).

The characteristics that were thought to be relevant were:

- age
- sex
- pregnancy
- serious physical disability
- recognised mental illness/psychiatric conditions.

Figure 18.2

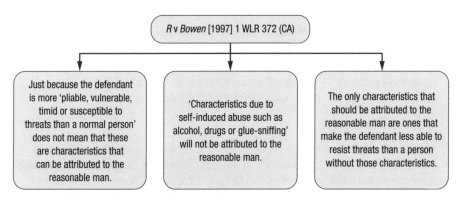

Availability of duress by threats

There are two factors that render duress unavailable:

1. voluntary association with a criminal gang; and
2. commission of murder or attempted murder.

Voluntary association with criminal organisations

Just as duress is denied to a defendant who did not take a reasonable opportunity to escape, it is also withheld from a defendant who put himself in a position where he might be pressurised into offending.

KEY CASE

R v Sharp [1987] QB 853 (CA)

Concerning: voluntary association with criminals

Facts

The defendant took part in several armed robberies. When he tried to leave the gang, another member held a gun to his head and threatened to blow it off. He took part in a further robbery in which someone was killed and he sought to rely on duress.

Legal principle

A person who voluntarily joins a gang, knowing of its nature, as an active member cannot avail himself of duress if pressure is put upon him to offend.

Case law has elaborated on this principle:

- Gang membership does not always remove duress; it depends on the nature of the gang and the sort of activities in which it engages. A defendant should not expect violence from a non-violent gang: *Shepherd* [1988] 86 Cr App R 47 (CA).
- Membership of an organised gang is not essential. It is enough that the defendant puts himself in the position where he will encounter criminals with a tendency to violence, e.g. by buying drugs from a dealer: *Hasan* [2005] 2 AC 467 (HL).

Duress and murder

Duress is not a defence to murder. Its basis is that a defendant commits an offence as 'the lesser of two evils' in comparison with the harm with which he has been threatened. As murder involves taking a life, there can be no greater harm. The House of Lords in *Howe* (see above) stated that an ordinary man would rather sacrifice his own life than take the life of another. This principle was extended to attempted murder in *Gotts* [1992] 2 AC 412 (HL).

 Make your answer stand out

A critical essay on this topic could require you to consider whether or not you agree with *Howe*. Would an ordinary person sacrifice his life (or that of a loved one) to save the life of another, who might be unknown to him? How should this principle operate if the threat is to kill five people (or 15, or 50) if the life of one person is not taken? How does this rule stand when you consider that self-defence is available to murder (see Chapter 17)? In order to address these difficult points, you could include the arguments put forward by Elliot (1989), whilst Loveless (2005) considers the rationale for denying duress to those who associate with criminals.

Duress of circumstances

Duress of circumstances evolved as a species of duress by threats, initially in relation to motoring offences. It differs from duress by threats in two ways:

1. The threat does not have to come from another person. It may come from the surrounding circumstances or from a naturally occurring event.
2. The offence is not nominated by another. The defendant commits an offence not because he is ordered to do so by another but because it seems to be the only way of avoiding the threat that he faces.

R v *Willer* (1986) 83 Cr App R 225 (CA)

Concerning: duress of circumstances

Facts

The defendant was the driver of a car that was being chased by a gang of youths who were threatening to kill him and his passenger. In order to escape them, the defendant drove through a pedestrian precinct.

Legal principle

It was held that the defendant should have a defence as he was 'wholly driven by the force of circumstances into doing what he did and did not drive the car otherwise than under that form of compulsion, i.e. under duress'.

The principles relating to duress of circumstances have evolved through a series of cases. The following are the key points to remember:

■ *The defendant's actions must be a reasonable and proportionate response to a threat of death or serious injury.* In *Martin* [1989] 1 All ER 652 (CA) the defendant's wife threatened to commit suicide unless he drove their son to work. This provided a defence of duress of circumstances to the charge of driving whilst disqualified.

■ *The threat of death or serious injury must come from an external source. Threats emanating from the defendant will not suffice.* In *Rodger and Rose* [1998] 1 Cr App R 143 (CA) the defendants were not able to rely on duress of circumstances for charges arising from their escape from prison. They argued that prison was making them suicidal, but it was held that internal threats would not suffice.

■ *The defendant's conduct is excused only whilst the threat exists.* Continuation after the threat has expired will not be covered by the defence. In *DPP v Bell* [1992] RTR 335 (DC) the defendant was able to rely on duress of circumstances to driving with excess alcohol as he only drove far enough to escape his attackers. In *DPP v Jones* [1990] RTR 33 (DC), in similar circumstances, the defendant drove all the way home and was not permitted to rely on the defence once the threat of death or serious harm had passed.

■ Putting it all together

Answer guidelines

See the problem question at the start of the chapter. A diagram illustrating how to structure your answer is available on the companion website.

Approaching the question

The facts give rise to potential liability for property offences but also allow scope for liability to be avoided on the basis of duress by threats. It should not be difficult to identify the duress issue as there is clear evidence that Debbie has been threatened in order to compel her to commit offences. It would be important to limit your discussion to duress by threats as there is no suggestion of duress of circumstances.

Important points to include

- Always start by establishing liability on the basis that there is no point in dealing with defences until it has been established that the defendant has committed an offence.

- The first point to consider here is Debbie's liability for theft of the mobile phone. Insufficient information is provided about the way that the offence is committed but you are told that the offence of theft is complete so little is required here other than a reference to section 1(1) of the Theft Act 1968 (see Chapter 12) as the issue is not complicated.

- Is Debbie able to rely on duress by threats? It is important to consider each of the elements of the offence in turn and establish this by reference to the facts:

  - ☐ *Nature of the threat:* it is arguable that a cut to the face that would leave a scar would be regarded as a serious injury so could form the basis of a defence of duress.

  - ☐ *Immediacy:* Jenny is with Debbie in the park so it does not seem that she has an opportunity to escape the threat and it seems that it was operating on her mind at the time of the offence.

  - ☐ *Causal nexus:* Jenny has nominated the offence that Debbie commits.

  - ☐ *Test for duress:* apply the two-stage test from *Graham* – clearly Debbie felt compelled to act and it is possible that a sober person of reasonable firmness would act in the same way if they were threatened with a knife.

  - ☐ *Voluntary association with criminals:* references to offending in the company of a group of older girls should trigger a discussion of the implications of gang membership (*Shepherd*).

■ Next, discuss Debbie's liability for burglary. Does she have a defence of duress? Follow the stages outlined in the previous point to reach a decision. There should be some consideration of whether John's threat is serious, given that Debbie has refused initially and presumably was not beaten. Take into account the relationship between them and the other options open to Debbie (telling her mother, perhaps) to consider whether this is a situation in which she can rely on duress.

 ## Make your answer stand out

This is a set of facts that gives rise to far more potential liability than the question asks you to discuss. John and Jenny could both be liable either for inchoate offences (see Chapter 4) or as an accessory to Debbie (see Chapter 5). Equally, Debbie has committed other offences, such as common assault. It is common for some students, in the pressure of the exam room, to discuss all the potential defendants and offences. This would be a waste of time, as the question specifies a discussion of property offences and Debbie's liability so there is no credit to be gained for including any other points. Make sure that your answer is not one that makes this common mistake.

Stronger answers would spot that taking a mobile phone probably involves the use of force, so there is scope for a discussion of robbery contrary to section 8 of the Theft Act 1968 (see Chapter 13). There is also scope to impress the examiner by making a distinction between section 9(1)(a) and section 9(1)(b) burglary when discussing Debbie's liability in relation to her elderly neighbour.

There is scope for a good discussion of whether duress is available to Debbie in relation to the burglary on the basis of voluntary association with criminals. Explain that *Hasan* has broadened the rule about gang membership to association with criminals outside of a gang situation in order to speculate on Debbie's association with John who, given his threats and insistence of burglary being committed, may be a criminal. Stronger answers will consider whether this rule can apply to a sibling relationship, as Debbie, presumably, has little choice about this association, especially if John still lives in the family home.

READ TO IMPRESS

Clarkson, C.M.V. (2004) Necessary Action: A New Defence. *Criminal Law Review*, 81.

Elliot, D.W. (1989) Necessity, Duress and Self-Defence. *Criminal Law Review*, 611.

Loveless, J. (2005) Duress, Voluntary Association and Confession Evidence. *Law Teacher*, 39: 375.

www.pearsoned.co.uk/lawexpress

Go online to access more revision support, including quizzes to test your knowledge, sample questions with answer guidelines, podcasts you can download and more!

And finally, before the exam . . .

By using this revision guide to direct your work, you should now have a good knowledge and understanding of the way in which the various aspects of the criminal law work in isolation and the many areas in which they overlap or are interrelated. You should also have brushed up the skills and techniques needed to demonstrate that knowledge and understanding in the examination, regardless of whether the questions are presented to you in essay or problem format.

Check your progress

☐ Look at the **revision checklists** at the start of each chapter. Are you happy that you can now tick them all? If not, go back to the particular chapter and work through the material again. If you are still struggling, seek help from your tutor.

☐ Attempt the **sample questions** in each chapter and check your answers against the guidelines provided.

☐ Go online to **www.pearsoned.co.uk/lawexpress** for more hands-on revision help:

   ☐ Try the **test your knowledge** quizzes and see if you can score full marks for each chapter.

   ☐ Attempt to answer the **sample questions** for each chapter within the time limit and check your answers against the guidelines provided.

   ☐ Listen to the **podcast** and then attempt the question it discusses.

   ☐ Evaluate sample exam answers with **you be the marker** and see if you can spot their strengths and weaknesses.

   ☐ Use the **flashcards** to test your recall of the legal principles of the key cases and statutes you have revised and the definitions of important terms.

◼ Linking it all up

Check where there are overlaps between subject areas. (You may want to review the 'revision note' boxes throughout this text.) Make a careful note of these, as knowing how one topic may lead into another can increase your marks significantly. In essence, a problem question could combine any number of offences and defences, not to mention involving multiple parties, so it is important that you cover as much of the syllabus as possible in your revision so that you are equipped to tackle any question that you may encounter. Selective revision can leave you in the difficult position of being able to tackle only part of a problem question. Consider these combinations to determine whether you can deal with them all:

✔ murder, rape, robbery and intoxication;

✔ involuntary manslaughter, criminal damage, self-defence and duress;

✔ accessories, fraud, non-fatal offences and insanity.

◼ Knowing your cases

Make sure you know how to use relevant case law in your answers. Use the table below to focus your revision of the key cases in each topic. To review the details of these cases, refer back to the particular chapter.

Key case	How to use	Related topics
Chapter 1 – Elements of criminal liability		
Fagan v *Metropolitan Police Commissioner*	To demonstrate coincidence of *actus reus* and *mens rea* as a continuing act	*Actus reus; mens rea*
R v *Miller*	To demonstrate coincidence of *actus reus* and *mens rea* in relation to a failure to act	*Actus reus; mens rea*
R v *Church*	To demonstrate coincidence of *actus reus* and *mens rea* as part of a single transaction	*Actus reus; mens rea*
Chapter 2 – *Actus reus*		
R v *White*	To show the 'but for' test in factual causation	Homicide
R v *Pagett*	To show the operation of legal causation where there are multiple causes	Homicide

Key case	How to use	Related topics
R v *Roberts*	To illustrate that the victim's act can break the chain of causation	
R v *Pittwood*	To show that a contractual duty to act can give criminal liability for omission	

Chapter 3 – *Mens rea*

R v *Woollin*	To illustrate the test for oblique intention	Homicide
R v *Cunningham*	To show the test for subjective recklessness	All recklessness offences except criminal damage
R v *Caldwell*	To show the test for objective recklessness	Criminal damage
R v *G*	To set out the test for recklessness in criminal damage	Criminal damage

Chapter 4 – Inchoate offences

R v *Griffen*; *R* v *Geddes*	To explain the notion of 'more than merely preparatory'	All offences
R v *Jackson*	To illustrate contingent plans are still plans to commit an offence	All offences
R v *Shillam*	To show that conspiracy requires a shared criminal purpose to which all conspirators have agreed	All offences
R v *Saik*	To show the *mens rea* for conspiracy requires the parties to intend every element of the principal offence	All offences

Chapter 5 – Accessorial liability

R v *Bainbridge*	To show that an accessory must have some knowledge of the criminal purpose of the principal	All offences
Maxwell v *DPP for Northern Ireland*	To illustrate the extension of the principle from Bainbridge to include 'one of a range of offences' within the principal's contemplation	All offences

▶

Key case	How to use	Related topics
R v *Rook*	To show how a defendant might withdraw from participation	All offences
R v *Becerra*	To show what a defendant must do to withdraw from participation	All offences
R v *Robinson*	To show how withdrawal works in spontaneous offences	All offences
R v *Powell; R* v *English*	To set out the criteria for departure from the common plan	All offences
R v *Gnango*	To show that the intended victim of a murder can be liable as an accessory to another's murder even when they do not cause the death or serious injury	Murder

Chapter 6 – Murder

No key cases in this chapter

Chapter 7 – Voluntary manslaughter

R v *Dietschmann*	To illustrate the position where an abnormality of mind is not the sole cause of killing	Diminished responsibility; homicide
R v *Clinton, Parker and Evans*	To show that sexual infidelity may be taken into account when considering qualifying triggers for loss of control	Homicide

Chapter 8 – Involuntary manslaughter

R v *Lamb*	To show that involuntary manslaughter requires a criminally unlawful act	
R v *Lowe*	To show that the criminally unlawful act must be positive	Omissions; *actus reus*
R v *Church*	To set out the test of dangerousness in constructive manslaughter	
R v *Newbury and Jones*	To show that a defendant need not recognise the dangerousness of his or her act	

Key case	How to use	Related topics
R v Adomako	To illustrate breach of duty in gross negligence manslaughter	
Chapter 9 – Non-fatal offences		
R v Ireland	To demonstrate words and silence as a basis for common assault	
R v Ireland	To show that only apprehension of immediate violence would suffice for assault	
R v Constanza	To show the requirement for immediacy in common assault	
R v Brown	To demonstrate that consent is only a defence to battery and not to bodily harm unless in the public interest	
R v Ireland; R v Burstow	To show that psychiatric injury can amount to bodily harm	
R v Savage	To illustrate the operation of half mens rea in relation to ABH	Mens rea
DPP v Parmenter	To set out the test of recklessness applicable to section 20 OAPA	Mens rea
Chapter 10 – Sexual offences		
R v Jheeta	To illustrate the relationship between conclusive presumptions and broader definition of consent in the Sexual Offences Act 2003	
R v Bree	To demonstrate the relationship between consent in rape and intoxication	
Chapter 11 – Criminal damage		
R v Hunt	To show the operation of lawful excuse in relation to protection of property	
R v Steer	To show the meaning of endangerment of life in relation to aggravated criminal damage	

▶

Key case	How to use	Related topics
Chapter 12 – Theft		
R v *Hinks*	To illustrate the meaning of appropriation in relation to gifts	
R v *Ghosh*	To set out the test for dishonesty	
R v *Lloyd*	To show when borrowing can amount to outright taking	
Chapter 13 – Theft-related offences		
R v *Hale*	To show that appropriation can be a continuing act in relation to robbery	Theft
R v *Walkington*	To illustrate what constitutes 'part of a building' for burglary	Theft
R v *Collins*	To show the requirements for trespass in burglary	
R v *Jones and Smith*	To show that trespass can include exceeding permission to enter	
Chapter 14 – Fraud		
No key cases in this chapter		
Chapter 15 – Insanity and automatism		
R v *Clarke*	To show what is meant by 'defect of reason' in insanity	
R v *Sullivan*	To illustrate the meaning of 'disease of the mind' in insanity	
R v *Windle*	To show that 'wrong' means 'contrary to law' for the purposes of insanity	
Broome v *Perkins*	To show that automatism requires a complete loss of control	
Chapter 16 – Intoxication		
A-G for Northern Ireland v *Gallagher*	To illustrate that intoxication through 'Dutch courage' cannot be used to avoid criminal liability	

Key case	How to use	Related topics
DPP v *Majewski*	To show that the effect of intoxication on a defendant's mind is relevant only to crimes of specific intent	
R v *Hardie*	To set out that consumption of non-dangerous drugs amounts to involuntary intoxication unless that consumption was reckless	Recklessness
R v *Kingston*	To show that involuntary intoxication is successful only if the defendant is incapable of forming mens rea	*Mens rea*

Chapter 17 – Self-defence

R v *Williams (Gladstone)*	To show that honestly held mistaken belief is sufficient for self-defence to be available	
Beckford v *R*	To show that the use of pre-emptive force may be lawful	

Chapter 18 – Duress

R v *Hudson and Taylor*	To show that threats must be operating on a defendant at the time of the threat	
R v *Cole*	To illustrate that there must be a link between the threat made and the offence committed	
R v *Howe*	To set out the two-stage test for duress	Homicide
R v *Sharp*	To show that an active gang member cannot use duress if they are pressured to offend	
R v *Willer*	To exemplify duress of circumstances	

■ Sample question

Below is an essay question that incorporates overlapping areas of the law. See if you can answer this question drawing upon your knowledge of the whole subject area. Guidelines on answering this question follow it.

ESSAY QUESTION

There is an increasing shift towards subjectivity as the basis for liability in criminal law.

Discuss the accuracy of this statement.

Answer guidelines

Approaching the question

This is the sort of question that often frightens students, as it is not immediately obvious what it requires. However, if you take a little time to work out what it requires, you will see that the question actually offers a great deal of scope to pull together a selection of different points and to create a clever answer that will impress the examiner. The mention of subjectivity is likely to make you think about states of mind and, as a result, *mens rea*; but do not forget to include a discussion of defences that raise issues of subjectivity and objectivity, such as provocation (or the new defence of loss of control that replaces it) and self-defence. A good way to get started might be to make a list of the forms of *mens rea* and defences that you could include and divide them into two categories: those that support the statement (such as recklessness) and those that go against it (the shift to a requirement for a reasonable belief in consent in sexual offences). Not only will this help you to generate points to include but it will also help you to create a structure for your answer.

Important points to include

- The starting point must be an explanation of the statement at the heart of the question, as this will set the focus for your essay and demonstrate to the examiner that you have understood what is required. You should explain that the subjectivity-versus-objectivity debate is often thought of in relation to *mens rea* but that it is also relevant to certain defences; and you should include within this a brief explanation of subjectivity and objectivity to make it clear that you understand the difference between the terms.

- You could start by introducing issues that tend to support the statement. The most obvious area of focus here would be on the move away from an objective test of recklessness, since the House of Lords in *R* v *G* overruled *Caldwell* and replaced it with a subjective test of recklessness. You could support this by reference to other areas where an honestly held belief is the touchstone for establishing *mens rea* or a defence, such as section 2 of the Theft Act 1968 in relation to dishonesty and as the trigger for the use of force in self-defence. Remember that you should not only describe these examples but comment on the rationale for their existence.

Make your answer stand out

Follow this up by introducing areas that indicate a shift away from subjectivity. A good example would be the reformulation of the *mens rea* of rape in the Sexual Offences Act 2003. The introduction of a requirement that a belief in consent must be reasonable (rather than just honestly held as was the case under the old law of rape: *DPP* v *Morgan*) represents a shift towards objectivity. You should consider why there was a move in this direction in relation to this offence and discuss how it fits with a more general shift towards subjectivity.

There are areas where a combined objective and subjective test is used: dishonesty (the *Ghosh* test) and defences, such as duress, self-defence and the old defence of provocation and its replacement, loss of control. You could strengthen your answer by considering whether such dual tests offer an effective compromise.

■ Further practice

To test yourself further, try to answer these three questions, which also incorporate overlapping areas of the law. Evaluate your answers using the answer guidelines available on the companion website at **www.pearsoned.co.uk/lawexpress**

Question 1

To what extent is causation in the criminal law a satisfactory mechanism for apportioning blame for harms in which persons or events (other than the defendant's actions) have contributed to the ultimate harm?

Question 2

Daniel has booked a day at a luxury spa. He has had a massage and a swim and is just wandering into the coffee shop in his swimming trunks and robe when he spots his ex-wife, Louise. He puts his hand on her shoulder and says, 'What are you doing here?' Startled, Louise jumps up and spills a fruit smoothie down the front of her robe. Her new husband, Kurt, sees what has happened and rushes towards Daniel, who runs away and hides in the ladies' changing room. Daniel rummages through some of the lockers, hoping to find a tracksuit that he can put on over his trunks. He has no success, so he changes his plan and goes into the mixed-sex sauna that is situated between the male and female changing rooms, planning to relax for a while and then go into the men's changing room to find his own clothes. The sauna is empty and dimly lit, so Daniel is confident that Kurt will not spot him, even if he looks in. After about ten minutes, when Daniel is relaxed and half-asleep, he is joined by Jennifer. They chat for a while and then Jennifer takes off her bikini top and invites him to touch her. Daniel fondles Jennifer's breasts and they kiss passionately, but when Daniel tries to remove Jennifer's bikini bottoms, she pushes him away and bursts into tears. Daniel tries to comfort her and is horrified when Jennifer explains that she is only 13 and that this was her first sexual experience, so she did not want to go too far. Daniel is horrified to learn Jennifer's age and asked how she came to be in an adult-only spa. Jennifer explained that her mother, Susan, works on reception and often gives her a day pass so that she can use the spa in the school holidays. Daniel decides to abandon his day at the spa. He changes into his own clothes and is just leaving when he is grabbed by Kurt, who tells him to keep away from Louise. Daniel struggles to get away and, in doing so, he stumbles and falls through the glass door at the front of the spa, severing an artery in his leg, which has to be amputated.

Discuss the criminal liability that arises on these facts.

Question 3

Lucy is upset following the break-up of her relationship with George. She thinks that if he would just talk to her then she could persuade him to go back out with her, so she goes for a walk through some woods where she knows that he takes his daily run every day, hoping to bump into him. One evening, just as it is getting dark, she notices that a large marquee has been erected in a field bordering the woods and goes to have a look at it, ignoring the 'private property' sign on the fence. The marquee is set up for a wedding reception, which upsets Lucy, who had hoped that George would want to marry her one day. She rampages around the marquee, overturning tables and smashing plates and glasses and then she starts to tear open the wedding presents. She is just holding a crystal vase that she has unwrapped when an elderly man comes into the marquee and demands to know what she is doing. Horrified, Lucy tries to run away, but the man grabs her arm. Lucy pushes him hard and he falls over, hitting his head on the corner of a table. Lucy runs through the dark woods in a state of panic, still holding the crystal vase. She bumps into George, who takes her in his arms and tries to calm her. Lucy kisses him passionately and they make love in the grass. Afterwards, they walk out of the woods together and Lucy realises that it is not George, but his cousin, Brandon, with whom he shares a close family resemblance. That evening, Lucy hears on the local news that a local farmer was found dead in a wedding marquee from a head injury.

Discuss the criminal liability that arises on these facts.

Glossary of terms

The glossary is divided into two parts: key definitions and other useful terms. The key definitions can be found within the chapter in which they occur as well as in the glossary below. These definitions are the essential terms that you must know and understand in order to prepare for an exam. The additional list of terms provides further definitions of useful terms and phrases that will also help you answer examination and coursework questions effectively. These terms are highlighted in the text as they occur, but the definition can be found only here.

■ Key definitions

Abetting	Form of assistance that implies consensus but not causation.
Aiding	This requires actual assistance but does not require consensus or causation.
Automatism	An act done by the muscles without any control by the mind.
Battery	Any act by which a person intentionally or recklessly inflicts unlawful personal violence on another.
Chain of causation	The link between the initial act of the defendant and the prohibited consequence.
Common assault	An act by which a person intentionally or recklessly causes another to apprehend immediate and unlawful violence.
Conduct crime	An offence in which the *actus reus* is concerned with the prohibited behaviour rather than its consequences, such as careless driving.
Counselling	A form of assistance that implies consensus but not causation.
Direct intention	This corresponds with the ordinary meaning of intention as purpose or aim.
Factual causation	A link between the defendant's act and the prohibited consequence that is established using the 'but for' test.

Grievous bodily harm (GBH)	Really serious harm.
Insanity	A defect of reason arising from a disease of the mind such that the defendant did not know the nature and quality of his act or that what he was doing was wrong.
Intervening act	Something that happens after the defendant's act that breaks the chain of causation.
Malice aforethought	Intention to kill or cause GBH.
Murder	Unlawful killing of a reasonable person within the Queen's peace with malice aforethought.
Procuring	A form of assistance that implies causation not consensus.
Recklessness	A term used to describe culpable risk-taking.
Result crime	An offence in which the *actus reus* prohibits a particular consequence irrespective of how it was brought about, e.g. murder.
Thin-skull rule	'Take your victim as you find them', even if they are particularly susceptible to harm.
Wound	A break in the continuity of the skin.

◼ Other useful terms

Accessory	Individuals who assist the commission of the principal offence in some way.
Actus reus	The guilty act or the conduct element of a crime.
Basic intent	Crimes in which the *mens rea* is intention or recklessness.
Deception	Words or actions that induce a man to believe that a thing is true when it is false.
Homicide	The killing of a human being by another.
Inchoate	Incomplete.
Mens rea	The guilty mind or the mental element of a crime.
Oblique intention	Includes foreseeable and inescapable consequences of achieving a desired result, even if the consequence itself is not desired.
Specific intent	Crimes in which the *mens rea* is intention only.
Strict liability	An offence that does not require *mens rea* in relation to all parts of the *actus reus*.
Transferred malice	A means of imposing liability for the unplanned consequences of deliberate wrongdoing.

Index

Emboldened entries refer to terms in the glossary